THE
DYNAMICS
OF LAW

THE DYNAMICS OF LAW

FOURTH EDITION

MICHAEL S. HAMILTON and GEORGE W. SPIRO

M.E.Sharpe
Armonk, New York
London, England

Library of Congress Cataloging-in-Publication Data

Hamilton, Michael S.
  The dynamics of law / by Michael S. Hamilton and George W. Spiro. — 4th ed.
    p. cm.
  Rev. ed. of: The dynamics of law / George W. Spiro. 3rd ed. 1992
  Includes bibliographical references and index.
  ISBN 978-0-7656-2086-6 (cloth : alk. paper)—ISBN 978-0-7656-2087-3 (pbk. : alk. paper)
  1. Justice, Administration of—United States. 2. Courts—United States. 3. Law—United States.
I. Spiro, George W. II. Spiro, George W. Dynamics of law. III. Title.

KF8700.S6 2008

347.73—dc22   2007022832

Our nation is founded on the principle
that observance of the law is the eternal safeguard of liberty
and defiance of the law is the surest road to tyranny.
—John F. Kennedy, September 30, 1962

* * *

To the memory of George W. Spiro
and
to our loving families

Contents

Preface

It is with great sorrow that I note the untimely passing of Dean George W. Spiro. This edition of *The Dynamics of Law* is dedicated to his memory. Since my first exposure to this text in graduate school, I have admired the ability of Dean Spiro, and before him Professor James L. Houghteling Jr., to present a subject as complex as law with clarity and precision. In this edition, I have attempted to maintain as much of that basic style as possible.

Like previous editions, this fourth edition of *The Dynamics of Law* is designed for use in social science and business administration courses that are concerned with our legal environment. New cases have been added to help students in their efforts to understand the institution of law. We continue to provide study problems and review questions at the end of each chapter. Chapter problems are drawn from the legal literature, as well as from articles and books of a more general nature. All the materials are designed to stimulate classroom discussion.

I wish to express my appreciation to Lucia Spiro for her support in reviving this text, which we hope will provide an economical and succinct alternative to the weightier compendiums published by others on the same subject. I gratefully acknowledge the assistance of Zip Kellogg, a remarkable librarian, in locating some obscure references, and Amelia Golden in preparing revised graphics. Special thanks also go to Professor Larry Luton of Eastern Washington University for his suggestion that I bring the project to M.E. Sharpe, and to Harry Briggs of M.E. Sharpe who was so patient, encouraging, and helpful to me during development of the project. I appreciate the generosity of those authors who permitted us to quote from their writings.

No small portion of the inspiration for my part in this project came from memories of my father, Harry Seymour Hamilton, an old-fashioned small-town civil lawyer who did the best he knew how for every client and was sometimes compensated for his efforts with a bushel of apples or a few dozen eggs, graciously received. Finally, my boundless appreciation goes to Carol Jean Boggis for her continuing tolerance and encouragement.

Michael S. Hamilton

THE
DYNAMICS
OF LAW

CHAPTER 1

The Nature and Function of Law

Law is an important part of our lives. Consequently, many people have a vague feeling that they ought to know more than they do about the law. They suspect that knowledge of legal rules might help them in their jobs or keep them out of trouble.

You could make no greater mistake, however, than to convince yourself that by simply memorizing legal rules from a book you will gain the knowledge you need to handle your own legal problems. Such rote learning is a waste of time, even for lawyers, for several reasons:

1. There are simply too many rules.
2. The same rules are not applied in all states. We can make a good many generalizations that will hold true for most states, but without investigation we can never be sure that a particular generalization is true for any one state.
3. The rules are constantly being modified by legislators, judges, and administrative agencies.
4. Most rules are not simple and categorical. To state a legal rule with accuracy is likely to require a surprising number of qualifications and exceptions. Many situations are not neatly covered by any single rule. Indeed, a lawyer—that is, an expert on legal rules—can often do no better than venture a prediction about which rule a court of law will apply in a given situation.

The proposition that underpins this book is that law must be viewed not as a body of static rules but as a *dynamic process by which rules are constantly changed, created, and molded to fit particular situations.* We shall describe and analyze the processes of the law in the belief that no one can truly understand legal rules without understanding the processes from which they emerge.

WHY DO WE NEED A SYSTEM OF RULES?

All of us have grown up in a world in which there are established guides for social behavior. Our parents made rules for us as children that we were expected to obey. As we grew older, more was expected of us, and we had to follow more rules that regulated our behavior. The vast majority of these rules were not rules of law, but norms of conduct. It is impolite, for example, to speak with your mouth full, but you would never be convicted as a criminal for violating this norm.

Some forms of social behavior are more necessary and some are more desirable than others. In fact, this is a reason that people form groups such as clubs and religious or business organizations. These groups play an important role in our lives, helping shape our behavior and satisfying needs that we all share. One group of particular importance to us is the nation-state. In our country, members of this group are called citizens; in other nation-states they may be called subjects.

Conceivably, a society could allow sheer power—physical, economic, social, or political—to determine which forms of social behavior should be enforced. It has been suggested that the primary reason for having a state is to provide members of a society with security from the possibility of physical harm as different groups contend to exert their power. History would seem to support this conclusion. For example, archaeologists examining ancient cities of Mesopotamia have uncovered evidence that the concept of the state emerged there to regulate struggles between agricultural communities for control of land and water.

We still look to the state to regulate the exercise of private power and to provide security and safety. However, most civilized societies also recognize such concepts as "justice" and "social utility" as criteria for establishing priorities for their citizens. A major task of government is to create and enforce rules of law based on these criteria in order to maintain an orderly process for settling disputes, to structure cooperative relationships, and to facilitate orderly changes (Lipson 1989, 46–50). Consequently, most of our laws are designed to accomplish one or more of three objectives:

1. to protect people from people (e.g., to regulate behavior, such as criminal laws and economic and environmental regulations);
2. to protect people from government (e.g., to protect civil rights and civil liberties); and
3. to protect government from people, especially the wealthy and unscrupulous (e.g., through conflict of interest and anticorruption laws).

What are rules of law? *Legal rules are guides to human conduct in society, established and enforced by public officials.* In our nation, these laws are designed to achieve a balance among diverse interests in our society, and they are enforced by officials acting on behalf of the whole community. But rules are not, and can never be, unchanging. In societies in which new problems keep emerging, new rules are continually needed. So it is less important to know the rules than it is to understand the processes by which rules are created and applied. This is why we suggested above that it is best to think of law not as a body of rules, but as a dynamic process—a system of regularized, institutionalized procedures for the orderly decision of social questions, including the settlement of disputes.

PRIVATE RULES FOR SOCIAL ORDERING

Law establishes a framework within which private decision-making takes place. For example, we all know there is a law stating that you must stop at a stop sign. As an individual, you make a private decision either to observe this law or to disregard it and risk the possibility of having an accident or being ticketed. The decision is yours; the law merely gives you guidance.

Although the legal system is the most powerful mechanism for exercise of social control (since public officials can, if necessary, apply methods of enforcement not available to private persons), there are other sources of guidance. Private groups and group rules help satisfy needs that we collectively share. The needs that they address can be grand or trivial. We join religious groups for spiritual reasons, educational groups for learning, and clubs for social reasons. Each of us is part of any number of groups, and we add or change groups over our lives to attend to our ever-evolving needs. These groups can last a lifetime, but they need not be formal, and they may be quite transient—lasting no more than a few hours or minutes (as at a religious prayer or social party). But these groups and the needs they satisfy collectively create the pushes and pulls that provide substance for our system of law and government.

In addition, when distinctions between right and wrong are particularly subtle, when the facts are hard to obtain, or when rapid remedies (damage awards, court orders, and criminal penalties) are not readily applicable, the law is effectively helpless. Courts and judges can do little to make people kinder to their spouses, to prevent students from cheating on exams, or to induce people to be more devoted or more truthful. Consequently, most social control in these areas must be exercised privately or not at all.

There is, then, a clear need that is filled by private groups. These groups create rules that in many ways resemble laws passed by the state or federal government. Your college or university, for example, probably has a student conduct code that outlines the rules concerning student discipline. The only real distinctions between these rules and those that we call laws are that the college rules govern a relatively small society (students in the school) and they are enforced not by public officials, but rather by officials of the school.

Many contemporary scholars would argue that our earlier definition of law is too narrow. They would object to limiting law to those rules enforced by public officials. Why do we need the force of the state to have law? Why not define law as a guide to human conduct in society established and enforced by any official, thereby including rules created by private organizations?

While it is possible to define law that broadly, the vast majority of legal scholars take a narrower view. Both for this reason and because this text examines the U.S. legal system as a model, we shall use the narrower definition. In Chapter 9, however, we shall discuss a direct and important link between private organizations' rules and those of the formal U.S. legal system.

CUSTOMS AND MORALS VERSUS LAW

Legal rules are distinguished from other rules by the fact that public officials create them and are supposed to enforce them. Behind legal rules stands the authority of the state. Although many of a community's customs and moral rules eventually become law, a custom or moral rule is not in itself a rule of law; it does not become one unless adopted as such by officials who have the power to create legal rules.

Morality encompasses an individual's ability to distinguish right from wrong and to act accordingly. The ideas of right and wrong, good and bad, are value judgments as determined and generally accepted by some reference group. Moral behavior may or may not coincide with a legal rule. It may, for example, be morally right to come to the aid of a person who is drowning, but it is not a legal necessity.

Problem

SAN DIEGO, Jan. 17 (AP)—A 75-year-old man in a wheelchair apologetically robbed a bank of $70 here on Tuesday so that he could buy heart medicine.

The man, William Hart, pleaded not guilty at his arraignment on Wednesday, contending that anyone in his position would have acted as he did. He was allowed to remain free without bail until a court appearance in two weeks.

The office of the United States Attorney here said it had not yet decided whether to prosecute Mr. Hart.

Mr. Hart, who has no criminal record, said he suffered a stroke and two heart attacks three years ago and had been on medication ever since. His right side is partly paralyzed and his speech is slurred.

On Tuesday he entered a branch of the bank, where he had $4 in his account, and apologized while demanding $70 from a teller, telling her he would blow up the bank if she did not comply. He said a bottle he was carrying was filled with explosives, but it actually contained a heart medication.

After the teller had turned over the money, a security guard followed Mr. Hart out of the bank and called the police. Mr. Hart was arrested minutes later when he tried to buy a $69 bottle of heart medicine at a drugstore near the bank.

Source: Excerpted from *New York Times* (1991).

Do you see any moral problems in this case? Are there any value conflicts? How would you handle this problem if you were the judge trying Mr. Hart's case?

The problems faced by Mr. Hart's judge are typical of those that intrigue philosophers and bedevil policymakers. Although it is obviously necessary to have a law against stealing, it may seem unfair to apply the law in the same way to Mr. Hart as to someone who is well off and commits a robbery just for the fun of it or as an occupation. Mr. Hart has broken the law, but it is a matter of argument whether he has also done wrong. In order to be a good citizen, should people obey the law, no matter how much the law offends their sense of morality? Conversely, should they do what they think is right under the circumstances, even if it means breaking the law? Perhaps the important thing is that any person considering these questions must understand the consequences, both legal and moral, of following each course of action.

You will notice in even the relatively objective account of the incident involving Mr. Hart that the question of moral judgment is affected by the use of value-laden words and phrases. Mr. Hart is "a 75-year-old man in a wheelchair" who is "partly paralyzed" and who robbed a bank "apologetically," terms that may make the bank and the police sound heartless in contrast. Such words influence our perception of the legal and moral issues involved in the case. In analyzing cases throughout this text, you should make every effort to analyze conflicting values and recognize value-laden words.

Custom, like moral behavior, may or may not coincide with legal behavior, yet custom is different from morality. It is customary to eat lunch at noon, but eating lunch at eleven cannot be said to be immoral (or illegal). A custom is a course of action that people have chosen to repeat when faced with a particular circumstance; it is usually enforced only by private methods of social approval and disapproval. Sometimes, though, a custom can become a law, as, for example, when the custom of driving on the right side of the road was written into a statute by legislators.

THE VARIOUS PERSPECTIVES OF LAW

To resolve such problems as finding the proper relation between law, custom, and morality, many people have spent a great deal of time trying to find one perfect legal theory. Two classic formulations of legal theory are *natural law* and *positivist law*. One positivist, John Austin (1875), suggests that law is any command that can be enforced. For positivists, a law is law so long as it can be enforced by the sovereign or legislator, quite independent of its moral content. Law is command and sanction as exercised by the state or other rulemaker, and it is the values of the rulemaker that are enforced. Positivists would argue that judges cannot impose their values on the law, but must apply the rules as provided by the state. Legal philosophers other than Austin who can be described as positivists are John Stuart Mill (1866) and H.L.A. Hart (1961).

The ancient Greek philosopher Aristotle is an example of a natural law theorist. For Aristotle, society is organized by *cosmic* or *natural law*. This cosmic law is an ideal form of law, higher than that made by mortals. Natural law theorists see as key components of law certain values and ideals that we aspire to attain. Natural law therefore reflects what ought to be rather than what is. Many natural law theorists begin from a religious base by suggesting that ideal values are God-given. Others suggest that it is through reason that we come to know true law. Natural law theory is reflected in our own system of government. In the Declaration of Independence, Thomas Jefferson wrote:

> We hold these truths to be self evident, that all men are created equal, that they are endowed by their creator with certain unalienable rights, that among these are life, liberty and the pursuit of happiness. That whenever any form of government

becomes destructive of these ends it is the right of the people to alter or abolish it, and to institute new government, laying its foundation on such principles and organizing its powers in such form, as to them shall seem most likely to effect their safety and happiness.

Would this justification for revolution be just as valid today as it appeared in 1776? Difficult personal choices may emerge when an individual's values and view of law clash with the prevailing perspective of society. For example, another Greek philosopher, Socrates, was charged with worshipping foreign gods and corrupting the young people of Greece. The people of Athens found him guilty and sentenced him to death in 399 B.C. His friend Crito offered to help him escape from jail, but Socrates declined to run, suggesting instead that he would submit to the laws of the state: "In war and in the court of justice, and everywhere, you must do whatever your state and your country tell you to do or you must persuade them that their commands are unjust."

You might ask yourself if you agree with Socrates. What if you thought the laws of the state were wrong and even potentially dangerous? Would you do whatever your country told you to do, or would you commit an act of rebellion? In the United States, Martin Luther King Jr. faced the difficult choice about what to do when state law conflicted with his own values. He chose a route of *civil disobedience:* he violated laws made by humans in the segregated South of the 1960s and accepted the consequences of his actions in order to follow laws that he felt were God-given and therefore of a higher order. His actions were intended to persuade others to reform and improve society by changing human laws.

New models of law are constantly being developed and tested in the hope they will clarify our understanding of the social processes of law. For example, many contemporary scholars have developed theories as part of a critical legal studies movement rooted in various perspectives of jurisprudence, such as legal realism and relativist epistemology (e.g., Hutchinson 1989; Zinn 1990). As you advance in your study of law and as you face particular legal problems, you should ask yourself which of the many theories would be most useful to you in resolving your particular concern. Right now, your job is to learn about our legal system and the interaction of its elements.

SOME REQUIREMENTS FOR AN EFFECTIVE LEGAL SYSTEM

Once you have a reasonable definition of law, your next job is to assemble a legal system that operates effectively. As you can imagine, there are an infinite number of ways in which a legal system can be put together. Every nation in the world has a slightly different legal system. In fact, legal scholar Karl Llewellyn developed the concept of a law-government continuum to illustrate just that point (see Figure 1.1).

The *government pole* of this continuum represents a legal system in which all decisions are left to the judgment of a leader of the system. Totalitarian political systems, such as Iraq under the leadership of Saddam Hussein, approach the government pole. The *law pole* represents the opposite situation, in which the set of rules is so complete that

Figure 1.1 **The Law-Government Continuum**

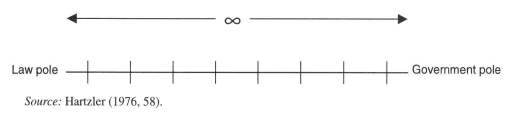

Source: Hartzler (1976, 58).

human judgment is unnecessary: every conceivable contingency is covered by specific laws. While no legal system exemplifies the law pole completely, the U.S. legal system is closer to it than most. Obviously, societies merely approach the extreme positions. It is possible to conceive of a viable legal system at any point along this continuum. Our own legal system is but one model among many; it contrasts in varying degrees with others. Since it is closer to the law pole than to the government pole, it contrasts most sharply with a highly autocratic system, such as an absolute monarchy or a dictatorship, which would be nearer to the government pole.

Whatever legal system is adopted, certain requirements must be met in order for it to be effective:

Most rules must be obeyed voluntarily. One objective of a legal system is to set forth guides for human conduct that will cause people to behave by choice as society wants them to behave. This is the preventive function of law. The most important legal rules (sometimes known as the primary rules) are those designed to channel the conduct of private persons and groups into patterns that will keep conflict to a minimum. Without a large measure of voluntary compliance with the primary rules, social life would be impossible: no community can afford to employ a large enough number of officials to compel everyone to obey the law.

Inevitably, though, some people do not comply, either deliberately or through carelessness or ignorance. Consequently a legal system must have officials such as police and judges to apply *secondary,* or *remedial,* rules. These are rules that determine what happens to people who have violated the primary rules. Again, recourse to officials and to remedial rules must always be the exception if a legal system is to be effective. Most people, most of the time, must observe the speed limits, live up to their contractual obligations, pay their taxes, and in other ways comply with the law if a law enforcement system is not to be overburdened.

The rules must seem just and reasonable. Why do most people comply with rules most of the time? To be sure, remedial rules are partly responsible: People do not want any trouble with the officials. They do not want to be arrested and prosecuted or to be sued; they do not want to be punished or to have to pay damages to somebody they have harmed. This is the *deterrence* effect of rules. But we probably tend to overestimate the importance of these fears. Most people obey legal rules both out of force of habit and because they feel, at least dimly, that doing so is right.

It does not follow from this that people will accept just any set of rules. People must believe that rules are relatively fair and reasonable. Circumstances sometimes arise, of course, in which it is desirable to establish a rule even though many people do not like it: antidiscrimination laws adopted in many communities may well be examples. Such laws are designed to raise the prevailing moral standards of the community. However, a rule that any considerable part of the community finds unjust or unreasonable will be difficult to enforce. The classic example of a law found unreasonable by society was the Eighteenth Amendment's prohibition of alcohol in 1919. This unpopular prohibition was widely, even flagrantly, violated and was ultimately repealed by the Twenty-First Amendment in 1933. An unpopular law may even cause harm that outweighs any possible good that the law might accomplish. Prohibition during the 1920s and many of our current gambling laws are often cited as evidence to support this proposition.

The rules must be flexible. Since the material circumstances of community life and thus the values and attitudes of a community are continually changing, the system of rules under which a community lives must be flexible and adaptable. There must be ways to mold existing rules to meet new, unexpected situations, and ways to make more substantial changes in the rules when such changes seem necessary. In our legal system, the task of interpreting rules to meet new situations has traditionally been assigned to the courts, while more substantial changes are usually made by legislative bodies.

The rules must be knowable. It is obviously not necessary for every citizen to know all the rules, but experts on the rules—lawyers—must be able to advise their clients on the probable legal consequences of their acts, and citizens must have a general idea of the most important laws. As a famous judge, Benjamin N. Cardozo, once said, "Law as a guide to conduct is reduced to the level of mere futility if it is unknown and unknowable" (1924, 3).

Under some circumstances, the requirement that laws be knowable may conflict with other requirements. The most certain and knowable rules tend to be those that are relatively simple and categorical and that have no qualification or exceptions ("Thou shalt not kill"). To make a rule seem reasonable and just, however, qualifications and exceptions have to be added. Thus, killing in self-defense is permitted in some circumstances, as is killing in times of war. Conversely, flexible and changing rules are less certain in their application—and less knowable—than are inflexible and unchanging rules. One of the hardest tasks for lawmakers is to balance these competing requirements.

THE CREATION AND APPLICATION OF LAW:
AN INTRODUCTION

We have stated that this book deals with processes and institutions by which legal rules are created and applied in particular cases. Following is a brief overview of how these subjects are covered.

When we speak of applying rules in particular cases, we are referring primarily to the process known as *adjudication*. Adjudication involves deciding exactly what happened—what the facts were in the particular case—and then deciding what legal rules should be applied to those facts. This process is considered in Chapters 2 and 3.

When we speak of creating and modifying rules—of *lawmaking*—we are referring to several processes. The best known of these is *legislative lawmaking,* a term that refers to enactment of legislation (that is, statutes) by popularly elected legislative bodies. Many people are aware of no other kind of lawmaking; indeed, to most of us a "law" means a legislative act.

Another great lawmaking process is *decisional lawmaking.* The notion that judges "make law" is much less familiar than the concept of legislative lawmaking. Nonetheless, law is made in the course of adjudicating cases. Whenever a question arises about the proper rule of law to apply in a particular case, the answering of that question by a judge is a creative act—an act of lawmaking. Judges make law for the future, because their decisions become potential precedents that may influence other judges deciding future cases involving similar factual situations. Law created by judicial decisions is variously called decisional law, case law, and judge-made law.

Chapter 4 describes how judges create new rules out of old ones by building on prec- edents. Chapter 5 discusses the manner in which legislators make law. Then, Chapters 6 and 7 return to judicial lawmaking: Chapter 6 describes how judges interpret statutes in the course of applying them in particular cases, and Chapter 7 describes how judges interpret the U.S. Constitution.

Legislators and judges have been making law and adjudicating cases for hundreds of years, but in the last century we have seen a vast increase in the role of administrators in the legal system. Today, administrative officials and agencies like the Federal Trade Commission or the Internal Revenue Service both adjudicate cases and make law. Their lawmaking is in part decisional (when they decide cases) and in part legislative (when they exercise powers delegated to them by legislatures to issue rules and regulations that have the force of law). In Chapter 8 we consider the role of administrators in the legal system.

We have defined legal rules to refer only to rules created by officials. However, private persons and groups make important contributions to official lawmaking and, in addition, create rules of their own that supplement the rules of law. These contributions are the subject of Chapter 9.

CHAPTER PROBLEM: PRACTICING RELIGION OR CHILD ABUSE

What happens when the legal system clashes with religious systems? In just such a case, members of the Christian Science faith confronted the Massachusetts legal system. The page one article that follows tells the story of two Christian Scientists who were convicted of manslaughter by a Boston jury because they turned to prayer and not to physicians when their son became ill; the boy subsequently died.

Verdict Seen as Fueling National Debate

The eyes of religious leaders, child advocates, and attorneys around the country were trained upon a Suffolk County courtroom yesterday as a Boston jury convicted two Christian Scientists who relied on prayer rather than medicine in their son's death. . . .

Because Christian Scientists believe that disease results from a lack of understanding of God's purpose for individuals and the world, they believe that prayer, not medical treatment, is curative. . . .

The Twitchells . . . relied solely on prayers to heal their 2½-year-old son Robyn, rather than seek medical care. They are charged with involuntary manslaughter . . . after Robyn Twitchell died of complications from a bowel obstruction. . . .

But church authorities said the trial, and the verdict, will bring the Christian Science Church closer together.

"The prosecutor has said no more spiritual healing, and our response is more and more spiritual healing," said Norman Talbot, a spokesman for the Church.

[Religious experts say] . . . Traditional churches . . . will perceive the verdict as an attack on religious freedom. . . .

Martin T. Marty, a professor of religious history at the University of Chicago [said], "there is a principle at stake—religions should define religions, not governments."

Source: Excerpted from Wong (1990, 1).

Questions

1. In your opinion, is the law the appropriate device for solving problems such as the one described above?
2. What value judgments underlie the premises of the various parties?
3. Do you think that the legal system has an appropriate role in regulating religious practice? What happens when religious practice may lead to death or serious illness?

QUESTIONS FOR REVIEW

1. One possible definition of law states, "Law is what the strongest person says it is." Evaluate this statement. What would be a better definition of law? Why?
2. Can you think of an example of a custom that later became law? Can you think of a custom that you believe *should* become law?
3. Parents and representatives of television networks and the toy industry are currently debating a significant question concerning the amount and form of advertising directed toward children. Parents often argue that such advertising is deceptive and that youngsters are unable to make informed judgments about products they see on TV; children thus become victims of profit-seeking corporations. Do you think television advertising should be regulated? Is law the appropriate device for resolving this problem?

4. One requirement of a legal system is that rules seem just and reasonable. One law states that the sanction for murder is that a murderer will be put to death. Is this law just and reasonable? Must *all* laws be just and reasonable? Explain.

5. It was stated in this chapter that laws must be flexible. Does this mean that there should be different standards for different people? Explain.

BIBLIOGRAPHY

Austin, John. 1875. *Lectures on Jurisprudence or, The Philosophy of Positive Law*. Edited by Robert Campbell. New York: J. Cockcroft.

Cardozo, Benjamin N. 1924. *The Growth of the Law*. New Haven: Yale University Press.

Hart, H.L.A. 1961. *The Concept of Law*. Oxford, UK: Clarendon Press.

Hartzler, Richard. 1976. *Justice, Legal Systems and Social Structure*. Port Washington, NY: Kennikat Press.

Hutchinson, Allan C., ed. 1989. *Critical Legal Studies*. Totowa, NJ: Rowman & Littlefield.

Lipson, Leslie. 1989. *The Great Issues of Politics: An Introduction to Political Science,* 8th ed. Englewood Cliffs, NJ: Prentice-Hall.

Mill, John Stuart. 1866. *The Positive Philosophy of Auguste Comte*. Boston: W.V. Spencer.

New York Times. 1991. "Bank Robber in Wheelchair Has an Alibi: Costly Medicine." January 18.

Wong, Doris Sue. 1990. "Christian Science Couple Convicted in Son's Death." *Boston Globe,* July 5, p. 1.

Zinn, Howard. 1990. *Declarations of Independence: Cross-Examining American Ideology.* New York: Harper Collins.

CHAPTER 2

The Courts and Adjudication

Only a tiny fraction of the innumerable infractions that take place every day in our society ever come before courts of law. But the few cases that do are of particular importance to the legal system and to the student of law. For one thing, these cases furnish the best documentation we have of the legal system at work. Even more important, they provide occasions on which judges make authoritative restatements of the scope and content of legal rules.

When courts decide cases, they perform two distinct, though interrelated, functions. First, they settle a controversy between the parties: they determine what the facts were and apply appropriate rules to those facts. This is the function commonly known as *adjudication.* We discuss adjudication in this chapter and the next.

Whenever there is any question about what rules to apply, the courts also perform a second function. They decide what the appropriate rules are and how they fit the particular case. Deciding what rules are applicable often requires the courts to reformulate and modify the scope of existing rules. Some of these reformulations become precedents that determine the future scope and content of rules. One significant result of the precedent-creating activity of courts is to keep many disputes from coming before the courts at all. The position a court takes in one case often makes possible a relatively reliable prediction of how it would view a similar case that might come before it. This predictability may deter the parties in the later case from taking the time and trouble to bring their case to court. This second function of the courts is sometimes referred to as *judicial lawmaking.* We examine judicial lawmaking in Chapters 4, 6, and 7.

This chapter begins by briefly distinguishing between civil law and criminal law. Next, we describe the categories of courts that make up a court system and the limits placed on their jurisdiction. Finally, we trace the sequence of steps that make up the adjudicative process. Chapter 3 is devoted entirely to one of those steps: the trial.

CRIMINAL LAW AND CIVIL LAW

The classification of legal rules and court proceedings as either criminal or civil is basic to our legal system, yet it is so confusing to many people that the distinction should be clarified at once.

If somebody has performed an act that probably violates some rule of law and you want to make a preliminary guess as to whether her violation is criminal or civil, ask yourself this question: what is likely to happen to the wrongdoer? If you decide that she is probably subject to official punishment—to a fine or imprisonment, for instance—then she has probably violated a criminal rule. If, on the other hand, you think that she will probably be sued and ordered to pay damages to whomever she has harmed or ordered to do or desist from doing some act, then she has probably violated a civil rule.

This is only a rule of thumb, however; we need some definitions.

Rules of *criminal law* impose duties on people (and sometimes on associations of people) and specify that any violation of those duties is a wrong not merely to the individuals who are harmed, but to the community at large. Since the whole community has been wronged, public officials take the initiative in bringing the wrongdoer to justice, prosecuting him before a court, and urging the judge and jury to convict and punish him. Any redress received by the individuals wronged as a result of a criminal proceeding is purely incidental. Criminal wrongs are usually classified as either *felonies* or *misdemeanors*, depending on their gravity. To give two examples at opposite extremes, a murder is a felony, while disorderly conduct is a misdemeanor.

Rules of *civil law* also impose duties on people and associations of people. In addition, they establish liberties and powers; however, in distinguishing civil from criminal rules, we are concerned here only with the civil rules that impose duties. Violation of a duty created by a civil rule is, of course, a wrong, but it differs from a criminal wrong in that it does not constitute a wrong against the community at large. When a wrongful act is merely a civil wrong, therefore, public officials will not take the initiative in prosecuting and punishing the wrongdoer. Instead, the injured person must bring a civil suit against the wrongdoer. All civil wrongs except breaches of contract are more commonly known as *torts* (from the French word meaning "wrong"). For example, trespass, libel, and negligence are torts.

The problem of definition is made more difficult because, as you may have guessed by now, a particular act may be both a criminal wrong and a civil wrong. For example, if SPEEDER, while driving recklessly and in violation of the speed limit, sideswipes CAREFUL DRIVER and damages his car, she is guilty of both a crime and a tort. The state is likely to prosecute SPEEDER for her criminal conduct, and CAREFUL DRIVER may sue her for the tort, asking payment for the damage done. Under the U.S. legal system, a criminal prosecution and a civil suit cannot be combined, even though both are based on the same act, so SPEEDER may face two separate trials.

Many wrongful acts, however, are *only* criminal wrongs. For instance, if SPEEDER drives recklessly and too fast, but harms no one, she is guilty only of a crime. By the same token, many wrongful acts are *only* civil wrongs, simply because lawmakers have decided that the acts do not endanger the public welfare. For example, if HOMEOWNER carelessly leaves a roller skate on his front porch and VISITOR steps on it and falls, injuring her back, HOMEOWNER will probably not be subject to prosecution by the state, because such negligence is usually considered a civil tort, not criminal. Similarly, if BUYER refuses to go through with his contract to purchase SELLER's lawn mower, he will not be prosecuted, since breach of contract is not a crime. But VISITOR and SELLER probably have grounds for bringing civil suits.

There is, unfortunately, no basis for wholly reliable prediction as to whether a particular act that appears wrongful is a crime or a civil wrong, or both. This is because lawmakers are free (within the broad limits imposed by constitutions) to make almost any sort of act a criminal or civil wrong, just as they can "legalize" acts that have in the past been legal wrongs. For instance, nothing prevents a legislature from passing a law tomorrow declaring that failure to keep a front porch safe for visitors will henceforth be a misdemeanor punishable by a fine or that henceforth possession of cocaine is not a crime.

To recapitulate, some wrongful acts violate both criminal and civil rules of law and may result in either criminal prosecution or civil proceedings, or both. Some wrongful acts violate only criminal rules, usually because no private person can claim to have been harmed, while other wrongful acts violate only civil rules, because they are not considered to affect the public interest. Incidentally, once a wrongful act has come before a court, the character of the court action can usually be identified by the label given to the proceeding. If the label is something like "STATE (or PEOPLE) versus SPEEDER," the case is usually criminal. But if the label is "CAREFUL DRIVER versus SPEEDER," the case is civil. Only governments prosecute crimes, but individuals sue other individuals for civil wrongs.

In this book we are concerned primarily with civil rules of law. Our generalized discussion of courts will not cover criminal courts or proceedings specifically, important though they are. However, everybody is subject to criminal law and thus should be familiar with the distinctions discussed above.

COURT SYSTEMS: ORGANIZATION AND JURISDICTION

People outside the legal profession have no need for a detailed knowledge of the numerous types of courts that make up the court system of any given state, but a general familiarity with the structure of a typical court system is indispensable to an understanding of the cases that are presented in this book.

Each of the fifty states of the United States has its own court system, in addition to the federal (e.g., national) court system. No two systems are alike. Indeed, the differences in both the functions and labels given to our state courts are many and bewildering, and no generalization is absolutely reliable for all of them. Court systems have rarely been the product of long-range planning; nearly all represent a series of patchwork accommodations to changing needs.

At the outset, it is necessary to recognize a basic distinction that prevails in all court systems between *trial courts* and *appellate courts*. Trial courts are the courts in which cases are first heard and decided; here the opposing parties present evidence on the facts and arguments on the law. Ordinarily, a single judge hears any given trial-court proceeding.

The great majority of cases go no further than a trial court. But if one of the parties is dissatisfied with the outcome of a trial, the law usually allows that party to make an appeal—that is, to ask an *appellate court* (a court of appeal) to review the rulings of the trial court. An appellate court consists of a number of judges, several or all of whom hear each appeal.

Figure 2.1 **The State Court System of Massachusetts**

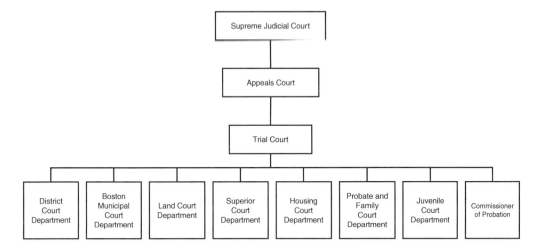

State Court Systems

The typical state court system consists of a considerable number of trial courts of limited jurisdiction, a smaller number of general trial courts, and a single appellate court for the whole state. Figure 2.1 illustrates the hierarchy of state courts in Massachusetts.

Trial Courts of Limited Jurisdiction

The vast majority of cases that come to our courts are tried by *trial courts of limited jurisdiction*. These cases are usually routine in character and of little importance except to the parties involved. The trial courts of limited jurisdiction fall into three classes: minor courts, intermediate courts, and specialized courts. As we shall see, they may be limited in a number of ways: for example, by money amount or by subject matter.

The Minor Courts. This lowest tier of trial courts, which are also referred to as local, petty, or inferior courts, are those staffed by rural justices of the peace (JPs) and their urban counterparts, often known as aldermen or magistrates. The JP is heir to centuries of tradition, dating back to English knights and country squires who were commissioned by the crown to keep the peace in rural areas. The modern namesakes of these knights and squires have authority to try petty criminal offenses and to hear civil cases involving claims not exceeding a few hundred dollars, such as minor contractual disputes. The remuneration that the JPs receive, consisting of fees for each case tried, is rarely their primary source of income. JPs are elected to the office; few have had legal training. The traditional minor courts are often criticized for the incompetence and bias of their magistrates. On their behalf, it may be said that the justice they dispense is readily accessible, speedy, and relatively inexpensive.

Many states have replaced the numerous JP courts and their urban counterparts with a smaller number of courts staffed by full-time, salaried, professionally trained judges. Even where this change has not occurred statewide, it has often taken place in the large towns and cities, or at least part of the original authority of the petty magistrates has been assigned to courts with full-time, legally trained judges. In the criminal sphere, the traffic and police courts are examples of the modernized minor courts. Courts that hear civil cases (or both civil and criminal cases) often bear such labels as city, town, municipal, or district courts.

In many ways, these modernized minor courts resemble intermediate-type trial courts (to be discussed below) more closely than they do the older type of minor court. But the trial courts in the minor-court classification do have some features in common. One is that, with occasional exceptions, they do not provide for a trial before a jury. Another is that appeals from their decisions are taken to the general trial courts (or occasionally to special courts of appeal) rather than to the regular appellate courts. Furthermore, such appeals often consist of complete new trials rather than mere reviews of errors alleged to have been made in the original trial.

Intermediate Trial Courts. In those states in which modernization of the minor courts has proved constitutionally or politically impossible, an intermediate tier of trial courts has sometimes been established between the JPs and the general trial courts, particularly in urban areas. These intermediate courts are often called county courts. As one might expect, they usually perform the same functions as the modernized minor courts. They try less serious criminal cases, and civil cases involving claims not in excess of a few thousand dollars. But their sphere of authority is much greater than that of the JPs. Most of these intermediate courts were created to take over part of the work formerly done by general trial courts. They provide jury trials, and appeals from their decisions go to regular appellate courts.

Specialized Courts. On the whole, there is strikingly little subject-matter specialization in the American court system. But a few subject-matter fields are frequently assigned to special courts, especially in urban areas. A number of cities, for instance, have special juvenile and domestic-relations (i.e., family) courts. Perhaps the specialized courts with the longest tradition are those that deal with such matters as the disposition of property left by deceased persons and with guardianships and adoptions. These are variously called *probate, orphan's,* and *surrogate courts.*

Why have certain kinds of cases been taken away from the regular courts and assigned to specialized courts? Usually the reason has been that handling numerous similar cases requires judges to perform functions markedly different from the trial judge's ordinary function of adjudication. Probate court judges, for instance, spend much of their time supervising the distribution (by executors and administrators) of property left by deceased persons—a task that involves adjudicating disputes only in exceptional cases. A major responsibility of a juvenile court judge is to search for a means of preventing a young offender from becoming a hardened criminal. An important part of the job of a domestic-relations judge is to see if it is possible to keep estranged couples from dissolving their marriages. Performing these tasks requires knowledge and skills quite different from those usually required for adjudication. Hence there are important advantages to assigning such cases to judges who have, or can attain, a special competence and whose courts can be staffed with specialized personnel, such as accountants, psychiatrists, and social workers.

General Trial Courts

The most important cases—those involving major crimes and large sums of money—are tried in general trial courts, also called courts of general jurisdiction. The cases you will read in this book virtually all began in general trial courts. When we speak of trial courts hereafter, we shall be referring to these courts unless we state otherwise. These courts are labeled *general* because they have authority to hear all types of cases not specifically assigned to courts of limited jurisdiction. Some small states have only one general trial court for the whole state, though that court usually consists of several judges who sit separately and hear cases in different cities in the state. Most states, however, are divided into a number of judicial districts, each consisting of one or more counties and each having its own general trial court.

General trial courts bear such varied labels as circuit, district, and common pleas courts. But labels can be deceptive: these same titles are used in some states to designate courts of limited jurisdiction or even appellate courts. New York State's general trial courts are called supreme courts, although this is the title usually given to the highest, final courts of appeal in other states.

Appellate Courts

All states have at least one appellate court, usually known as the *supreme court*. This is the "court of last resort"; it hears appeals from all trial-court decisions, criminal and civil, except those of minor courts. In a few states, however, the volume of appeals is so great that one or more intermediate appellate courts have been established to hear appeals in less important cases. Alternatively, a single appellate court may be divided into several subdivisions that hear appeals as if they were separate courts.

The Federal Court System

The federal court hierarchy, illustrated in Figure 2.2, is comparatively simple. The basic unit of jurisdiction is the *district*. Each district has a U.S. District Court. These are the general trial courts of the federal system (the system has no minor courts). There are ninety-four federal district courts in the fifty states and U.S. territories, including at least one district in each state, the District of Columbia, Puerto Rico, Guam, the Virgin Islands, and the Northern Mariana Islands. Many states constitute a single district, but some states are divided into two, three, or four districts. New York, for instance, has four districts.

Each district forms part of a larger judicial area known as a *circuit*. There are twelve

Figure 2.2   **The United States Court System**

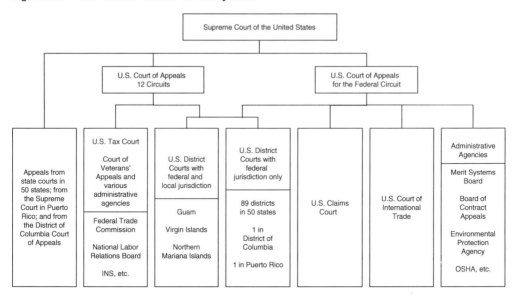

Source: Based on Administrative Office of the U.S. Courts (1989); National Archives and Records Administration (2006).

judicial circuits with Courts of Appeals, including the District of Columbia. A major responsibility of each court of appeals is to hear appeals from decisions of the district courts in its circuit. Because it hears most appeals of federal administrative law cases (e.g., those involving regulations and adjudicatory decisions of national government agencies), the District of Columbia Circuit Court of Appeals has developed special expertise in this area.

A so-called thirteenth-circuit Court of Appeals for the Federal Circuit, also located in Washington, DC, has nationwide jurisdiction defined by subject matter (e.g., patent laws, cases decided by some administrative agencies, and specialized federal trial courts such as the Court of International Trade and the U.S. Claims Court). The U.S. Claims Court generally has jurisdiction over claims against the United States. Typical of cases it hears are claims against the national government for the taking of property or claims that grow out of construction contracts. The Court of International Trade, as its name implies, deals with import transactions and customs issues. Lastly, there is a U.S. Court of Military Appeals, independent of the rest of the court system, which is the final appellate court in which individuals may review courts-martial proceedings.

The nation's highest appellate court is the Supreme Court of the United States, whose nine justices sit in Washington, DC. Contrary to a widespread belief, the national Supreme Court is not available as a court of last resort for any appellant with the perseverance to take a case "all the way to the top." The truth is that the Supreme Court reviews only a limited number of cases that are considered to be particularly important to the legal system, and it chooses which ones it will review.

Limitations on Jurisdiction

We have already said quite a bit about the jurisdiction of courts, but we have not really defined *jurisdiction*. Although this term is used in several different ways, the root concept has to do with the boundaries of a court's authority to hear and decide cases.

Subject-Matter Jurisdiction

No court has unlimited jurisdiction to hear and decide all kinds of cases. One type of limitation on jurisdiction is based either on the subject matter of the controversy or on the nature of the parties. For example, as discussed earlier, probate courts deal only with cases involving property left by deceased persons, and juvenile courts handle only those cases in which children are involved.

Territorial Jurisdiction

Every court serves some specified geographical area, which is known as its *territory of jurisdiction*. The territorial jurisdiction of the Supreme Court of the United States, the Court of Appeals of New York, and the Boston Municipal Court, for instance, is indicated in the official title of each court. If the judges on a court are elected, residents of the territory of jurisdiction vote to elect them. If a court is empowered to grant jury trials, jurors are selected from among persons living within the territory. Past decisions of a court are in a sense "law" within the territory, and cases brought before the court ordinarily have some connection with the territory.

This geographical connotation of jurisdiction accounts for a common practice of speaking of a jurisdiction as if it were a particular area. When we say, for instance, that a decision of the Massachusetts Supreme Judicial Court is a binding precedent "throughout the jurisdiction," we mean that it is binding throughout Massachusetts or, more literally, throughout the territory of jurisdiction of the Massachusetts Supreme Judicial Court. In general, states are the most significant territorial units of jurisdiction in the U.S. legal system.

Jurisdiction over Particular Persons and Property

Let us suppose that BUYER institutes a lawsuit against SELLER in the Superior Court of Massachusetts, asking for $10,000 in damages for breach of contract. Let us suppose, too, that the Superior Court has jurisdiction over this type of controversy and that BUYER and SELLER signed the contract now at issue in Suffolk County in Massachusetts. It is still quite possible that the court may not have jurisdiction to try BUYER's lawsuit.

This is because another rule on jurisdiction requires that a court have jurisdiction over the physical person of the defendant who is being sued or over some of the defendant's property. This is, first, a matter of the court's ability to exercise some control over the defendant. Officials who serve a state court never have power to act outside the state, and frequently they even lack power to act outside the court's judicial district. Hence the court wants to be shown, before it hears a case and renders a decision, that there is some chance to make its decision effective. It is also important to make sure that defendants know that they are being sued. And a plaintiff's efforts to prove that a court has jurisdiction will most likely make the defendant aware of what is happening.

How can BUYER demonstrate to a court that it has jurisdiction over SELLER? The most common procedure is for her to ask the court clerk to issue a *summons* (a document notifying SELLER that BUYER is suing him) and then to arrange to have the summons served on SELLER. There are a number of alternative methods for serving SELLER with a summons, but ordinarily it is delivered to him in person or, if he is a resident of the district, to his residence or place of business. Except under limited circumstances we need not consider here, summonses usually cannot be served outside the state in which they are issued. If BUYER succeeds in having a summons validly served on SELLER, a court will assume that a sufficient connection has been established between SELLER and the court's territory of jurisdiction to warrant its proceeding to hear the case.

If BUYER were suing SELLER in connection with property owned by SELLER located in Suffolk County, it might under some circumstances be sufficient for BUYER to prove to a court that it has jurisdiction over the property. In that event, the court could make a decision affecting the property even though it never asserted its jurisdiction over SELLER'S person.

State versus Federal Jurisdiction

The great majority of cases can be tried only in state courts, since they do not involve subject matter or parties that would bring the cases within jurisdiction of the federal courts. A much smaller number of cases fall exclusively within jurisdiction of the federal courts. And between these two groups is a sizable class of cases for which jurisdiction of the state and federal courts overlaps.

Most cases over which the federal courts have jurisdiction fall into one of two categories:

Cases Involving Diversity of Citizenship. A large proportion of cases in the federal district courts are there solely because the respective parties are citizens of different states. The authors of the U.S. Constitution, apprehensive of state-court bias against out-of-state parties, gave Congress authority to allow such cases to be brought to federal courts. Congress has decided that when the parties in a lawsuit are citizens of different states and when the amount in controversy exceeds $50,000, a party may bring the case to the federal courts.

All such cases may also be tried in state courts but, for various reasons, including the impression that federal judges are more competent and broader in their views than their state counterparts, one party or the other in a lawsuit often chooses to take advantage of the privilege to be heard in federal court.

Cases Involving Federal Questions. There are a number of subjects over which Congress has decided the federal courts should have *exclusive* jurisdiction. Their jurisdiction is exerted even if diversity of citizenship does not exist and the amount in controversy does not exceed the $50,000 level. Trademarks, copyrights, patents, bankruptcy, and admiralty actions are all examples of the sort of cases over which federal courts exert exclusive jurisdiction. There are, however, many federal questions that have not been categorized as exclusively the domain of federal courts, and these may routinely be heard in state courts.

Conflict of Laws

Once a court has decided it has authority to hear a case, it may also have to decide whether to apply local rules of law or those of some other territorial jurisdiction. Many people take it for granted that the courts of State X always apply the legal rules of State X in deciding cases, but this is not necessarily true. Let us suppose, for instance, that BUYER and SELLER make a contract in Illinois in which they agree that SELLER will sell to BUYER some machinery located in Indiana and that the machinery will be delivered to BUYER's plant in that state. Instead, SELLER sells the machinery to someone else, and BUYER is now preparing to sue her for breach of contract. SELLER currently lives in Pittsburgh, Pennsylvania, and BUYER decides that it will be simplest to bring his suit in the Allegheny County Court of Common Pleas in Pennsylvania.

Assume that Illinois, Indiana, and Pennsylvania have slightly different rules with respect to sales contracts. Which state's rules should be applied in this case? Although the Allegheny County Court ordinarily applies Pennsylvania rules, there are perhaps reasons for not applying them in this particular case. For one thing, it seems likely that BUYER and SELLER, if they gave the matter any thought at all when they entered into the contract, contemplated that the law of Illinois (where the contract was made) or of Indiana (where it was to be performed) would apply.

For us to examine here the principles by which problems of this sort are solved would carry us far afield. The body of legal principles governing such situations is known as *conflict of laws,* and it is sufficiently complex that you will need to complete law school to understand it.

Federal courts also have problems in deciding what set of rules to apply to a case. Since BUYER is not a citizen of Pennsylvania but of Illinois and since his claim exceeds $50,000, he can exercise his right to sue SELLER in the federal district court in Pittsburgh. What rules of contract law will the federal court apply? Will it apply Pennsylvania, Illinois, or Indiana rules, or will it apply some sort of federal rule? In general, the federal court in Pittsburgh will try to apply the same contract rules as the state court in Pittsburgh would have applied if the case had been brought before it.

THE PROCESS OF ADJUDICATION

Now that we know something about the courts and their jurisdictions, we can begin to discuss the process by which a civil suit is adjudicated in the courts. Again, *adjudication* refers to proceedings in which a controversy (either a civil case or a criminal prosecution) is judged. In civil suits, the parties are often called litigants in a process of *litigation*, or contesting a lawsuit in a court. First we must distinguish between two classes of issues that the courts are called upon to resolve.

Issues of Fact and Issues of Law

The basic tasks of courts in adjudication are (a) to appraise the *evidence* presented by the parties to support their allegations about the facts, and (b) to appraise the *arguments* presented by the parties to support their assertions about which rules of law should be applied to the facts. Conflicting evidence creates *questions* (or *issues*) *of fact*; conflicting arguments create *questions* (or *issues*) *of law*.

Three kinds of cases come before the courts. First are cases in which there is no doubt about what rules to apply once the facts have been established. Second are cases in which there is no dispute over the facts but a very real dispute over the proper rules to apply to those facts. Third are cases in which there is disagreement about both the facts and the applicable rules.

At first, the distinction between questions of fact and questions of law seems perfectly obvious. A question of fact concerns what happened (or, in some cases, what is happening or will happen). To be more precise, it may involve an event, a relationship, a condition, or a state of mind. In the BUYER-SELLER example above, such factual questions as these might arise:

> What words did BUYER address to SELLER? (*event*)
> Had BUYER and SELLER previously been on friendly terms? (*relationship*)
> Was BUYER over twenty-one years old? (*condition*)
> Was BUYER speaking seriously when he made his proposal? (*state of mind*)

To answer a pure question of fact should require no knowledge of the law. However, a question of law involves determining what legal rule to apply to a given set of facts, and clearly requires knowledge of the law. A convenient way of formulating a question of law is: "Given this combination of facts, what is the applicable rule?" How a court answers a question of law is important not only to the parties concerned but to the legal system as a whole, because the court's ruling may become a precedent affecting decisions in similar cases in the future. Answers to questions of fact have no such significance.

All this seems simple and straightforward. Unfortunately, however, some of the questions that arise in cases cannot be classified neatly as pure questions of fact or pure questions of law. Consider, for instance, these questions: "Was DRIVER driving negligently?" "Is HUSBAND still married to WIFE?" "Did BUYER make SELLER a valid offer?"

None of these questions can be characterized as purely factual or purely legal. Each contains both an element of "what happened?" and an element of "what are the rules?" Moreover, the elements must be considered together: To try to isolate a pure question of fact would simply not be worthwhile, for in each case the factual element is stated in terms of legal concepts. We must know something about the law (of negligence, marriage, and contract) to know which facts matter. When the rule is that "all who drive over sixty miles per hour are guilty of the offense of speeding," then the question to be answered is one of pure fact: "Was John driving over sixty miles per hour?" No knowledge of law is needed to answer this.

But when the rule is that "all who drive negligently may be liable for harm they do," the question "Was DRIVER driving negligently?" can be answered only by someone who knows what legal negligence is. Further, we cannot transform this question into a pure question of fact by substituting for the definition of negligence. For instance, we cannot answer the question "Was DRIVER driving with less care than a reasonably prudent person would have shown under the same circumstances?" unless we know how a court goes about measuring DRIVER's conduct against that of "a reasonably prudent person."

Similarly, the question "Are HUSBAND and WIFE still married?" cannot be answered without reference to legal rules about the formation and dissolution of marriages. Nor can we say whether BUYER made SELLER a valid offer without knowing something about the various combinations of circumstances that the law says may constitute a valid offer, to which the circumstances of BUYER's proposal must be compared. In short, the factual and legal elements in these questions are inextricably intertwined. Consequently, writers about the law recognize a class of questions that they call *mixed questions of law and fact.*

You may ask why it matters how a particular question is classified. It matters because questions of fact and questions of law are handled quite differently in the courts. As we shall see in Chapter 3, when a case is tried before a judge and jury, the jury's basic function is to find the facts, which are usually disputed by the parties (e.g., the parties offer conflicting versions of what happened). Determining which version of the facts is most credible is the province of the jury. Doing so is supposed to require no knowledge of law. The trial judge, on the other hand, rules on issues of law. Moreover, courts of appeal normally accept the trial jury's findings of fact as conclusive, and they review only answers that the trial court has given to questions of law.

Significantly, no special provision is made for mixed questions. Over the years, judges have put some questions that were really mixed into the fact category and others into the law category. Their classification has depended on tradition and on policy judgments as to what juries and judges do best, rather than on logic. The question of whether DRIVER was driving negligently is normally treated as a question of fact; in other words, it is answered by a jury whenever a jury is hearing a case. The legal component of the question is dealt with by the judge when explaining the rules of negligence to the jurors and then instructing them to apply those rules to the facts they find.

The classification of the question of whether BUYER made a valid offer to SELLER may depend on whether the proposal was oral or written. If BUYER simply made an informal oral proposal, the question of whether he intended his words to be a legal offer is usually treated as a question of fact. But if BUYER wrote SELLER a letter, the question of whether he made an offer is much more likely to be treated as a question of law. This difference in the treatment given to oral utterances and to written communications seems to be largely a matter of policy, representing perhaps a decision that jurors are well qualified to decide what a person meant by spoken words, in light of evidence as to tone and demeanor, whereas judges should be left to interpret the more calculated intent behind a letter. Often the distinctions are fine ones.

Defining and Resolving the Issues

Using an actual case for illustration, we shall now trace the steps that make up the process of adjudication. The case involves the concept of *employment-at-will.* According to this long-standing concept, employers may fire for *any* reason employees who are not under contract. Of course, we know that today an employer may not fire someone for reasons that discriminate, for example, on the basis of race, gender, or national origin. But can an employer fire you for refusing to follow an order to violate a law?

In our example, Judy Boyle brought a lawsuit against Vista Eyewear and David Baker, the president of Vista. In legal terminology, the parties were adversaries. Judy Boyle was the plaintiff (the party who sued) in the lower courts of Missouri, while Vista Eyewear and David Baker were the defendants (the people being sued). Although Boyle's name appears first on the appellate court decision, the trial court plaintiff's name is not always listed first. In an appellate decision, the first name is often that of the person who loses in the trial courts and appeals—the appellant. This person may have been either the plaintiff or the defendant in the trial court. The person against whom an appeal is made is called the appellee.

The decision shown here is that of the Missouri Court of Appeals. (Nearly all the decisions you will read in this book are decisions of the appellate courts, for reasons that will be explained shortly.) The report of the decision is taken from an official *reporter*, the report that each state publishes of its judicial decisions. In addition, these reports are published by Thomson/West Publishing Company, which has organized its National Reporter system by regions.

The report consists of excerpts from the opinion written by Judge Nugent. An opinion not only announces the court's decision, but also presents a justification of it. Note the reasons given justifying the decision in this case.

Boyle v. Vista Eyewear

Missouri Court of Appeals
700 S.W. 2d 859 (Mo. App. 1985)

NUGENT, JUDGE: Vista Eyewear, Inc. and David A. Baker, defendants, appeal from a judgment for plaintiff Judy A. Boyle following a jury verdict awarding Mrs. Boyle $1.00 in actual damages and $15,000 punitive damages for furnishing her a service letter which falsely states the reasons her employment was terminated. Mrs. Boyle cross-appeals from dismissal of the wrongful discharge count of her petition. We affirm the circuit court's judgment on Counts I (dealing with overtime compensation) and II (dealing with her service letter) and reverse its judgment on Count III (wrongful discharge) and remand that count.

Plaintiff, Judy A. Boyle, worked as a lab helper for Vista Eyewear, an optical manufacturing company, from September, 1977, to January 9, 1979, in Vista's bench department. Her duties included hand-edging, hardening and testing eyeglass lenses produced by defendant. The regulations of the United States Food and Drug Administration require all eyeglass manufacturers to test all glass lenses for their resistance to breaking or shattering before such lenses may be sold or distributed to the public.

Plaintiff's evidence tended to establish that the standard industry procedure is to submit all lenses to either a hardening chemical treatment or heat treatment.

Plaintiff and her witnesses testified that the drop ball impact test was never used by Vista and that on all rush jobs and on some other lens jobs the hardening treatment was skipped. Nevertheless, plaintiff was required to initial a form for each set of eyeglasses stating that she had heat or chemically treated and impact tested the lenses.

Mrs. Boyle complained to her supervisor and to defendant David Baker, president and part owner of Vista, about the company's practice of not hardening and testing lenses. When she spoke to Mr. Baker expressing concern about potential injuries to customer's eyes, he said that it was not her worry, that he had insurance that would take care of it if he got sued. Plaintiff told Mr. Baker that "money was a poor substitute for somebody's eyesight." She testified that Baker "was very aggravated with me. He told me . . . 'Just go do what you're told. I don't want to hear any more about it.'"

She warned her employer that she would report the violations of the law to governmental authorities, but defendant continued their practice. During her tenure with Vista, she repeatedly urged her employer to make certain that the lenses were hardened and tested in a manner consistent with what she believed to be the law.

After months of such fruitless urgings . . . she complained to the federal Food and Drug Administration (FDA). She told Mr. Baker what she had done and again he was aggravated. Then Mrs. Boyle told Mr. Baker that she would perform the required eyeglass lens hardening and testing.

Mr. Baker asked Mrs. Boyle to withdraw the complaints and to tell the FDA that she had lied. He also instructed other employees to throw broken glass into the bottom of the drop ball testing machine, apparently to give the FDA the false impression that drop ball testing was being done. A few weeks later in November, 1978, OSHA conducted an investigation of defendant's premises.

About two months after the complaints to the FDA, on January 9, 1979, David Douglas, plaintiff's supervisor let plaintiff know that something was wrong. He told her that nothing was wrong with her production or work. He said that the problem was that she had reported to Mr. Baker, the president, that Douglas was using drugs. Mrs. Boyle asked Douglas to go with her to Mr. Baker to prove that she had not so accused him. Douglas refused and fired her on the spot. On cross-examination plaintiff quoted Douglas as saying the problem was not with her work but, "I am mad because you have turned me in on drugs to Mr. Baker." He then yelled, "You are fired. Get out." When she protested that she had not told Mr. Baker that he was using drugs, Douglas said, "Yes, you did. You are fired."

Plaintiff went immediately to Mr. Baker's office to protest. She told him what had happened and of Douglas' accusation of her. Baker said nothing—he just looked at the floor—when she challenged him, asserting that he knew Douglas was not telling the truth. She asked Baker if the reason she was being fired was that she had gone to the federal agencies, but Baker, she testified, just stood there and said nothing. . . .

In due time, Mrs. Boyle made a written request to David Baker and Vista for a service letter stating the true reason for her discharge. In his answer, Mr. Baker wrote that the reason for her discharge was her arguing with her departmental supervisor.

Thereafter, Mrs. Boyle filed her petition for unpaid overtime compensation (Count I) and for damages for failure to issue a service letter that correctly stated the true reasons for her discharge (Count II). She alleged that she was fired for the complaints made to OSHA and the FDA and not, as defendants stated in their service letter, for arguing with her supervisor. Later she added Count III alleging that she was wrongfully discharged from her employment for filing complaints with OSHA and FDA.

Defendants filed a motion to dismiss Count III on the ground that she was an at-will employee and that Missouri law does not recognize a cause of action for wrongful discharge of such an employee absent a contract of employment or statutory authority. . . . The trial court granted defendants' motion and dismissed Count III for failure to state a claim.

On her cross-appeal, Mrs. Boyle asserts that the trial court erred in dismissing Count III of her petition for failure to state a cause of action. [The court went on to affirm counts I and II.]

III. Public Policy Exception to At-Will Employment Doctrine

On her cross-appeal, plaintiff Boyle claims that the trial court erred in dismissing her Count III for failure to state a cause of action. She asserts that *Count III states a claim for wrongful discharge of an at-will employee in violation of public policy* as expressed in the federal statute and regulation governing manufacture of eyeglasses [emphasis added].

Count III sounding in tort, alleges in its pertinent part, that the defendants violated certain public policies by (a) manufacturing unsafe eyeglasses, the lenses of which had not been hardened and tested in compliance with the regulations of the Food and Drug Administration; (b) taking reprisals against an employee for reporting violations of law to the authorities; (c) failing to protect citizens against dangerous, nonshatterproof eyeglasses; and (d) falsely attesting to prescribing physicians that lenses had been hardened and tested. It further alleges that the defendants fired plaintiff because she warned them that she would notify the authorities of their practices if they did not stop them and because the defendants chose to continue their practice of falsely attesting to the hardening and testing of lenses. Count III finally alleges lost wages and mental anguish and seeks actual and punitive damages.

Count III is based upon an exception to the employment-at-will doctrine, a rule most recently re-enunciated in *Dake v. Tuell*, 687 S.W.2d 191 (Mo. 1985) (en banc) filed April 2, a decision we have been anticipating in the belief that the Supreme Court might furnish us additional guidance on the most recent developments in the law pertaining to discharge of at-will employees.

Although in *recent years the courts in twenty-eight states have to one degree or another recognized a new public policy exception to the at-will employment doctrine*, the plaintiffs in *Dake* chose not to invoke that exception but proceeded on the theory of prima facie tort.

Dake, as the Supreme Court noted, in its opening paragraph, involved the "sole issue . . . whether discharged at will employees can maintain a suit for wrongful discharge against their former employers by cloaking their claims in the misty shroud of prima facie tort." Predictably, the court said, "No," as have other courts to which this particular prima facie tort question has been presented. See, *Murphy v. American Home Products* 58, N.Y.2d 293, 448 N.E.2d 86, 90–91. In *Dake* the court held that the prima facie tort theory is not available for use in circumventing the well-established employment-at-will doctrine. That doctrine simply provides that an employer can discharge for cause or without cause an at-will employee who does not otherwise fall within the protective reach of a contrary statutory provision. *Dake*, 687 S.W.2d at 193.

The Supreme Court, therefore, chose not to answer the unasked question whether in that case the public policy exception was available to those two Missouri at-will employees. In its tautly written opinion the court deliberately confined its decision to the prima facie tort question presented.

B. "Public Policy"

[5] The public policy exception is a narrow exception to the at-will employment doctrine. It provides that an at-will employee who has been discharged by an employer in violation of a clear mandate of public policy has a cause of action against the employer for wrongful discharge.

[6] "Public policy" is that principle of law which holds that no one can lawfully do that which tends to be injurious to the public or against the public good. . . . It finds its sources in the state constitution, in the letter and purpose of a constitutional, statutory or regulatory provision or scheme, in the judicial decisions of the state and national courts, in "the constant practices of the government officials," and in certain instances, in professional codes of ethics. The at-will employment doctrine itself is judicially enunciated public policy.

In this case the public policy alleged to have been violated is set out in the federal Food and Drug Administration's regulation found in 21 C.F.R. §801.410. In summary, that regulation first notes that the data "available on the frequency of eye injuries resulting from the shattering of ordinary crown class lenses constitutes an avoidable hazard to the eye of the wearer." The physician or optometrist has the option of ordering glass, plastic or laminated lenses made impact resistant by any method, but all such "lenses shall be capable of withstanding the impact test" described in paragraph (d) (2) of §841.410.

The regulation then requires that each finished impact-resistant glass lens for prescription use, with certain specified exceptions, be individually tested and shown to be capable of withstanding the impact test described in paragraph (d) (2).

C. Application of the Public Policy Exception

[7] We turn now to the application of the public policy exception to Mrs. Boyle's case. First, the federal regulation in question, 21 C.F.R. §801.410, is a clear mandate of public policy. It is a set of specific directives to eyeglass manufacturers by the Food and Drug Administration, the federal agency charged with statutory responsibility in the area that includes the manufacture of eyeglasses. This regulation, promulgated by the Secretary of Health and Human Services, "has the force and effect of law to the same extent as though written into the statute." *Archambault v. United States*, 224 F.2d 925, 928 (10th Cir. 1955).

The clear mandate of the law and the public policy enunciated in the federal statute and regulation was to prescribe a process of manufacturing eyeglasses which was designed to give eyeglass wearers maximum protection against eye injuries and blindness.

Second, the federal regulation clearly imposes upon defendants as manufacturers a positive duty to harden and test each glass lens they manufacture, but in this case that duty also fell on plaintiff as an employee engaged in the very part of the manufacturing process in which hardening and testing and the mandated record keeping is done. In addition, as the person who conducted the tests, she had the positive duty under regulation to maintain records of the tests.

Defendants rely on *Bell v. Faulkner*, 75 S.W.2d 612 (Mo. App. 1934) as authority for the proposition that defendants could without liability fire plaintiff, an at-will employee, at any time with or without reason. There defendants fired Bell because he would not vote for certain candidates in city election and would not force members of his family to do so. He sued for wrongful discharge, contending that defendants' conduct was a direct violation of a state penal statute regarding voting and that such violation gave him a cause of action. In reversing the judgment for *Bell*, the court did not address the question whether the public policy of the state had been violated. It simply said that the penal statute did not itself create a cause of action in plaintiff for damages. The court did not discuss and apparently did not consider whether, aside from the statute, Bell might have had a common law action for wrongful discharge, the issue we are considering.

Plaintiff Boyle was fired, according to Count III, because she warned defendants that she would notify the FDA of their illegal practices if they did not stop and because, despite her warnings, defendants chose to continue to violate the positive duty laid upon them by the federal regulation and to continue to insist that their employees do the same. She might have added, as the record clearly indicates and the jury apparently believed, that she was also fired for refusing to violate FDA regulation, for persisting in hardening and testing lenses in compliance with the regulation and for actually reporting defendants' violations to the FDA. Under the public policy exception, any one of those allegations, including those now in Count III would state cause of action. She should be permitted to amend her petition accordingly.

Conclusion

[8] Although employers generally are free to discharge at-will employees with or without cause at any time, they are not free to require employees, on pain of losing their jobs, to commit unlawful acts or acts in violation of a clear mandate of public policy expressed in the constitution, statutes and regulations promulgated pursuant to statute. The at-will employment doctrine does not depend upon

the employer having such a right. The employer is bound to know the public policies of the state and nation as expressed in their constitutions, statutes, judicial decisions and administrative regulations, particularly, as here, those bearing directly upon the employer's business.

As many of the decided cases illustrate, the burden of the at-will employment doctrine seems to be falling most heavily and harshly upon professional and upper and middle level employees. They have the least protection. Most are at-will employees and few have job security through union or individually negotiated contracts. They have the most to lose, frequently being the long-term employees who have the greatest responsibility and substantial investment in and the highest expectations from their careers. They are the most vulnerable to the improper demands of employers who find it profitable to take chances with antitrust and consumer fraud violations, environmental pollution, health-related misconduct, defense procurement fraud, and the like. The at-will employment doctrine does not include, contemplate or require a privilege in the employer to subject its employees to the risks of civil and criminal liability that participation in such activities entails.

Accordingly, *where an employer has discharged an at-will employee because that employee refused to violate the law or public policy* as expressed in the constitution, statutes and regulations promulgated pursuant to statute, or because the employee reported to his superiors or to public authorities serious misconduct that constitutes violations of the law and of such well established and clearly mandated public policy, *the employee has a cause of action in tort for damages for discharge.*

In this case plaintiff Boyle has stated a cause of action for wrongful discharge against the defendants in alleging that they fired her for threatening to report their activities and practices to the Food and Drug Administration. Upon remand she should be permitted if she wishes to amend Count III of her petition to incorporate those allegations the evidence seems to support and which, when liberally construed, Count III seems to imply. Accordingly, we reverse the judgment of the circuit court on Count III of the petition and remand that count to the circuit court for further proceedings; in all other respects we affirm the judgment of the circuit court.

KENNEDY, J. concurs.
BERREY, J. dissents by way of separate opinion.

BERREY, JUDGE, dissenting:
I respectfully dissent from the majority opinion. In view of the recent pronouncement regarding discharge of at-will employee as set forth in *Dake v. Tuell*, 687 S.W.2d 191, 193 (Mo. banc 1985) I must dissent.

The answer to a question of law is sometimes referred to as the *rule of the case*, since it is likely to affect the decision of future cases. As we shall learn in Chapter 4, however, the precise content and breadth of such a "rule" become clear only as later cases arise and the courts decide them. Although you may not understand every word and phrase in this opinion, the question of law facing the court and the court's answer to that question should be clear enough. Try to restate them in your own words.

Does the decision in this case provide legal protection for a whistleblower turning in an employer who violates the law? If a worker does blow the whistle on an employer, is the protection enough to avoid disruption to the worker's employment and career? These are important questions, because the answers (yes and no) suggest employees may at times be required to seek other employment if they wish to behave in a professional and ethical manner in some workplaces. Although highly desirable in most work settings, acting in a professional manner may be inconvenient in some situations.

Note Judge Nugent's reference to a "professional codes of ethics" as a source of public policy that might protect actions of a whistleblower like Boyle, and his suggestion that some employees are more vulnerable than others to "improper demands of employers who find it profitable to take chances with antitrust and consumer fraud violations, environmental pollution, health-related misconduct, defense procurement fraud, and the like." Consider the following Code of Ethics of the National Association of Environmental Professionals (NAEP), whose members are mostly individuals employed by privately owned consulting firms and corporations engaged in environmental management and impact assessment activities (see Exhibit 2.1).

Is there anything in the NAEP code of ethics that might protect employees who refuse to break the law from discharge by their employer, similar to Boyle? In 1990, a federal district court jury in Newark, New Jersey, awarded over $1.3 million to Dr. Valcar Bowman Jr., a former environmental manager for Mobil Chemical Corporation, for wrongful discharge after he refused to change environmental audit reports and remove environmental records from a Mobil plant in Bakersfield, California (Marcus and Adler 1990). Dr. Bowman was certified by NAEP as an environmental professional and referred to its code of ethics at trial. An appeal by Mobil was rejected (*Bowman v. Mobil*, 945 F.2d 394, Cir. 3, 1991; Geyelin 1991).

Although Congress enacted the Whistleblower Protection Act of 1989 (5 *U.S. Code* §1221), it is widely viewed as ineffective in protecting employees from retaliation by employers (Kohn, Kohn, and Colapinto 2004) due to the disruption caused to employees' careers and the expense of defending their rights in court. As a result, public interest groups such as Public Employees for Environmental Responsibility (PEER 2007) have emerged to provide support for whistleblowers and encourage accountability in government organizations.

Pretrial Efforts to Define the Issues

The first stage of *Boyle v. Vista Eyewear* took place in the trial court. What happened there? The answer to this question is nearly always to be found near the beginning of the appellate-court report. Judge Nugent's opinion tells us that Vista Eyewear Inc. and David Baker appeal from a judgment for plaintiff Judy Boyle. The meaning of these words will become clear as we consider the steps in a lawsuit that preceded trial.

When the plaintiff (Boyle) first decided to bring suit, she had her lawyer send the defendant (Vista Eyewear) a legal document known as a *complaint*. This complaint consisted of a brief summary of Boyle's version of what had happened and stated what remedies she was asking. A complaint normally accompanies the summons, discussed a few pages back. Once Vista Eyewear received the summons and the complaint, it was obliged either to make some sort of response or else lose the suit by default.

A defendant's response to a complaint may take several forms:

1. *Answer.* If the defendant thinks he can contest the plaintiff's version of the facts, he will send the plaintiff a document known as an *answer.* In this answer he may deny all the plaintiff's important allegations of fact. (For instance, Vista might simply have denied that it had terminated Boyle.) Denying an allegation in the complaint immedi-

Exhibit 2.1
Code of Ethics and Standards of Practice for Environmental Professionals

The objectives of Environmental Professionals are to conduct their personal and professional lives and activities in an ethical manner. Honesty, justice and courtesy form moral philosophy which, associated with a mutual interest among people, constitute the foundation of ethics. Environmental Professionals should recognize such a standard, not in passive observance, but as a set of dynamic principles guiding their conduct and way of life. It is their duty to practice their profession according to this Code of Ethics.

As the keystone of professional conduct is integrity, Environmental Professionals will discharge their duties with fidelity to the public, their employers, clients, with fairness and impartiality to all. It is their duty to interest themselves in public welfare, and to be ready to apply their special knowledge for the benefit of mankind and their environment.

Creed

The objectives of an Environmental Professional are:
1. To recognize and attempt to reconcile societal and individual human needs with responsibility for physical, natural, and cultural systems.
2. To promote and develop policies, plans, activities and projects that achieve complementary and mutual support between natural and man-made, and present and future components of the physical, natural and cultural environment.

Ethics

As an Environmental Professional I will:
1. Be personally responsible for the validity of all data collected, analyses performed, or plans developed by me or under my direction. I will be responsible and ethical in my professional activities.
2. Encourage research, planning, design, management and review of activities in a scientifically and technically objective manner. I will incorporate the best principles of the environmental sciences for the mitigation of environmental harm and enhancement of environmental quality.
3. Not condone misrepresentation of work I have performed or that was performed under my direction.
4. Examine all of my relationships or actions, which could be legitimately interpreted as a conflict of interest by clients, officials, the public or peers. In any instance where I have financial or personal interest in the activities with which they are directly or indirectly involved, I will make a full disclosure of that interest to my employer, client, or other affected parties.
5. Not engage in conduct involving dishonesty, fraud, deceit, or misrepresentation or discrimination.
6. Not accept fees wholly or partially contingent on the client's desired result where that desired result conflicts with my professional judgment.

Guidance for Practice as an Environmental Professional

As an Environmental Professional I will:
1. Encourage environmental planning to begin in the earliest stages of project conceptualization.

2. Recognize that total environmental management involves the consideration of all environmental factors including: technical, economical, ecological, and sociopolitical and their relationships.

3. Incorporate the best principle of design and environmental planning when recommending measures to reduce environmental harm and enhance environmental quality.

4. Conduct my analysis, planning, design and review my activities primarily in subject areas for which I am qualified, and shall encourage and recognize that participation of other professionals in subject areas where I am less experienced. I shall utilize and participate in interdisciplinary teams wherever practical to determine impacts, define and evaluate all reasonable alternatives to proposed actions, and assess short-term versus long-term productivity with and without the project or action.

5. Seek common, adequate, and sound technical grounds for communication with and respect for the contributions of other professionals in developing and reviewing policies, plans, activities and projects.

6. Determine that the policies, plans, activities or projects in which I am involved are consistent with all governing laws, ordinances, guidelines, plans and policies to the best of my knowledge and ability.

7. Encourage public participation at the earliest feasible time in an open and productive atmosphere.

8. Conduct my professional activities in a manner that ensures consideration of technically and economically feasible alternatives.

Encourage Development of the Profession

As an Environmental Professional I will:

1. Assist in maintaining the integrity and competence of my profession.

2. Encourage education and research and the development of useful technical information relating to the environmental field.

3. Be prohibited from lobbying in the name of the National Association of Environmental Professionals.

4. Advertise and present my services in a manner that avoids the use of material and methods that may bring discredit to the profession.

Source: Reprinted with permission of the National Association of Environmental Professionals, 389 Main Street, Suite 202, Malden, MA 02148, www.naep.org.

ately raises an issue of fact; the court will have to decide whose allegation is correct. Alternatively, the defendant may admit some of the plaintiff's allegations but go on to allege additional facts that throw new light on the situation. (For instance, Vista might have admitted that it terminated Boyle, but then explained that she had been consistently late for work.)

If the defendant alleges new facts, the plaintiff sometimes responds with a document known as a *reply*. If the reply denies the defendant's allegations, further exchanges, or amendments to the original documents, may be called for.

2. *Counterclaim.* The defendant may respond to the plaintiff's complaint by entering a *counterclaim*; in other words, the defendant may make a claim of his own for dam-

ages against the plaintiff. (For instance, in addition to justifying its firing of Boyle, Vista might have claimed that she had harassed Baker.) A counterclaim may raise issues of fact, issues of law, or both.

3. *Demurrer.* Finally, the response may say, in effect, "Even if all the plaintiff has alleged were true, it would still not provide the basis for a legal claim." This is what is known as a *demurrer* (or a *motion to dismiss.*) A demurrer raises an issue of law. For the sake of completeness, we should note that the plaintiff may demur to the defendant's answer, or a portion of it, and that the defendant may likewise demur to the reply.

This action is in no sense an admission that all the charges made against the defendant by the plaintiff are true. A demurrer admits allegations only for the purpose of argument. It merely says, "Even if these allegations *were* true, they would not constitute a basis for legal action." If the defendant is confident that the complaint states no basis for legal action, a demurrer is the simplest way to dispose of the whole matter.

A simple motion to dismiss, if granted, may allow a plaintiff to bring essentially the same case again with additional allegations, unless it is dismissed "with prejudice" against a recurrence. A defendant who wishes to avoid a recurrence may in some circumstances use a demurrer to move for *summary judgment*, a court judgment that will prevent a repeat trip to court on the same facts.

Standing to Sue

Does being a taxpayer automatically confer on anyone the key to a courtroom door? A threshold consideration in every civil lawsuit concerns whether the plaintiff has *standing to sue*: eligibility to bring a particular case to court. The following decision illustrates the use of a motion for summary judgment that raises this question. Determining standing to sue is one way in which the courts manage their workload, by refusing to hear evidence about allegations that do not represent a real case or controversy. In this case, the court established new criteria restricting who is eligible to bring a case to court.

The National Wildlife Federation (NWF) sued the U.S. Bureau of Land Management (BLM) and other federal parties in federal district court, alleging they had violated the Federal Land Policy and Management Act of 1976 (FLPMA) and the National Environmental Policy Act of 1969 (NEPA) in the course of administering the land withdrawal review program and that their actions should be set aside. Under this program, BLM makes various decisions affecting the status of public lands and their availability for private uses such as mining, grazing cattle, cutting timber, and exploring for oil and gas. The trial court granted a BLM motion for summary judgment, holding that NWF lacked standing to seek judicial review of BLM actions. The Court of Appeals reversed, holding that affidavits of two NWF members were sufficient to establish standing. Excerpts from the decision of a closely divided U.S. Supreme Court ruling that NWF lacked standing appear below. We have italicized certain key passages.

Lujan v. National Wildlife Federation

Supreme Court of the United States
497 U.S. 871 (1990)

JUSTICE SCALIA delivered the opinion of the Court.

In this case we must decide whether respondent, the National Wildlife Federation (hereinafter respondent), is a proper party to challenge actions of the Federal Government relating to certain public lands. . . .

I. In 1976, Congress passed the FLPMA, . . . and established a policy in favor of retaining public lands for multiple use management. . . . It provided that existing classifications of public lands were subject to review in the land use planning process, and that the Secretary [of the Interior] could "modify or terminate any such classification consistent with such land use plans." 1712(d). It also authorized the Secretary to "make, modify, extend or revoke" withdrawals. 1714(a). Finally it directed the Secretary, within 15 years, to review withdrawals in existence in 1976 in 11 western States, 1714(1)(1), and to "determine whether, and for how long, the continuation of the existing withdrawal of the lands would be, in his judgment, consistent with the statutory objectives of the programs for which the lands were dedicated and of the other relevant programs," 1714 (1)(2). Activities undertaken by the BLM to comply with these various provisions constitute what respondent's amended complaint styles the BLM's "land withdrawal review program," which is the subject of the current litigation. . . .

II. In its complaint, respondent averred generally that the reclassification of some withdrawn lands and the return of others to the public domain would open the lands up to mining activities, thereby destroying their natural beauty. . . . Respondent . . . alleged that all of the above actions were "arbitrary, capricious, an abuse of discretion, or otherwise not in accordance with law," and should therefore be set aside pursuant to 10(e) of the APA, 5 U.S.C. 706.

III. A. . . . [R]espondent claims a right to judicial review under 10(a) of the APA, which provides:

"A person suffering legal wrong because of agency action, or adversely affected or aggrieved by agency action within the meaning of a relevant statute, is entitled to judicial review thereof." 5 U.S.C. 702.

This provision contains two separate requirements. First, the person claiming a right to sue must identify some "agency action" that affects him in the specified fashion; it is judicial review "thereof" to which he is entitled. . . . When, as here, review is sought not pursuant to specific authorization in the substantive statute, but only under the general review provisions of the APA, the "agency action" in question must be "final agency action." See 5 U.S.C. 704. . . .

Second, the party seeking review under 702 must show that he has "suffer[ed] legal wrong" because of the challenged agency action, or is "adversely affected or aggrieved" by that action "within the meaning of a relevant statute." Respondent does not assert that it has suffered "legal wrong," so we need only discuss the meaning of "adversely affected or aggrieved . . . within the meaning of a relevant statute." . . . [W]e have said that to be "adversely affected or aggrieved . . . within the meaning" of a statute, the plaintiff must establish that the injury he complains of (his aggrievement, or the adverse effect upon him) falls within the "zone of interests" sought to be protected by the statutory provision whose violation forms the legal basis for his complaint. See *Clarke v. Securities Industry Assn.*, 479 U.S. 388, 396–397 (1987). . . .

B. Because this case comes to us on petitioners' motion for summary judgment, we must assess the record under the standard set forth in Rule 56 of the Federal Rules of Civil Procedure. Rule 56(c) states that a party is entitled to summary judgment in his favor "if the pleadings, depositions, answers to interrogatories, and admissions on file, together with the affidavits, if any, show that there is no genuine issue as to any material fact and that the moving party is entitled to a judgment as a matter of law." Rule 56(e) further provides:

> When a motion for summary judgment is made and supported as provided in this rule, an adverse party may not rest upon the mere allegations or denials of the adverse party's pleading, but the adverse party's response, by affidavits or as otherwise provided in this rule, *must set forth specific facts showing that there is a genuine issue for trial.* [emphasis added] If the adverse party does not so respond, summary judgment, if appropriate, shall be entered against the adverse party.

As we stated in *Celotex Corp. v. Catrett*, 477 U.S. 317 (1986), "the plain language of Rule 56(c) mandates the entry of summary judgment, after adequate time for discovery and upon motion, against a party who fails to make a showing sufficient to establish the existence of an element essential to that party's case, and on which that party will bear the burden of proof at trial." 477 U.S., at 322. Where no such showing is made, "[t]he moving party is 'entitled to a judgment as a matter of law' because the nonmoving party has failed to make a sufficient showing on an essential element of her case with respect to which she has the burden of proof." Id., at 323.

These standards are fully applicable when a defendant moves for summary judgment, in a suit brought under 702, on the ground that the plaintiff has failed to show that he is "adversely affected or aggrieved by agency action within the meaning of a relevant statute." *The burden is on the party seeking review* under 702 *to set forth specific facts* (even though they may be controverted by the Government) showing that he has satisfied its terms. [emphasis added] *Sierra Club v. Morton*, 405 U.S. 727, 740 (1972) . . .

C. We turn, then, to whether the specific facts alleged in the two affidavits considered by the District Court raised a genuine issue of fact as to whether an "agency action" taken by petitioners caused respondent to be "adversely affected or aggrieved . . . within the meaning of a relevant statute." . . .

As for the "agency action" requirement, we think that each of the affidavits can be read, as the Court of Appeals believed, to complain of a particular "agency action" as that term is defined in 551. . . .

We also think that whatever "adverse effect" or "aggrievement" is established by the affidavits was "within the meaning of the relevant statute" i.e., met the "zone of interests" test. . . . The only issue, then, is whether the facts alleged in the affidavits showed that those interests of Peterson and Erman were actually affected. . . .

There is no showing that Peterson's recreational use and enjoyment extends to the particular 4500 acres covered by the decision to terminate classification to the remainder of the two million acres affected by the termination. All she claims is that she uses lands "in the vicinity." The affidavit on its face contains only a bare allegation of injury, and *fails to show specific facts* supporting the affiant's allegation." 699 F. Supp., at 331. . . .

The District Court found the Erman affidavit "similarly flawed." . . .

The Court of Appeals disagreed with the District Court's assessment as to the Peterson affidavit (and thus found it unnecessary to consider the Erman affidavit). . . .

As set forth above, Rule 56(e) provides that judgment "shall be entered" against the nonmoving party unless affidavits or other evidence *"set forth specific facts showing that there is a genuine issue for trial."* [emphasis added] The object of this provision is not to replace conclusory allegations of the complaint or answer with conclusory allegations of an affidavit. Cf. *Anderson v. Liberty Lobby, Inc.*, 477 U.S. 242, 249 (1986) . . . Rather, the purpose of Rule 56 is to enable a party who believes there is no genuine dispute as to a specific fact essential to the other side's case to demand at least one sworn averment of that fact before the lengthy process of litigation continues.

At the margins there is some room for debate as to how "specific" must be the "specific facts" that Rule 56(e) requires in a particular case. But where the fact in question is the one put in issue by the 702 challenge here—whether one of respondent's members has been, or is threatened to be, "adversely affected or aggrieved" by Government action—Rule 56(e) is assuredly not satisfied by averments which state only that one of respondent's members uses unspecified portions of an immense tract of territory, on some portions of which mining activity has occurred or probably will occur by virtue of the governmental action. It will not do to "presume" the missing facts because without them the affidavits would not establish the injury that they generally allege. . . .

IV. We turn next to the Court of Appeals' alternative holding that the four additional member affidavits proffered by respondent in response to the District Court's briefing order established its right to 702 review of agency action.

A. It is impossible that the affidavits would suffice, as the Court of Appeals held, to enable respondent to challenge the entirety of petitioners' so-called "land withdrawal review program." That is not an "agency action" within the meaning of 702, much less a "final agency action" within the meaning of 704. The term "land withdrawal review program" (which as far as we know is not derived from any authoritative text) does not refer to a single BLM order or regulation, or even to a completed universe of particular BLM orders and regulations. It is simply the name by which petitioners have occasionally referred to the continuing (and thus constantly changing) operations of the BLM in reviewing withdrawal revocation applications and the classifications of public lands and developing land use plans as required by the FLPMA. . . .

The case-by-case approach that this requires is understandably frustrating to an organization such as respondent, which has as its objective across-the-board protection of our Nation's wildlife and the streams and forests that support it. But this is the traditional, and remains the normal, mode of operation of the courts. Except where Congress explicitly provides for our correction of the administrative process at a higher level of generality, we intervene in the administration of the laws only when, and to the extent that, a specific "final agency action" has an actual or immediately threatened effect. *Toilet Goods Assn.*, 387 U.S., at 164–166. . . .

For the foregoing reasons, the judgment of the Court of Appeals is reversed.

REHNQUIST, C.J., AND WHITE, O'CONNOR, AND KENNEDY, J.J., CONCUR
BLACKMUN, J., filed a dissenting opinion, in which BRENNAN, MARSHALL, and STEVENS, J.J., joined.

Questions

1. What criteria did the court apply in this case to determine if a plaintiff has standing? Is a general interest in or concern about something of value sufficient to give one standing to sue?
2. Must the harm alleged to have been suffered by the plaintiff be of a financial nature?
3. Do you think the outcome in this case may have been due to poor preparation of the complaint and supporting documents by plaintiff's attorney?

The documents exchanged by the plaintiff and the defendant—the plaintiff's complaint; the defendant's answer, demurrer, or counterclaim; and, if necessary, the plaintiff's reply—are known collectively as the *pleadings*. They have three purposes: to narrow the issues to those really in dispute, to let the parties know beforehand what issues they must be prepared to deal with at trial, and to inform the trial judge (who receives copies) what the case is about before the trial begins.

For many years the exchange of pleadings was the only means used to narrow the issues in dispute prior to trial. Yet the pleadings were often too brief to reveal all the details of the charges and countercharges that the parties intended to make against one another in the trial. Delays were often caused, and injustice sometimes done, when some element of the allegations of fact or of the legal arguments presented by one party caught the other party by surprise during the trial. Today most courts rely on various procedures, known as *discovery procedures*, to eliminate the element of surprise from the trial of a lawsuit. One of these procedures, for instance, calls for the use of depositions—sworn statements made by parties or witnesses before a court officer in response to questions put by the attorneys of the opposing parties. Still another procedure for clarifying issues before the trial is the *pretrial conference*, at which opposing lawyers review in the judge's presence their legal arguments and the evidence they propose to produce. In many courts this procedure has proved remarkably effective not only in narrowing the issues but in bringing about out-of-court settlements before any trial takes place.

The Trial Stage

A surprisingly large proportion of lawsuits initiated actually do get settled out of court. But what does a trial court do with those cases that come to trial?

How a case is handled in the trial court depends in part on whether the facts are in dispute. In cases where the only issues in dispute are issues of law raised by demurrers and other types of *motions* (for instance, motions challenging the court's jurisdiction), a relatively simple procedure can be used. No jury is needed (since jurors, being laypersons, have nothing to do with interpreting the law), and no witnesses have to be heard. The judge, who has read the lawyers' written arguments about the applicable rules (known as *briefs*), conducts what is often known as a *hearing on motions*, in which he or she listens to oral arguments and sometimes asks questions. At the conclusion, or at a later date if the problem is difficult, the judge hands down a decision either granting or denying the motion. This decision is often accompanied by a short opinion (these opinions, unlike those of appellate judges, are usually not published). Cases that may be disposed of on the basis of such pretrial motions are generally heard and decided expeditiously.

When there are disputed questions of fact in a case, however, a full-dress trial must be held to give the parties a chance to present evidence in support of their respective versions of the facts. Sometimes trials are held before a judge alone, in which event the judge decides both legal and factual issues. But cases involving claims for damages must ordinarily be tried before a jury if either party so desires.

As we have mentioned, the jury's task is to "find the facts"—that is, to decide from the evidence presented which party's version of the facts is, on the whole, more convincing. This is not because jurors are regarded as expert fact finders; indeed, most jurors have had no previous experience in weighing conflicting evidence introduced in a trial. Rather, it is because jurors are ordinary citizens who are presumed capable of making common-sense judgments. Jurors are, in a sense, surrogates for the mythical "reasonably prudent person" the courts would like to believe resides within the typical citizen, reflecting the collective moral standards of the community. In most trials the jury is also responsible for applying the rules, as outlined by the judge, to the facts it has found.

The judge's task in a trial is to rule on motions made by the opposing attorneys during the proceedings. Each motion raises an issue of law. An attorney may contend, for instance, that there has been an irregularity in the conduct of the trial; or that a particular item of evidence that the opposing attorney wishes to present should be excluded; or that the judge's instructions to the jury are incorrect; or that since the opposing side has failed to present a case that could conceivably be regarded as convincing, a verdict should be entered for the attorney's client at once. (Each of these motions is considered further in Chapter 3.) The trial judge's ruling about the law on any one of these motions may provide a basis for appeal.

The Appellate Stage

Most cases that come before a trial court are never appealed. But if one of the parties is dissatisfied with the outcome, he or she has the right to make an appeal within a specified time.

Why is an appeal allowed? There are two reasons. First, since trial judges often have to decide questions of law rapidly and with little time for reflection, they inevitably make mistakes. Especially in complex cases combining issues of law and technical facts, the expertise of many judges is limited. So it is only fair to give the loser a chance to ask an appellate court, which is under less pressure, to review rulings of a trial judge. If the appellate court finds an error serious enough that it may have affected the outcome of the trial, it will reverse the decision of the trial court and send the case back to that court with instructions to take further action in accordance with the appellate decision.

The second reason that an appeal is allowed is that in most jurisdictions there is more than one trial court, and different trial courts faced with cases raising essentially the same question of law may give different answers to that question. This means that the same rules may not be applied throughout a jurisdiction, a situation that is hardly conducive to public confidence. When confusion of this sort arises, an appellate court can produce uniformity by deciding once and for all what the "correct" rule is.

What does the appellate court review? It reviews the trial court's disposition of issues of law, some of which were raised by the types of motions that lawyers made before and during a trial.

An appellate court does *not* reevaluate the evidence itself. An appellate review is not a new trial. Appellate judges do not sit with juries, nor do they rehear testimony or consider new evidence. (If new evidence is discovered after a decision in a trial court, it must normally be submitted to the trial court with a petition for rehearing.) All that the appellate judges know about the evidence is what they can read in a transcript of the trial that is submitted to them. Consequently, they are in no position to decide whether the trial court has drawn the right conclusions from the evidence. The only question about the facts that appellate judges feel at liberty to ask themselves is whether there is sufficient evidence in the record to make it possible for a reasonable person to reach the conclusion that the trial jury (or judge) actually reached. Once in a while, it is fairly obvious to an appellate court that a trial court has been wrong in its finding on the facts (perhaps because the jury had a strong prejudice against one of the parties). Reversals on such grounds are rare, however, and appellate courts nearly always accept as conclusive the trial court's finding on the facts.

Each appeal is heard by several appellate judges sitting together. The opposing lawyers submit written briefs spelling out their arguments, citing precedents and statutes, and then usually supplement these briefs with oral arguments before the court. The judges may, in turn, question the lawyers. The appellate courtroom atmosphere is quite different from that at a trial: with no witnesses and no jurors, it is usually quiet and undramatic. Unlike trial judges, appellate judges are not acting as referees in a hard-fought tactical contest; their function is to decide fine legal questions in the light of past decisions, scholarly writings, and their own perceptions of the law's ultimate objectives. After they have arrived at a decision, they do what most trial judges have no time to do: they write opinions spelling out at length their reasons for deciding as they have the issues of law brought before them.

Unless the parties in a case can obtain a rehearing, which is rarely granted, they are obliged to accept the appellate decision as the last word. The so-called principle of *res judicata* ("the matter having already been judged") prevents the loser from bringing a new suit against the winner on the same set of facts, either in the same court or in another court. With few exceptions, even if the appellate court later comes to believe that its own decision on the issues in the case was wrong, and even if it reverses its position on the legal issue involved in the course of deciding a similar case later on, the original decision will not be reviewed or overturned.

Trial-court decisions on legal issues lack the finality of appellate decisions and are only occasionally accompanied by published opinions, so they are seldom cited as precedents. The reputation of a particular trial judge or the cogency of a judge's reasoning may give some of these decisions considerable influence with appellate courts; officially, however, their authority as precedents does not extend beyond the court jurisdiction in which they originate.

Appellate decisions are important to the parties involved, but even more important to the legal system itself. Because these decisions represent the fruits of extensive judicial study and reflection, they assume great persuasive authority as declarations of the scope and meaning of legal rules. Their usefulness as precedents is particularly enhanced by the reasoning in opinions that accompany them, for in these opinions the appellate judges try to explain and justify their decisions to judges and lawyers who may in the future be confronted with similar cases.

HOW TO READ AND ABSTRACT AN APPELLATE DECISION

Why should anyone who is neither a lawyer nor training to become one read judicial decisions? The lawyer reads decisions partly to be able to prophesy for a client what the courts are likely to do and partly to try to influence judges by citing precedents in support of the arguments he or she later presents in court. Law school students, for whom reading cases is both an intellectual exercise and a means of learning about legal rules and the judicial process, spend a great deal of their time in exhaustive analysis and comparison of decisions involving closely related issues of law. But even for the student who is not studying to become a lawyer, there is no better way of learning about legal rules and the judicial process than by seeing how rules emerge from decisions of courts in actual cases. Also, reading judicial decisions is less expensive than hiring an attorney to satisfy your curiosity, and if you think you have been wronged, it may assist you in deciding whether to hire an attorney, which is always advisable when pursuing litigation.

One general observation must be made at the outset. As you read the judicial decisions in this book, you will encounter many unfamiliar words and phrases. Those that are essential to your understanding of the case are explained below either in footnotes, in parenthetical insertions, or in the text. But the language of judges contains so many technical words that if you tried to understand every one of them before proceeding, the flow of your reading and understanding of the whole would be needlessly impeded.

Probably the best way to understand a case is to prepare an *abstract* of it. An abstract of a case is a brief summary stating what were the irreducibly essential facts, what happened in the trial court, what was the question of law that the appellate court faced, how it answered that question, and how it justified its answer. Anyone who reads a well-prepared abstract should be able to get a clear, accurate idea of what the case was all about without having to refer back to the original report. This is what lawyers do with every case they find that they expect to refer to in court, and it is what law students (at least those who are prepared to answer questions posed by law professors using the Socratic method) do for every case they read before they go to class.

There is no one right way to abstract a case, but the outline below suggests a useful approach:

Title of Case

Name of appellate court, year of decision

1. *Facts.* What were the events leading up to this lawsuit? Leave out nonessentials. For instance, P and D are usually sufficient designations for Plaintiff and Defendant, and place names can usually be omitted. Be sure, though, that you have included every fact essential to an understanding of the legal problem.

   Important note: The facts included in the appellate court's report do not necessarily represent what *really happened.* They are merely the facts that the appellate court has *assumed* to be true. If the appeal is based on the trial judge's ruling on the defendant's demurrer, for instance, then the facts before the appellate court are merely those that the plaintiff alleged in his or her complaint, since a demurrer says, in effect, "Even if these alleged facts were true, they would not be a basis for legal action." In disposing of the legal question that a demurrer raises, the trial judge and the appellate court must treat the alleged facts *as if* they were true. Appellate courts also act on the assumption that a jury's findings on the facts are correct, even though the jury might very well have misinterpreted the facts. It makes no difference; although they may not be the true facts, these are the facts on which the appellate court based its decision and therefore the ones that must be summarized.

   The final sentence in this first section of the abstract should indicate what remedy the plaintiff is seeking. For instance, "P then sued D to recover damages for breach of contract."

2. *What happened in the courts below this one?* What rulings were made on motions? Was there a jury verdict?

3. *Question(s) of law raised on appeal.* This is the most difficult and important item in the abstract. Here are some suggestions: (a) Always frame the questions in such a way that they can be answered yes or no. The appellate court must formulate the issues in this way in order to deal with them. (b) Do not include any questions that the court did not have to answer in order to dispose of the case. (c) Be sure you have not inadvertently included questions about the facts. (d) Do not frame the question too broadly. For instance, "Did P and D make a contract?" usually does not narrow the issue sufficiently. "Did D's letter constitute a valid offer?" would probably be more useful. It is normally best to word the question so that it refers to the parties. "Must a contract be in writing?" is unlikely to be as useful as "Was the agreement between P and D invalid because not in writing?"

4. *Appellate court's answer to these questions, and its reasons.* Give the court's answer to each question asked. The first word of each answer should be yes or no, followed by a brief summary, in your own words, of the court's reasoning. This paragraph should, in short, contain a statement of the rule of law that emerges from the case.

You may wish to add one more item:

5. *Personal observations on this decision.* Ask yourself: All things considered, does this decision seem to produce "justice"? Does the court's reasoning seem sound? Does the decision seem to fit in with related rules and decisions with which you are familiar? Does the decision seem likely to provide a useful precedent on which courts faced with similar cases can build, or is it more likely to create difficulties? Is there any reason to believe that factors not revealed in the case report—for instance, the personal beliefs of the judge or unmentioned economic facts—may provide the best explanation for the decision?

Here is a sample abstract of the decision in *Boyle v. Vista Eyewear*:

Boyle v. Vista Eyewear

Missouri Court of Appeals
700 S.W. 2d 859 (Mo. App. 1985)

1. *Facts:* Judy Boyle claims to have been discharged from her job for threatening to report her employer's violation of a federal regulation requiring certain treatment and testing of eyeglass lenses. This is a tort action against Vista Eyewear, Inc., and its president, David Baker, to recover actual and punitive damages for wrongful discharge. Claims were also made for overtime compensation and for damages for failure to issue a service letter that correctly stated the true reasons for her discharge.

2. *In the court below:* A judgment was entered in favor of the employee with respect to overtime wages and with respect to her service letter. The trial court dismissed her wrongful discharge claim for failing to state a claim for which relief could be granted.

3. *Questions of law raised on appeal:* Was employee's allegation that she was discharged for threatening to report Vista Eyewear's violation of a federal regulation sufficient to state a claim for wrongful discharge under a "public policy" exception to the employment-at-will doctrine?

4. *Resolution:* Yes, her allegation was sufficient to state a claim. The public policy exception is a narrow exception to the at-will employment doctrine. It provides that an at-will employee who has been discharged by an employer in violation of a clear mandate of public policy has a cause of action against the employer for wrongful discharge. In this case, Boyle has stated an action for wrongful discharge against the defendants for alleging that they fired her for threatening to report their activities to the FDA.

CHAPTER PROBLEM: HANDLING CLAIMS OF THE POOR

A former dean of Harvard Law School, Roscoe Pound, said:

> A ... problem is to make adequate provision for petty litigation, to provide for dispos-
> ing quickly, inexpensively, and justly of the litigation of the poor, for the collection
> of debts in a shifting population, and for the great volume of small controversies
> which a busy, crowded population, diversified in race and language, necessarily
> engenders. It is here that the administration of justice touches the greatest number
> of people. (Pound 1913, 315)

One way to handle these claims in our society is through small-claims courts. Legal
scholar Alexander Domanskis proposed a Model Small Claims Court Act, outlined
below:

Model Small-Claims Court Act

Section 1 *Small claims division; judges*
    A small claims division is established in each (district) as a division of the (district
court). Judges of the (district court) are the judges of the small claims division.

Section 2 *Jurisdiction*
    The jurisdiction of the small claims court shall extend to all civil actions, other
than actions for injunctive relief, brought by any person (association, corporation,
or other legal entity) where the amount involved, exclusive of costs, does not exceed
($500–$1,000). . . .

Section 5 *Pleadings; service of process*
    a. No formal pleadings shall be necessary. A claimant must prepare a complaint,
which adequately informs the defendant of the nature of the claim.
    b. Service of the complaint upon the defendant shall be by registered or certified
mail with return receipt requested from the addressee. If return receipt shows that
there has not been effective service, the court may direct that service on the defendant be completed by personal service. . . .

Section 7 *Time for appearance; order for plaintiff to appear*
    The date for the appearance of the defendant shall not be more than 30 days or
less than 10 days from the date of filing. If the complaint is not served upon the
defendant at least 5 days prior to the appearance date, the clerk shall set a new date
for the appearance of the defendant which shall be not more than 30 days or less
than 10 days from the date of the issuance of the new notice and the clerk shall
inform both parties thereof. When the date for appearance is fixed, the plaintiff shall
be informed of said date and ordered to appear.

Section 8 *Fees*

Fees shall be levied for filing and service of process. (The fees charged will be the same as those in the district court.) The judge may waive prepayment or payment of fees upon the plaintiff's sworn statement or evidence of the inability to pay fees.

Section 9 *No trial by jury*

There shall be no trial by jury in the small claims division. Trial by jury may be had on appeal [to a trial court of general jurisdiction].

Section 10 *No attorney to take part*

No attorney at law or other person than the plaintiff and defendant shall take any part in the prosecution or defense of litigation in the small claims division. Either party may present witnesses at any small claims proceeding.

Source: Domanskis (1976).

Questions

1. How does this model compare to your community's technique for handling small claims?
2. Is there any reporter system in your area that indexes small-claims reports?
3. What is the jurisdiction of the small-claims court of your area?
4. Can one appeal the decision of your area's small-claims court? If so, to which court?

QUESTIONS FOR REVIEW

1. What is the difference between civil and criminal law?
2. What types of courts exist, and what types of case does each handle?
3. Describe and diagram the court system of your state. Diagram the federal court system.
4. Why do we define the boundaries of courts' authority to hear and decide cases? What are some of these boundaries?
5. What is the difference between an issue of fact and an issue of law? Give an example of such a difference.
6. In the United States, we have a dual system of courts, that is, courts at both the state and federal levels. Is this system a necessary condition for the efficient administration of justice? Describe some pros and cons of the dual system.
7. What are the pretrial pleadings? What is their purpose?
8. Why do we need appellate courts? Why not let trial courts act as the court of last resort?
9. Assume that a party loses a case based on some principle of law that is later changed. May the decision then be appealed?

BIBLIOGRAPHY

Administrative Office of the U.S. Courts. 1989. *The United States Courts: Their Jurisdiction and Work, January 1, 1989.* Washington, DC: U.S. Government Printing Office.

Domanskis, Alexander. 1976. "Small Claims Courts: An Overview and Recommendations." *University of Michigan Journal of Law Reform* 9 (Spring): 590–619.

Geyelin, Milo. 1991. "Legal Beat: Mobil Corp." *Wall Street Journal*, September 19.

Kohn, Stephen M., Michael D. Kohn, and David K. Colapinto. 2004. *Whistleblower Law: A Guide to Legal Protections for Corporate Employees.* Westport, CT: Praeger.

Marcus, Amy Dockser, and Stephen J. Adler. 1990. "Jury Awards Ex-Mobil Manager $1.3 Million in Wrongful Discharge." *Wall Street Journal,* November 23.

National Archives and Records Administration. 2006. *The United States Government Manual, 2006–2007.* Washington, DC: U.S. Government Printing Office.

Pound, Roscoe. 1913. "The Administration of Justice in the Modern City." *Harvard Law Review* 26 (1913): 302, 315.

Public Employees for Environmental Responsibility. 2007. www.peer.org.

CHAPTER 3

The Trial Stage

We reviewed the whole adjudicative process in the last chapter, starting with the exchange of pleadings and ending with the disposition of the final appeal. In this chapter we shall focus on the trial, which, from the viewpoint of the litigants, is by far the most important stage in the adjudicative process.

The first part of the chapter consists of a step-by-step description of a civil trial before a jury. Many civil cases are tried without a jury—for instance, cases that involve the rules of equity (see Chapter 4) and any case in which the parties have agreed to waive their right to a jury trial. But a trial without a jury is not sufficiently different from a jury trial to warrant a separate description. The principal difference is that in a trial without a jury, the judge is both the formulator of the legal rules (including the rules of trial procedure) and the finder of the facts. The second part of this chapter consists of a critical appraisal of some problem areas in the trial process.

TRIAL PROCEDURE IN A CIVIL CASE BEFORE A JURY

The following is a generalized description of the sequence of events in a trial, from selection of a jury to the recording of a judgment. It is generalized because there are many variations in the details of procedure from one court to another.

The Jury Is Selected

As you will remember from Chapter 2, every trial court serves a judicial district. (The district of a state trial court is often a county; a federal district court may serve an entire state.) Officials in each district maintain a list of residents who are available for jury duty. Periodically, the names of enough jurors to meet the trial court's needs for its current session are chosen by lot from this list, and the prospective jurors are then summoned to the courthouse. Some of them may be excused if they have a good reason, but the rest must report to the courthouse every day for several weeks, standing ready to serve if they are assigned to a case. In an effort to lighten the burden of having to serve for weeks at a time, many states have instituted a system of one day/one trial. Very few people are exempt from service under this new system, which requires individuals to appear for jury duty for one day or one full trial. Serving for the full day or full trial fulfills their obligations.

When the case is ready for trial, traditionally twelve of the prospective jurors are chosen by lot to fill the jury box. Often two additional prospective jurors are chosen to allow for two alternate jurors, who hear the whole case and are available to replace jurors who become incapacitated during the trial. Prospective jurors are then questioned   collectively or individually, by the judge or by the lawyers, according to local practice—on whether they have any connection with any of the participants in the trial (parties, lawyers, or witnesses) or any biases on the issues involved. In an accident case, for instance, the prospective jurors may be asked whether they have ever been involved in an accident suit.

The lawyers may demand the exclusion of any prospective juror for a specified cause. For example, bias may exist for many reasons. A potential juror may admit that he or she cannot be totally fair in a particular case. An implied bias sufficient for elimination might exist if one of the potential jurors is related to one of the parties or the lawyers. Such people are excused even if they believe that they can be fair. The lawyers may also make a limited number of *peremptory challenges*, exclusions made without giving any reason. This privilege enables a lawyer to exclude jurors who he feels intuitively may be unfriendly to his client's cause. For example, he may have a hunch that farmers, or plumbers, would be hostile to his client, so he would challenge any prospective jurors in these categories. The rejected jurors go back to the jury room to await assignment to other cases. Their places are taken by other prospective jurors, chosen by lot, who are also questioned. In a case that has aroused strong public interest or emotions, selecting a jury may take days or even weeks. Lawyers may call upon experts from other disciplines (such as psychologists) to help them decide upon the best jurors.

The Plaintiff's Case Is Presented

The lawyer representing the plaintiff (or P) now makes her opening statement to the court. She outlines the version of the facts that she expects to prove and makes clear what she is asking the court to do for her client. Next she presents her evidence in whatever order she thinks best. She calls each of her witnesses to the stand and subjects them to *direct examination*, phrasing questions in a way that will elicit answers favorable to her client's case. (She will almost certainly have interviewed these witnesses beforehand in an effort to prepare them for the witness stand, but attempts to have witnesses "memorize their lines" usually backfire.) The lawyer representing the defendant (or D) has the right to object to any of P's questions, or to any answer from P's witnesses, on the grounds that the question or answer is improper under the rules of evidence; the judge must either accept or reject D's objections.

When P has finished her direct examination of each witness, D may, if he wishes, *cross-examine* the witness. D may try to bring out facts that P has preferred not to touch upon, or he may try to cast doubt on testimony by revealing the witness to be confused, forgetful, misled, self-contradictory, deliberately untruthful—or simply ridiculous. Cross-examination at its best is a high art.

After D's cross-examination of each witness, P has another chance to question the witness. This *redirect examination* allows P to try to repair any weakening of the witness's original testimony caused by the cross-examination.

When P is finished presenting her evidence, she "rests her case." At this point, D is likely to move that P's suit be thrown out, on the grounds that even if all P's evidence were true and even if it were interpreted as favorably to P's position as possible, P has still failed to prove her case. This is known as a motion for a *directed verdict* or for a *nonsuit* (similar to summary judgment, discussed previously). If the judge accepts D's contention, P's suit is thrown out and the trial is over. Of course, P probably would not have brought her suit to court in the first place unless she had some basis for believing that she could establish the elements of a case; hence, the chances are that D's motion will be denied. But occasionally a plaintiff's witnesses fail to give the testimony expected, or else their testimony is completely discredited on cross-examination. Then the plaintiff's case may simply collapse, and D's motion may be granted. If, however, it is denied, the trial continues.

The Rules of Evidence

Before we go on with our trial, let us look for a moment at the rules that govern the admissibility of evidence.

Why are there restraints placed on what lawyers may introduce in evidence and on what witnesses may say? Would it not be better to let the judge and jury get the whole story, including every bit of evidence that any participant might possibly consider relevant?

The answer is clear: First, such a procedure could mean that the trial of even a fairly simple case might drag on for weeks. And second, no finder of fact—least of all a jury—should have to extract the truth from the tangle of irrelevant, misleading, and unreliable evidence that such a freewheeling procedure would produce.

Our rules of evidence have been largely shaped with the jury in mind. Most jurors have little experience in analyzing evidence objectively, and many of them have prejudices that are not easy to suppress. They are apt to become confused, forgetful, and, in a long trial, bored and inattentive. The rules of evidence are designed to keep the jury from hearing items of evidence that are (a) irrelevant and immaterial to the questions of fact at issue, (b) repetitious of evidence already admitted, (c) of a sort shown by experience to be of dubious reliability, (d) not readily testable by cross-examination, and (e) in violation of certain confidential relationships.

The rules of evidence have been developed piecemeal over the years, mostly by judges faced with novel problems of proof. They are numerous and complex, and we shall do no more than touch on a few of them to give some idea of their purpose and operation.

Suppose that BUMPED is suing TRUCKER (a small furniture-moving company) for damage resulting from an accident in which BUMPER, a truck driver employed by TRUCKER, collided with BUMPED's automobile. BUMPED's lawyer starts to introduce evidence designed to show that BUMPER was involved in another accident three years before. TRUCKER's lawyer immediately objects to the evidence. The question that the judge must decide is whether a showing that BUMPER had an earlier accident would increase the probability that he is at fault in the accident with BUMPED, thus justifying admission of the evidence. Most courts have answered no to this question, holding that the evidence is not really relevant and that there is a risk that some jurors will jump to the unwarranted conclusion that a driver with one past accident must be accident-prone and therefore at fault in the present case. So the judge will probably rule that BUMPED's lawyer may not present this evidence.

May BUMPED's lawyer mention before the jury that TRUCKER carries liability insurance? Carrying insurance makes TRUCKER neither more nor less responsible for the accident, but knowledge of that fact might lead some jurors to favor passing the repair bills along to the rich insurance company, regardless of who was at fault. So the evidence is usually excluded. However, many plaintiffs' lawyers have discovered various ways of hinting to the jury that the defendant is insured.

Should the court admit testimony from a seven-year-old boy about what he saw of the accident? The answer used to be no, but in many courts now a child's testimony will be admitted if the judge is satisfied, after questioning the child outside the courtroom, that the child is a competent witness: that he has the ability to observe, recollect, and communicate and that he understands the importance of telling the truth.

Should a witness be allowed to express her opinion about whether BUMPER was driving carelessly when the accident occurred? Probably not. Unless a witness is an acknowledged expert on some subject that demands expertise, the court wants to hear only her factual observations, not her opinions or the inferences she has drawn from those observations. The task of drawing inferences and of forming opinions is for the jury.

How about the testimony of someone who did not see the accident himself, but who was told about it by an eyewitness? If the eyewitness is not available to testify, should the court hear his account at second hand? Such *hearsay* is normally excluded, because the eyewitness, whose perception of the accident is what really matters, cannot be put under oath or subjected to the crucial test of cross-examination. That is, the reliability of the eyewitness's perception of the event cannot be tested by cross-examining the person to whom he described it. Since a great deal of valuable evidence would be lost if the courts excluded all hearsay, however, numerous exceptions to this exclusionary rule have been made to cover particular situations in which the hearsay evidence is likely to be trustworthy.

Finally, suppose that BUMPED's lawyer has reason to believe that BUMPER told his physician shortly after the accident that he had had one of his dizzy spells at the moment the accident occurred. May the lawyer insist that BUMPER's doctor take the stand and reveal what BUMPER told her? No, unless BUMPER consents. Confidential communications of patient to doctor, client to lawyer, confessant to confessor, and spouse to spouse, and in a few other relationships, are privileged; that is, the person to whom the communication was made cannot be compelled to testify as to its contents if the communicator raises an objection.

The Defendant's Case Is Presented

Now to return to our trial. P has rested her case, and D now makes his opening statement, outlining what he intends to prove. He then presents his evidence. D may concentrate on rebutting the implications of P's evidence, or he may introduce new facts that alter the legal significance of what P has proved. In BUMPED's suit against TRUCKER, for instance, TRUCKER's lawyer may try to show that BUMPER was *not* driving negligently or that, even if he was, his negligent driving did not cause the accident. Or D may show that BUMPED was also negligent, since *contributory negligence* by the plaintiff will usually prevent his recovering damages. The examination of D's witnesses follows the usual sequence: direct examination by D, cross-examination by P, and redirect examination by D if desired.

The Plaintiff's Rebuttal Is Presented

After D has rested his case, P is permitted to introduce further evidence in order to rebut D's evidence.

At this point, D may once again move for a directed verdict; that is, he may ask that P's suit be thrown out on the ground that P has failed to establish a case that the jury could decide otherwise than for the defendant. P may make a similar motion, contending that she has so clearly established her client's right to a judgment that no jury could reasonably decide otherwise. Once in a great while the judge will grant one of these motions, thus taking the case away from the jury. But even if the judge himself thinks that P has failed to prove her case or D his defense, he will often let the case go to the jury so it can decide.

The Lawyers Make Their Closing Statements

The lawyers (usually D first and then P) now sum up. Each reviews the evidence, stressing the strong points of his or her own case and the weaknesses of the adversary's case. These closing statements can be extremely important, for they may be what the jurors remember best when they retire to decide on a verdict.

The Judge Instructs the Jury

The judge's most important moment in the trial comes when he instructs the jury. He usually starts by spelling out the questions of fact that the jury must answer on the basis of the evidence presented. In the federal courts and the courts of some states, the judge may give the jury his own evaluation of the various items of evidence, but in most state trial courts the judge is not permitted to do this.

Ordinarily, the jury is instructed to decide what the facts are, to apply the rules to those facts, and to come up with a *general verdict*—that is, a decision in favor of one party or the other. If the jury decides for the plaintiff, its verdict will include an award of money damages in a specified amount. In order for the jury to arrive at a general verdict, the judge must first explain the rules that would apply to alternative findings of fact. In our auto accident case, for instance, the judge would have to explain to the jury what is meant by negligence, what would be the consequence of a finding of contributory negligence, and (in case the jury finds for the plaintiff) how damages are measured under the law.

Under some circumstances, the judge instructs the jury to bring in a set of answers to the questions of fact that he formulates for them. This is known as a *special verdict*. The judge then applies the rules to the facts found and assesses the damages.

In a trial without a jury, there is, of course, no need for instructions. But if the judge prepares a formal opinion, it usually contains a separate statement including "Findings of Fact" and "Conclusions of Law." These facilitate the task of the appellate court, which normally accepts the findings on the facts but must review the conclusions concerning the proper rules to apply.

After the judge has given his instructions, the lawyers may challenge the correctness of the instructions or may ask the judge to give the jury certain additional instructions. The judge then has to decide whether these proposed instructions correctly state the law and whether a useful purpose will be served in repeating them to the jury.

The Jury Deliberates and Brings in a Verdict

The jurors' deliberations in the jury room are secret. There is no officially sanctioned way of finding out, during or after the trial, how they went about performing their task. This means, of course, that jurors may willfully ignore the judge's instructions; they may even decide the case by flipping a coin. All evidence indicates, however, that most juries are conscientious and do the best job they can.

The judge has told the jury that under the law of the jurisdiction all twelve jurors, or some majority of them, must agree on the verdict. He has urged them to make every effort to reach agreement. But sometimes the jurors are unable to agree on a verdict, even after long deliberation. Then a jury is said to be *hung*. A mistrial is declared, and the whole case must be tried again.

If the jurors do reach a verdict, they return to the courtroom and report their decision. At this point the loser may move that the court award him a *judgment notwithstanding the verdict* (on the ground that no reasonable jury could have decided as this jury did) or that a new trial be granted because of some alleged irregularity in the trial just completed or because the verdict is contrary to the manifest weight of the evidence. And if the plaintiff has won a verdict for damages, the alleged excessiveness or insufficiency of the amount awarded may warrant a motion for a new trial.

A Judgment Is Entered on the Record

Unless the judge grants the motion for a new trial, he now orders that a *judgment* be entered on the record. In most cases this judgment is, in effect, a formal confirmation and recording of the jury's verdict. A dissatisfied party has a specified number of days in which to appeal. If no appeal is taken or if the appellate court affirms the trial court's judgment, that judgment stands on the record as the final disposition of the case. Under the rule of *res judicata*, the matter cannot be brought again before any court.

The Judgment Is Executed

Winning a judgment for damages is not always the end of the road for the plaintiff. If the defendant does not pay up voluntarily, the plaintiff must go to the sheriff to get her judgment *executed*. The sheriff has no power to act against the defendant's person to enforce an award of damages; in order to satisfy the judgment he must seize some of the property, if any can be found within the jurisdiction. As a result, valid judgments often prove impossible to execute. However, a judgment does remain on the record and may provide the basis for a later suit for payment in another court.

If, instead of a judgment for money damages, the plaintiff has won an equity judgment—if the judge had granted her an injunction, for instance—she would probably have much less difficulty in enforcing it. Equity judgments (or *decrees,* as they are usually called) are addressed to the defendant personally; they order him to do something or to stop doing something. If he fails to comply with such an order, he may be held in *contempt of court* for disobeying the court order and have to pay a fine or even go to prison.

THE ADVERSARY SYSTEM

At the heart of the adjudicative process are two basic principles. The first is that both sides to a controversy must have a chance to be heard—to have their "day in court." Closely related is a second principle, based on a belief that the best way to find the truth and do justice in a case is to make the parties themselves responsible for most of what happens at the trial. In U.S. trials, the judge is little more than a referee throughout most of the proceedings, while the jury merely observes and listens. The parties (acting through their lawyers) must plan and execute their own strategies, must find and present their own evidence and arguments. We call this an *adversary system.*

What are the practical implications of this system?

1. The facts on which a trial court bases its decision are those that the parties assert and substantiate with evidence. Important witnesses may go unheard and important items of evidence remain unrevealed simply because the parties did not discover them or chose not to introduce them. Moreover, the evidence that is presented may fail to influence the outcome, even though it is important, simply because it is ineptly presented. The court, in short, bases its decision not on all the true and relevant facts, but merely on those facts that were discovered and effectively presented to it.

Although we tend to take the concept of the party presentation of evidence for granted, there are alternative methods. For instance, the court could have a staff of its own investigate the facts and report its findings to the judge, as is the practice in some European court systems. And the judge and jurors could take a much more active part in initiating inquiries and in asking questions of the witnesses. But underlying our adversary system is a conviction that the court is more likely to learn all the facts it needs to know and to make a balanced appraisal of them if the initiative for producing them is left with the adversaries.

2. It is up to the parties' lawyers to object whenever they believe that an irregularity in the proceedings has occurred or is about to occur. Suppose one party tries to introduce

evidence that falls into one of the categories of evidence considered inadmissible under the exclusionary rules of evidence discussed previously. Although the judge would readily exclude such evidence if the other party objected to it, ordinarily she will not exclude it if no objection is made. Moreover, a lawyer who fails to object at the time the evidence is introduced loses the right to object to it later in appealing an unfavorable decision.

3. Although many trial judges have had years of experience in evaluating evidence, a majority of U.S. courts do not allow a judge to comment on the evidence when she makes her charge to the jury. Even in those jurisdictions in which judges may comment on the evidence, their discretion in doing so is more restricted than in the courts of many other countries.

4. In deciding what rules of law apply to a particular case, the trial judges rely heavily on the briefs and oral arguments of the lawyers. Ordinarily, trial judges simply do not have time to search out, on their own, past decisions, statutes, or relevant passages in scholarly treatises; they are obliged to rely on the citations brought to their attention by the lawyers. Although they are less pressed, appellate judges also tend to choose from among the arguments made and the precedents cited by the lawyers. Sometimes entire pages or sections of a lawyer's brief appear more or less intact in a judge's appellate decision.

THE TRIAL PROCESS: SOME PROBLEM AREAS

A major theme of this book is that a litigant often cannot be sure what rules of law govern her case until an appellate court has finally decided it. But we shall have little to say hereafter about another form of uncertainty that is just as unsettling for the litigant: can she actually prove her version of the facts in the trial court?

Critics of trials and trial courts claim that the hazards of litigation are greater than they need be. They complain that the adversary system puts the trial lawyer under too great a temptation to mislead the court, that juries of untrained citizens are too easily misled, that methods of recruiting judges too often discourage the best candidates, and that the delays in securing justice in many U.S. trial courts constitute a denial of justice.

Let us consider briefly each of these problem areas in the administration of justice in the United States.

The Role of the Lawyer

As we suggested in the preceding section, under the adversary system every trial is a contest. The contestants are the lawyers—experts in the art of *advocacy* (preparing and presenting evidence and arguments). The rules of the game are enforced by a referee—the judge. The jury (or the judge when there is no jury) decides who wins.

The lawyer's role is thus of crucial importance. The French novelist Balzac once described the jury as "twelve men chosen to decide who has the better lawyer" (Carson 1966, 565). And it is unfortunately true that the performance of a skilled lawyer often has a greater effect on the jury than the testimony of witnesses or even the instructions of the judge.

The adversary system is based on the notion that an injured party is the best advocate for his own interests, and every party is entitled to be represented by a skilled champion—or attorney—to fight for him. Although it may seem a bit melodramatic, hiring a lawyer is thus analogous to being represented by a knight in shining armor, jousting with lance and charging steed before the assembled court in a valiant attempt to protect a client's honor—or so some lawyers would have us believe.

Behind the adversary system is a presupposition that all lawyers will do their best to win. The expectation is usually justified. But not all lawyers are equally skillful, and the party with the stronger case, with "justice" on his side, does not necessarily have the better lawyer. Litigants with strong cases have lost because their lawyers were inept; apparently hopeless causes have been saved by brilliant advocacy.

There is no obvious way to eliminate this distortion from the administration of justice. Some critics have suggested that the advantage enjoyed by a superior lawyer could be offset by assigning a more active role to the judge, allowing her more freedom to put questions to witnesses and to comment critically to the jury on the evidence.

These difficulties are also applicable to the appellate courts. But appellate judges, free from the tensions and time pressures of the trial court, are better able than trial judges to prevent the unequal abilities of the two lawyers from distorting the outcome. Appellate judges also have the time to do their own research if they wish, which makes such tactics as misinterpretation or suppression of precedents less rewarding for the unethical lawyer.

In the case that follows, the Superior Court of Pennsylvania concluded that the plaintiff's attorney had failed to provide adequate representation for his client. The court went on to say that the ineffectiveness of counsel will, under some circumstances, entitle the litigant to a new trial. Few would argue that this plaintiff was entitled to a new trial, but where would you draw the line between an "ineffective" representation and one that is simply less skillfully presented than another?

Pennsylvania v. Napper

Superior Court of Pennsylvania
385 A. 2d 521 (1978)

SPAETH, JUDGE: This is a most unusual case. At a Post Conviction Hearing Act (PCHA) hearing, appellant's trial counsel all but admitted that he had been ineffective in failing to advise appellant fully on the advisability of accepting a plea bargain. Under the circumstances of this case, we agree with counsel; and while we regret his ineffectiveness, we commend his candor.

In 1970 appellant, who was then 18 years old, was convicted by a jury on two indictments for aggravated robbery and sentenced to two consecutive terms of five to twenty years. We affirmed *per curiam*.

On February 23, 1976, appellant filed a petition under the Post Conviction Hearing Act in which he alleged that his trial counsel had been ineffective. The petition was denied, after a hearing, on June 3, 1976. This appeal followed.

Appellant argues that his counsel should have advised him more fully of the advantages and disadvantages of a plea bargain offered by the Commonwealth. By trial counsel's testimony at the PCHA hearing, the facts surrounding the bargain were as follows. Before trial the district attorney offered to recommend a sentence of twelve or eighteen months (counsel was unsure which) to three years total sentence on both indictments. Counsel advised appellant of the terms of the offer, but neither recommended that appellant should accept it, nor gave any advice on the advisability of accepting it. Appellant told counsel that if the offered sentence would mean "state time" (more than two years) he didn't want to plead guilty. After pleading not guilty, appellant went to trial, with the consequences reviewed above.

In deciding whether counsel was ineffective, we first ask whether the action or strategy that counsel decided against or neglected had arguable merit. The question presents little difficulty here. A recommendation of twelve or eighteen months to three years is quite a "bargain" on indictments that could bring—and here did bring—a total sentence of ten to forty years. To be sure, if a defendant and his counsel think there is some chance of winning the case at trial, the bargain becomes less advantageous. In such a case we would have a difficult time reviewing the arguable merit of the bargain. Much would depend on the circumstances prevailing at the time and on counsel's judgment of the defendant's chances—factors on which an appellate court cannot and should not second-guess trial counsel. Here, however, we have the benefit of counsel's assessment of appellant's chances:

> Q. [PCHA Counsel]: Do you recall him [appellant] being aware that there was substantial incriminating evidence in this case?
> [Trial Counsel]: I'm aware that it was a stone cold loser.

Thus, in counsel's eyes the advisability of accepting the plea bargain had, not simply arguable, but considerable merit.

We next must ask whether trial counsel had a reasonable basis for doing what he did. *Commonwealth v. Hubbard, supra.* Since the case against appellant was very strong—in counsel's words, appellant "could not win it"—we would be hard pressed to imagine any good reason for counsel's failure to advise appellant that the case was very strong and the plea bargain offered therefore very advantageous. Here, as it happens, the reason for counsel's failure need not be imagined but is disclosed by the record; and not only is it not a good reason, it is a very bad one. Counsel testified as follows. Until he was assigned to this case he had tried only summary cases in Municipal Court. This case was his first assignment in the jury trial section of the Defender Association. In "offhandedly" presenting the plea bargain to appellant (N.T. PCHA 28) said counsel,

> I had two things to work with. I had the fact that I had a plea bargain, and if he accepted it I would not have my first jury. If he did not accept it, I would have my first jury.
> [1, 2] Defense counsel has a duty to communicate to his client, not only the terms of a plea bargain offer, but also the relative merits of the offer compared to the defendant's chances at trial.

See Amsterdam, Segal and Miller, *Manual for the Defense of Criminal Cases* (1967):

> The decision whether to plead guilty or contest a criminal charge is probably the most important single decision in any criminal case. This decision must finally be left to the client's wishes; counsel cannot plead a man guilty, or not guilty, against his will. But *counsel* may and *must give the client the benefit of his professional advice on this crucial decision,* and often he can protect the client adequately only by using a considerable amount of persuasion to convince the client that one course or the other is in the client's best interest. *Such persuasion is most often needed to convince the client to plead guilty in a case where a not guilty plea would be totally destructive.* Id. at 2–143 (emphasis added).

Here, counsel chose to neglect his duty "to give [appellant] the benefit of his professional advice on [the] crucial decision" whether to accept the plea bargain offer; his "offhanded" presentation, made for reasons entirely inappropriate to his client's interests, failed to make clear to appellant "the risks, hazards or prospects of the case." Under the circumstances, we must hold trial counsel ineffective, for we cannot conclude that he "made an informed choice, which at the time the decision was made reasonably could have been considered as advancing and protecting the appellant's interest."

The order of the lower court is reversed, and the judgments of sentence vacated. Before re-trial, appellant shall be afforded the opportunity to engage in plea bargain discussions, with advice of counsel.

The adversary system raises another problem: It subjects lawyers to conflicting loyalties. On the one hand they are expected to fight to win. In presenting a client's case, a lawyer must be one-sided and partisan, not neutral and objective. Not only is this the presupposition behind the system, it is also what the client who pays a lawyer expects her to do. And lawyers, being human, want to win. They know that their reputation and future income depend on victories. This is most nakedly evident when lawyers take cases on a *contingency* basis, meaning they will be paid an agreed percentage of any damages they win—and nothing if they lose.

On the other hand, lawyers can never forget that they are participating in a process that has as its object the doing of justice. Lawyers are often described as *officers of the court*, a reflection of the degree to which the court must depend on them. And yet some of the steps they may take in order to win may defeat the law's objective of arriving at a just decision.

A body of rules and principles has been developed to help lawyers reconcile these conflicting pressures. Some are official rules, enforceable with the aid of such sanctions as judicial reprimand, forfeiture of the lawyer's case, fine or imprisonment for contempt of court, and suspension or revocation of the lawyer's license to practice (known as *disbarment*). But some of the most important rules are unofficial and only persuasive in their force. Most of these latter rules, called canons, are embodied in the Code of Professional Responsibility and Code of Judicial Conduct adopted by the American Bar Association in 1908. They were subsequently taken over in their entirety or in substance by most state bar associations and even enacted into law in several states.

The canons are couched in general terms. Their tone and spirit are illustrated by the following excerpts, which have to do with the conflicting loyalties just discussed.

> Canon 7. *A lawyer should represent a client zealously and within the bounds of the law. . . .*
>
> 7–3. Where the bounds of the law are uncertain, the action of a lawyer may depend on whether he is serving as advocate or adviser. A lawyer may serve simultaneously as both advocate and adviser, but the two roles are essentially different. In asserting a position on behalf of his client, an advocate for the most part deals with past conduct and must take the facts as he finds them. By contrast, a lawyer serving as adviser primarily assists his client in determining the course of future conduct and relationships. While serving as advocate, a lawyer should resolve in favor of his client's doubts as to the bounds of the law. In serving a client as adviser, a lawyer in appropriate circumstances should give his professional opinion as to what the ultimate decisions of the courts would likely be as to the applicable law. . . .
>
> 7–27. Because it interferes with the proper administration of justice, a lawyer should not suppress evidence that he or his client has a legal obligation to reveal or produce. In like manner, a lawyer should not advise or cause a person to secrete himself or to leave the jurisdiction of a tribunal for the purpose of making him unavailable as a witness therein.

The Role of the Jury

We would have far less cause to worry about the courtroom tactics of lawyers if the finders of fact in most civil cases were trained judges, rather than untrained, easily misled jurors. Courts in the United States try a much higher proportion of cases before juries than do the courts of any other country. Most countries that use juries limit their use to major criminal cases. Only the United States uses them extensively in civil cases.

Even in this country, as we have seen, not all civil cases go before juries: Most minor-court trials and most equity cases are heard by a judge alone. But either party in an ordinary suit for damages normally has a right to insist on a jury trial. For the federal courts, this right is protected by the Constitution of the United States, and some form of jury-trial right is guaranteed, constitutionally or by statute, in all the states.

The reasons for this loyalty to the jury system are primarily historical. The right to a trial by a jury of one's peers—particularly in criminal cases—was one of the hard-won victories in the long struggle against abuses of power by the monarchs of England. On a number of notable occasions in the colonial period, juries stood up to oppressive royal judges. When our early constitutions were framed, therefore, the right to trial by jury was considered extremely important. In the nineteenth century, during the Jacksonian era and again later in the century, public confidence in the jury was further strengthened by the concept of *popular sovereignty*, which stressed popular participation in government and discounted the importance of training and expertise (such as that possessed by judges) in government service.

The average American probably continues to think favorably of trial by jury. But among students of our legal system, the institution has been a subject of controversy for years. Here are some frequent criticisms of the jury system and some answers to those criticisms:

1. Most jurors, say the critics, are not trained to draw objective conclusions from a body of factual evidence. They are all too often at the mercy of their emotions and prejudices. Except in very short trials, they tend to become confused, bored, inattentive, and forgetful. Eager to finish the job, they are often willing to abandon personal convictions or even to resort to the toss of a coin in order to reach agreement. These well-known frailties encourage lawyers to put on a show for the jurors—to appeal to their emotions and biases—instead of presenting the case in an orderly, logical manner as they would if a judge were trying it. Finally, if the plaintiff's lawyer (in an accident case, for instance) can win the jury's sympathy, the jury is likely to grant inordinately generous damages.

Defenders of the jury insist that these allegations are greatly exaggerated and that most juries are conscientious, serious, sensible, and even rather stingy in their awards. Defenders point to the testimony of a number of trial judges who have written about the high proportion of cases in which jury awards have been very close to what the judges would have awarded had they been sitting alone.

2. Jurors, the critics go on, are particularly ill qualified to apply the law to the facts. To be sure, this is not necessarily their fault. The judge is supposed to explain the relevant rules in language jurors can understand. But judges learn from bitter experience that ap-

pellate courts will scrutinize their instructions to make sure that they have stated the law correctly, and they know if they make any significant error an appellate court will reverse their judgment. Faced with the choice between addressing the jury in simple, everyday language and using impeccably correct technical language, many judges choose well-worn verbal formulas they expect will be acceptable to an appellate court even if they are virtually incomprehensible to jurors.

Once again defenders of the jury system charge exaggeration. In the great majority of cases—and notably in the personal-injury cases that take up so much of the time of our trial courts—the real controversy is over the facts; the rules are simple, and jurors ordinarily have no trouble understanding them. The defenders admit, however, that in more complex cases involving business arrangements and transactions, trial by jury does not always work particularly well. In these cases, in fact, more and more litigants are waiving their right to a jury trial.

The jury's defenders may even concede to the critics that our courts should make greater use of the special rather than the general verdict. When a judge asks the jury for a special verdict, he requires it to give yes-or-no answers to the questions of fact he has formulated. Then he applies the law to the jury's answers. The jury does not need to understand the rules of law that the judge will apply to his findings of fact.

3. Even when jurors understand the rules that the judge explains, retort the critics, they sometimes choose to ignore them. Take the contributory-negligence rule, for example. Some states still adhere to the common-law rule that contributory negligence prevents the plaintiff from recovering any damages. In an auto accident suit, for instance, even though the defendant was obviously driving carelessly, the plaintiff will not be awarded damages if she is shown to have been the least bit careless herself. If the defendant was driving very carelessly and the plaintiff was only a little bit careless, applying the rule is apt to seem grossly unfair, and in many verdicts it is clear that the jury has chosen to ignore it. This is easy to do when only a general verdict is required; the jurors have only to announce to the court that they find for the plaintiff and award her so much in damages. They are not required to specify—as they would in a special verdict—that they found the plaintiff to have been wholly without negligence. In effect, the jurors are thus able to defy the judge.

If the judge was sure that the jury had disobeyed her instruction, she could overturn the verdict. But proof of defiance is rarely available, and most judges are reluctant to overturn jury verdicts on the ground that they are contrary to the evidence. Furthermore, it seems probable that judges often tacitly approve of the jury's refusal to apply the contributory-negligence rule.

Defenders of the jury contend that the jury's power to alter the law in particular cases is a *virtue* of the system. The jury, they say, blunts the law's sharp edges and brings to the trial process the average person's sympathy with human frailty and sense of what is reasonable conduct. Judges are trained professionals, in the upper income brackets, and are likely to be somewhat insulated from the harsher realities of life; hence they are usually less qualified than jurors to apply the community's standards of what is justifiable. Moreover, there are twelve jurors to one judge: When the task is to appraise the credibility of evidence and apply vague standards, such as the *reasonable-care* standard of negligence law, the consensus of twelve persons of diverse origins and temperaments may be more valid than the decision of one person.

A judge, the defenders point out, cannot make exceptions to the rule in difficult cases because her interpretations of the law create precedents. Juries can make exceptions by interpreting the facts in order to reach the desired result, because their verdicts do *not* create precedents (e.g., their decisions about facts do not create law).

Critics of the jury system concede some merit to this argument, but they point out that it raises serious questions: Can juries always be counted on to bend the law in the right direction? Are they not capable of being shortsighted, irrational, and even vindictive? And what happens to the goals of predictability and equality before the law if different juries apply a rule differently in similar cases? Finally, when a rule is really unsatisfactory, might not public pressure on the legislature (rather than a jury's defiance of the judge's instructions) be an appropriate way to get a rule changed?

4. The critics argue that jury trials take too long and cost too much. As we shall see later in this chapter, long delays in obtaining justice pose a serious problem, particularly in metropolitan areas. And it is true that trials before a judge alone are generally shorter than trials held before a jury: No time is used in selecting the jury and instructing it, and presenting the facts to a trained judge normally takes considerably less time than presenting them to a jury. In short, reducing the proportion of jury trials would save time and reduce delays that now plague the administration of justice. It would also lower the costs of litigation (for the state as well as for the litigant, who pays court costs covering part of the actual costs), both because each trial would take less time and because jurors' fees would be eliminated.

Defenders of the jury reply, first, that the virtues of the jury system are worth the extra time and money it entails. They also note that litigants who wish to have their cases tried more speedily and at less cost may waive their right to a jury trial.

5. Defenders of the jury have one further argument: jury service, they insist, gives the people a chance to participate in government; it is education in citizenship; it increases respect for the judicial process and the law; and it makes the public share responsibility for decisions that may be difficult and unpopular.

One could be more enthusiastic about this argument, retort the critics, if the obligation to serve was more rationally distributed. Lists of eligibles from which jury lists are made up are rarely complete; members of many occupational groups (e.g., veterinarians, pharmacists) are automatically exempt, not always for good reasons; and many people who prefer not to serve can get excused. And unfortunately, those exempted or excused are often those who would make the best jurors.

This controversy over the merits of the jury system has been going on for decades and will doubtless continue. The pressure for change may lead to greater use of the special verdict and possibly to greater popularity for the *blue-ribbon jury* (drawn from a restricted list of citizens who have achieved a certain level of relevant expertise) in certain kinds of cases. Most promising, perhaps, are efforts made in many communities to speed up trials by inducing litigants to forgo their right to a jury trial. But in view of continued popularity of the jury system and the ample constitutional protection it enjoys, it is not likely to disappear.

Recruitment of Trial Judges

Another controversy centers on methods of recruiting trial judges. Many students of the U.S. legal system are convinced that we could do far more to secure the services of the best possible people for the trial bench.

What qualities should trial judges possess? They must have technical competence and a broad knowledge of many fields of law. Most important, probably, is their familiarity with the rules of trial procedure and evidence; hence some prior experience as a trial lawyer is invaluable. They must have a judicial temperament: capable of rigorous objectivity, firm, patient, and not easily flustered.

Trial judges must also be capable of independence of judgment. Central to the democratic tradition is the principle that judges should be immune to improper pressures both from private-interest groups and from other officials. In principle, the only influences that may be brought to bear on a judge are those exerted in the courtroom by the presentation of evidence and argument. But other influences are always in the background. Every judge has friends and former associates; every judge belongs to a variety of organizations; every judge knows that certain officials and party leaders played a part in placing him on the bench; every judge knows that certain acts will enhance his popularity, while other acts will diminish it. A judge must resist the temptation to take these influences into account in arriving at decisions.

This is not to say that a judge should be insulated from the currents of popular opinion —if, indeed, that were possible. As we shall see in later chapters, the judge frequently finds that no rule of law is clearly applicable to the case before her. She must make a choice, and her beliefs about what is *just* or what is best for the community inevitably affect her decision. If her personal philosophy and convictions are too different from those held by the community, her decisions will provoke conflict and frustration. In the 1920s, for example, antilabor judges freely granted injunctions against strikes and picketing at a time when public sympathy was swinging toward labor. The result was the Norris-LaGuardia Act and its state counterparts, which prohibited all labor injunctions. But to say that judges must share the dominant beliefs and aspirations of their time is not to say that they must court popularity by responding to every popular whim and sentiment.

Processes of Selection

In the early decades of the Republic, most judges were appointed. Then came the era of Jacksonian democracy, with its distrust of appointed officials and its tendency to minimize the importance of special competence and security of tenure for public officials. Today judges are selected in one of five principal ways. Jerome Corsi, a scholar who has done considerable research on judicial politics, has categorized these five techniques:

1. *Partisan elections:* candidates under political labels run for fixed terms.
2. *Nonpartisan elections:* candidates run restricted campaigns and political party is not designated on the ballot.
3. *Legislative election:* the full state legislature votes on candidates.
4. *Gubernatorial appointment:* the governor (with the advice and consent of another political body, such as the state senate or governor's council) selects individuals to fill vacancies.
5. *Merit plan:* a judicial nominating committee composed of members of the bar screens candidates for vacancies and nominates a small number to the governor, who makes the final selection from this list. (Corsi 1984, 107)

Qualifications for Eligibility

In most European countries, the judiciary is a career service. Young law school graduates who want to become judges take a special set of examinations; if they pass them, they enter the service and work their way up the ladder. Each promotion is decided upon by senior judges and other civil servants. In Great Britain, all trial judgeships (except in the minor courts) are filled by appointment from among the elite group of specialized trial lawyers known as barristers. In the United States, the only requirement is that the would-be judge be trained in law—and even that is not necessary for some minor judgeships.

Compensation

Compensation has a lot to do with who does, and who does not, decide to become a judge. Few jurisdictions today offer salaries as inadequate as those commonly offered in earlier days, but no judge earns an income comparable to those received by highly successful private attorneys. Prestige, a sense of power, and the opportunity for public service, rather than the level of compensation, account for the willingness of able lawyers to become judges.

Tenure

The length of the term of office also affects the attractiveness of a judicial position. Lawyers will hesitate to abandon a flourishing private practice for a judgeship if, after a brief term, they do not stand a good chance of being returned to office.

Federal judges and the judges in a few states enjoy life tenure. Most judges, however, have limited terms, frequently as short as four or six years. In some states in recent decades, terms have been lengthened; in others, reappointment or renomination has become more or less automatic for any judge who has served honorably. And under the so-called *sitting-judge* tradition followed in some states, a judge who has once stood for election is able to run for reelection without opposition (i.e., she is the nominee of both parties).

One reason for the reluctance of some states to grant judges extended tenure is that there is no effective way of getting rid of bad judges. In principle, judges can be impeached, and some states provide for their removal by popular vote, but these procedures have been invoked only in rare, extreme cases. Judges whose conduct on the bench is unworthy—because they are tyrannical, arbitrary, abusive, bigoted, or even drunk—are subject to no effective discipline from higher courts and are usually hard to get rid of.

Appointment versus Election

The respective merits of appointment and election are a subject of continuing debate. Some observers believe that in a democracy the people should play a direct part in choosing their judges; others are convinced that the best people cannot be persuaded to become judges if they have to act like politicians and campaign for office.

But the elective and appointive systems are not really as different as they seem, and there is no evidence that states using one system have better judges than those using the other. The truth is that under both systems the selection of judges falls pretty much to local political leaders. In filling an appointive post, the president or governor almost invariably takes the advice of the local chieftains of his or her party in the jurisdiction where the judge will serve. When the position is elective, party leaders pick the candidates who will appear on the party ticket. Their choice rarely fails to be ratified in the primary or by the party convention. Since voters are notoriously unable to appraise the professional qualifications of opposing judicial candidates, they vote by party label and the winners are swept into office along with the rest of the ticket.

In any case, campaigning for judicial office is no longer so distasteful a chore as it once was. In jurisdictions with a sitting-judge tradition, for example, the would-be judges know that they will not have to wage much of a campaign when they run unopposed for reelection. And even where there is a real contest, most communities no longer expect of judicial candidates the kind of aggressive, partisan campaign that they expect of other candidates. Furthermore, the lengthening of judicial terms in many states has meant that campaigns are less frequent. Longer terms have also meant more midterm vacancies, created by the death or retirement of incumbents, to be filled by interim appointments. Appointees must, of course, run for the office in the next election, but by that time their names are often well enough known to give them a clear advantage in the campaign.

Politics and the Judiciary

What part should partisan politics play in the recruitment of judges? Is it unwise to leave the selection of judges to the political parties, as is done under both the elective and the appointive systems? Or does party politics play a necessary and desirable role in the process of selecting judges?

The judiciary must be taken out of politics, says one group. Party leaders must not be permitted to choose the appointees and the candidates, because politicians are less concerned with finding the best person than they are with using judgeships as inducements to party loyalty and as rewards for those who have worked for the party or contributed to its treasury. These critics point out that lawyers who have stayed out of politics or who are affiliated with the party out of power stand almost no chance of becoming judges, no matter how well qualified they are.

Judges who owe their position to a political party, continue the critics, come to the bench with an indebtedness that may imperil their independence. Of course, they cannot openly serve the interests of that party or favor the lawyers who belong to it, but they are able to perform a host of small favors. They can pay their political debts, for example, by choosing party regulars for jobs as court employees. And they have the power to make appointments to a variety of temporary legal positions: receivers, trustees in bankruptcy, referees in foreclosure proceedings, administrators of estates, and special guardians, for instance. Some of these posts are quite lucrative. No judge is likely to appoint a dishonest or incompetent person, but it is customary to distribute these jobs as patronage—that is, to give them to people who have worked for the party in power.

Those who seek to take the judiciary out of politics have suggested several reforms. One is the so-called nonpartisan election of judges, in which candidates run in special elections without party labels. Whether calling an election nonpartisan makes it nonpolitical is open to doubt, however. Candidates nearly always have backers—either parties or private-interest groups—and the nonpartisan election may simply conceal from the voters who those backers are.

Another proposed reform is the Missouri Plan, so called because it was first used in choosing some of the judges in that state. Whenever a judicial vacancy occurs, a nonpartisan nominating commission—made up of appellate judges, representatives of the bar association, and laypersons—selects a panel of three candidates to fill it. The governor is obliged to appoint one of the three. The appointee serves for a year's probationary period and then stands for election to a much longer term, running unopposed on his or her record. The only question before voters is whether Judge X shall be retained in office. This plan combines nonpartisanship, the appointive principle, and the elective principle.

Opposed to this whole approach are those who insist that since judges are not merely technicians but wielders of power and makers of rules, their recruitment simply cannot be taken out of politics. Politics, they say, is the struggle to obtain and exercise power, and judgeships are bound to be prizes in that struggle. Efforts to make the selection process nonpolitical are doomed to failure. Whatever group chooses the appointees or candidates for judgeships will become the focus of political pressure. If the bar associations make the choice, they will be dragged into the arena of political struggle. If nominating commissions do it, pressure will be exerted on those who name the commissioners and then on the commissioners themselves. Since political influences are bound to affect the selection of judges, it is better to have those influences operate through the established political parties. Voters give their support to the party that comes nearest to standing for what they believe in, knowing that if that party wins, it will probably bring into office judges who share its general attitudes and philosophy. The public can hold the party responsible.

Those who defend present methods of recruitment recognize that each has its shortcomings. But these shortcomings have been lessened, they insist, by the adoption of longer terms and the sitting-judge tradition.

The evidence shows that the great majority of U.S. trial judges are competent, conscientious, and incorruptible. And so they will remain as long as the bar and the public hold them to a high standard of conduct—higher than that to which most other officials are held. True, voters are often confused and indifferent when they have to choose between competing candidates at the polls. But they know that they want judges of high caliber, and they are prepared to punish any party whose choices for the bench prove unsatisfactory. In addition, party leaders are not likely to risk having their selections for judgeships denied endorsement, or censured, by the local bar association.

The same forces operate on the judges themselves. The high standards that the public and the bar have set for the judiciary, together with the judges' concern for their reputations and their respect for the judicial office and the tradition surrounding it, impel nearly all new judges to do the best job they can, regardless of how they were chosen for the office.

Delay in the Courts

Fortunately, most disputes in our society do not have to be settled in the courts; if they did, the burden on our courts would be intolerable. Only a tiny percentage of disputes end up in lawsuits, and only a very small percentage of the suits initiated ever go to trial. Moreover, of the suits that do go to trial and on which a judgment is entered, only a small percentage is appealed.

The great majority of disputes are settled out of court, often "on the courthouse steps," as the saying goes. However, many people have expressed the opinion that this is a particularly litigious country, though the evidence on the subject is mixed. According to one major study of the court system produced by Marc Galenter, for example, in 1982 the United States had about 2,400 lawyers per million people, yet produced about the same per capita volume of litigation as Canada, which had only 890 lawyers per million (Galenter 1983, 4–71; Guinther 1988, 109). Virtually every study of the U.S. court system clearly demonstrates a dramatic rise in the amount of litigation actually getting to court. Although the volume of civil litigation has not risen as fast as the country's population, it has grown faster than the number of courts and judges available to handle it. The most striking increase is in personal-injury claims (particularly claims arising from automobile accidents), which have long been the greatest source of litigation. Not only are there more personal injuries today than there used to be, but the proportion of such injuries that leads to lawsuits is rising—perhaps because of the widespread impression that juries are prone to award very generous damages to personal-injury claimants.

Many explanations have been made for this rise in litigation: population growth in the

United States, an increased knowledge of the law, changes in the business climate, and changes in the law that open up new avenues for lawsuits (such as medical malpractice and product liability) (Guinther 1988, 117–140).

The number of cases that do reach the trial stage has become so great that many trial courts are unable to keep up with them. This is particularly true of courts serving large metropolitan areas, where there are sometimes delays of two or more years between the time a lawsuit is initiated and the time it is disposed of by a trial court. Recently, some of these courts have taken drastic measures that promise to bring them up-to-date gradually (or at least to keep the backlog constant), but others are still permitting new cases to pile up on the court calendar more rapidly than they can dispose of old ones.

Some delay between the date a lawsuit is filed and the date it comes to trial is probably desirable, because it gives time for strong feelings to subside and affords the lawyers a chance to sound out the possibilities for settlement. Delays of a few months are not serious, but delays of one or more years are. The truth of the maxim "Justice delayed is justice denied" is most dramatically illustrated in the cases of accident victims who are deprived of their earning power by the negligence of another but must wait several years before a court awards them damages, during which time they may exhaust their savings and be forced to go on relief. There may be other unfortunate consequences as well. The longer the delay, the higher the costs of litigation become (e.g., attorneys fees, compensation for expert witnesses, transportation of witnesses). Moreover, long delays often penalize one or both parties by depriving them of the testimony of witnesses who cease to be available. It is sometimes possible to obtain sworn statements from such witnesses while they can still be heard. But sworn statements are likely to be less effective than live testimony, just as testimony based on fresh recollection is likely to more persuasive than testimony relating to incidents dimly remembered from several years back.

The prospect of extended delays may, it is true, encourage the parties to reach a settlement out of court. But some people can better afford to wait than others. The party who finally gives in and accepts a settlement may be a plaintiff who deserved to receive more than he settled for—or a defendant, fighting a frivolous suit, who would in all likelihood have won in court had she held out. Delays encourage the defendant with a weak defense or the claimant with a frivolous claim to bluff in the hope of achieving an ill-deserved settlement. It may be that the prospect of long delays discourages people from bringing lawsuits, but those who are discouraged may be precisely those who most deserve aid from the courts.

Measures to Deal with Delays

One way of cutting down on delays would be to increase the number of courts or at least the number of judges, and many jurisdictions are adopting this solution. But officials hesitate to propose an increase in the number of judges until they are satisfied that nothing else can be done to speed up the disposition of cases. Here are some alternative corrective measures that are being tried or considered.

Improvements in the Management of Court Systems

The court system would probably be more efficient if all the general trial courts in a state were brought into an integrated, centrally administered system. This would allow judges with relatively light loads to be assigned temporarily to help out in overloaded courts. The federal court system has set the example here: its central administrative office compiles statistics comparing the caseloads of the various federal districts. These comparisons help the presiding judges of the higher federal courts exercise their authority in assigning district judges to temporary duty in districts other than their own. A few states have followed this example.

　　Another way of relieving congestion in the general trial courts would be to transfer part of their caseload down to the minor courts by raising the maximum amount that may be sued for in the minor courts. Some states have made this change. In others, though, the quality of justice dispensed by the minor courts is so poor—particularly in courts presided over by nonprofessional, part-time justices of the peace—that legislatures have been reluctant to increase their responsibilities.

More Efficient Judges

Trial judges are sometimes criticized for not working long enough or hard enough. As a generalization, the charge is certainly unjustified, but it is probably fair in some instances. Therefore, some critics feel that the appellate courts should have power to supervise the performance of trial judges. A related problem is retirement: how can judges with failing intellectual powers be eased from the bench with dignity and compassion? Some states still have a compulsory retirement age, though such arbitrary arrangements inevitably deprive the courts of the services of some judges who are still at the height of their powers.

More Efficient Trial Lawyers

Many trial lawyers take on more cases than they can handle and then have to ask the courts for repeated postponements. By its very nature, the operation of a trial court provides opportunities for time wasting—sometimes perhaps as deliberate strategy—by lawyers, litigants, witnesses, prospective jurors, and even judges. In addition, getting all these people into a courtroom at one time is a complicated matter that necessarily takes time to coordinate. Thus, no court can plan a daily schedule with precision, because it is impossible to predict exactly how long it will take to dispose of each case. In fact, some cases will not be tried at all: one of the participants may become ill, or there may be a last-minute settlement. But many of the postponements requested by poorly organized lawyers could be avoided if judges sternly denied their requests. Also, many trials could be shortened if the judge kept a tighter rein on the proceedings, strictly excluding irrelevancies, repetition, and mere showmanship.

Better Training of Trial Attorneys

In recent years the judiciary has become more vocal about its dissatisfaction with the training of lawyers for trial work. Judges argue that the courts would operate more efficiently and rapidly if trial lawyers demonstrated at least a minimum level of competence in the special skills required for courtroom defense. In fact, some federal courts now require lawyers who wish to practice there to demonstrate their competence by showing proof that they have taken a list of specialized courses. In effect, the judges have established more rigorous licensing requirements for lawyers who wish to practice in their courts.

Wider Use of Pretrial Techniques

Earlier we noted the value of various discovery techniques and of the pretrial conference. Narrowing the issues to true areas of controversy and letting each side know exactly what the other side expects to prove and what its evidence will be allows a trial to proceed more rapidly and efficiently. These techniques also improve the chances of pretrial settlement.

Shorter Trials

It has already been explained that trial judges can shorten trials by keeping a tighter rein on the proceedings. But certainly the best way to reduce the number of courtroom hours spent on each case is to curtail the proportion of cases tried before a jury.

As we have seen, a party in a suit for damages has a constitutionally protected right to a jury trial in the federal courts and in the courts of many states. In order to induce litigants to forgo that right voluntarily, some states require that a case be heard in a minor court or before a special tribunal before a jury trial can be demanded. Others set the court costs charged for a nonjury trial much lower than the costs charged for a jury trial, in the hope that the parties will accept the nonjury trial. But as long as plaintiffs in accident cases believe that a jury will treat them more generously than a judge will, they will probably insist on their constitutional right.

Trial judges can reduce the time they must devote to nonjury trials by appointing members of the bar to serve as their special fact finders, thus relieving themselves of the time-consuming task of hearing evidence. These special fact finders are variously referred to as masters, auditors, or referees. A master takes testimony at a formal hearing, not unlike an ordinary trial, and then prepares a report for a judge in which the evidence is summarized and a finding of fact is made on each factual issue the master has been asked to examine. If the entire case has been turned over to a master, he may also recommend how the case should be decided. Although the final judgment is the responsibility of the judge, she rarely inquires further into the factual issues examined by the master.

Special Administrative Tribunals

Certain kinds of cases have been removed from the regular courts for reasons unconnected with court congestion, but this practice has served incidentally to relieve that congestion. For example, special administrative tribunals (discussed in Chapter 8) have been set up to handle the claims of employees against their employers in connection with on-the-job injuries. Every state now has one or more tribunals of this sort, often called workers' compensation boards. They resemble ordinary courts in many ways, but they follow simplified procedures and apply quite different rules in determining and measuring liability. It has been suggested that the automobile accident cases that now swamp our courts might be tried before tribunals modeled on these workers' compensation boards. But since the suggestion has provoked a great deal of opposition from lawyers' organizations, it is not likely to be adopted in the near future.

These are some of the measures that have been taken or proposed to lessen delays in our courts. Although some jurisdictions are making progress, the problem of court congestion remains serious.

ALTERNATIVE DISPUTE RESOLUTION

Many individuals and corporations would gladly exchange long court delays for speedy resolution of their disputes. A burgeoning business of alternatives to the formal court system has thus come into being in the United States (see Chapter 9). These businesses provide dispute resolution services in a wide variety of areas, including retail sales disputes, domestic disputes, environmental controversies, and labor-management relations.

Typically disputes are handled in a manner similar to a courtroom proceeding but with less formality, emphasizing techniques of negotiation similar to those used to secure pretrial settlements. Often, rules of evidence are less rigidly adhered to in order to expedite decision-making. But this need not be the case. The parties are free to negotiate their own guidelines. For example, people may turn to the services of an arbitration service, such as the American Arbitration Association.

Many businesses today include an arbitration clause in their commercial contracts specifying that if a dispute should arise under the contract, it will be settled by arbitration (i.e., a binding decision by an independent third party) rather than in the courts. Arbitration is likely to be speedier and less expensive than litigation. Moreover, the dispute can be settled by arbitrators who have expert knowledge of the subject matter of the disputed contract—a knowledge that trial judges are unlikely to possess.

An interesting legal question has emerged regarding arbitration agreements: namely, how binding are these agreements? If a party agrees to arbitration but later reconsiders or is dissatisfied with the resolution, may that party then seek recourse in the courts? The Supreme Court of the United States recently addressed this issue and, in the case that follows, announced at least some retreat from years of hostility toward arbitration. The McMahons were customers of the large brokerage firm of Shearson/American Express. They signed a standard agreement that required arbitration in the event of a dispute. The

McMahons claimed that Shearson/American Express violated the Securities Exchange Act of 1934 by fraudulent excessive trading.

Shearson/American Express v. McMahon

U.S. Supreme Court
482 U.S. 220 (1987)

JUSTICE O'CONNOR delivered the opinion of the Court: This case presents questions regarding the enforceability of predispute arbitration agreements between brokerage firms and their customers. The first is whether a claim brought under §10(b) of the Securities Exchange Act of 1934 (Exchange Act), 48 Stat. 891, 15 U.S.C. §78j(b), must be sent to arbitration in accordance with the terms of an arbitration agreement.

Between 1980 and 1982, respondents Eugene and Julia McMahon, individually and as trustees for various pension and profit-sharing plans, were customers of petitioner American Express Inc. (Shearson), a brokerage firm registered with the Securities and Exchange Commission (SEC or Commission). Two customer agreements signed by Julia McMahon provided for arbitration of any controversy relating to the accounts the McMahons maintained with Shearson. The arbitration provision provided in relevant part as follows:

> Unless unenforceable due to federal or state law, any controversy arising out of or relating to my accounts, to transactions with you for me or to this agreement or the breach thereof, shall be settled by arbitration in accordance with the rules, then in effect, of the National Association of Securities Dealers, Inc. or the Board of Directors of the New York Stock Exchange, Inc. and/or the American Stock Exchange, Inc. as I may elect. 618 F. Supp. 384, 385 (1985)

In October 1984, the McMahons filed an amended complaint against Shearson and petitioner Mary Ann McNulty, the registered representative who handled their accounts, in the United States District Court for the Southern District of New York. The complaint alleged that McNulty, with Shearson's knowledge, had violated §10(b) of the Exchange Act and Rule 17 C.F.R. §240.10b-5 (1986) by engaging in fraudulent, excessive trading on respondents' accounts and by making false statements and omitting material facts from the advice given to respondents.

Relying on the customer agreements, petitioners moved to compel arbitration of the McMahons' claims pursuant to §3 of the Federal Arbitration Act, 9 U.S.C. §3. The District Court . . . found that the McMahons' §10(b) claims were arbitrable under the terms of the agreement, concluding that such a result followed from . . . the "strong national policy favoring the enforcement of arbitration agreements."

The Court of Appeals . . . reversed on the Exchange Act claims.

The Federal Arbitration Act, 9 U.S.C. §1 et seq., provides the starting point for answering the questions raised in this case. The Act was intended to "revers[e] centuries of judicial hostility to arbitration agreements" . . . by "plac[ing] arbitration agreements 'upon the same footing as other contracts.'" . . . The Arbitration Act accomplishes this purpose by providing that arbitration agreements "shall be valid, irrevocable, and enforceable, save upon such grounds as exist at law or in equity for the revocation of any contract."

. . . The Act also provides that a court must stay its proceedings if it is satisfied that an issue before it is arbitrable under the agreement, §3; and it authorizes a federal district court to issue an order compelling arbitration if there has been a "failure, neglect, or refusal" to comply with the arbitration agreement, §4.

[1] The Arbitration Act thus establishes a "federal policy favoring arbitration" . . .

When Congress enacted the Exchange Act in 1934, it did not specifically address the question of the arbitrability of §10(b) claims. The McMahons contend, however, that congressional intent to require a judicial forum for the resolution of §10(b) claims can be deduced from §29(a) of the Exchange Act, 15 U.S.C. §78cc(a) which declares void "[a]ny condition, stipulation, or provision binding any person to waive compliance, with any provision of [the Act]."

[3] First, we reject the McMahons' argument that §29(a) forbids waiver of §27 of the Exchange Act, 15 U.S.C. §78aa. Section 27 provides in relevant part:

> The district courts of the United States . . . shall have exclusive jurisdiction of violations of this title or the rules and regulations thereunder, and of all suits in equity and actions at law brought to enforce any liability or duty created by this title or the rules and regulations thereunder.

The McMahons contend that an agreement to waive this jurisdictional provision is unenforceable because §29(a) voids the waiver of "any provision" of the Exchange Act. The language of §29(a), however, does not reach so far. What the antiwaiver provision of §29(a) forbids is enforcement of agreements to waive "compliance" with the provisions of the statute. But §27 itself does not impose any duty with which persons trading in securities must "comply." By its terms §29(a) only prohibits waiver of the substantive obligations imposed by the Exchange Act. Because §27 does not impose any statutory duties, its waiver does not constitute a waiver of "compliance with any provision" of the Exchange Act under §29(a).

We do not read *Wilko v. Swan,* 346 U.S. 427, 74 S. Ct. 182, 98 L. Ed. 168 (1953) as compelling a different result. In *Wilko,* the Court held that a predispute agreement could not be enforced to compel arbitration of a claim arising under §12(2) of the Securities Act, 15 U.S.C. §77l(2). The basis for the ruling was §14 of the Securities Act, which, like §29(a) of the Exchange Act, declares void any stipulation "to waive compliance with any provision" of the statute.

Wilko must be understood, as holding that the plaintiff's waiver of the "right to select the judicial forum" . . . was unenforceable only because arbitration was judged inadequate to enforce the statutory rights created by §12(2).

In *Scherk,* the Court upheld enforcement of a predispute agreement to arbitrate Exchange Act claims by parties to an international contract.

The decision in *Scherk* thus turned on the Court's judgment that under the circumstances of that case, arbitration was an adequate substitute for adjudication as a means of enforcing the parties' statutory rights. *Scherk* supports our understanding that *Wilko* must be read as barring waiver of a judicial forum only where arbitration is inadequate to protect the substantive rights at issue. At the same time, it conforms that where arbitration does provide an adequate means of enforcing the provisions of the Exchange Act, §29(a) does not void a predisputed waiver of §27—*Scherk* upheld enforcement of just such a waiver.

The second argument offered by the McMahons is that the arbitration agreement effects an impermissible waiver of the substantive protections of the Exchange Act. . . . The McMahons argue, that §29(a) compels a different conclusion . . . they contend that predispute agreements are void under §29(a) because they tend to result from broker overreaching. They reason as do some commentators, that *Wilko* is premised on the belief "that arbitration clauses in securities sales agreements generally are not freely negotiated."

We decline to give *Wilko* reading so far at odds with the plain language of §14, or to adopt such an unlikely interpretation . . .

Section 29(a) is concerned, not with whether brokers "maneuver[ed customers] into" an agreement, but with whether the agreement "weaken[s] their ability to recover under the [Exchange] Act."

The former is grounds for revoking the contract under ordinary principles of contract law: the latter is grounds for voiding the agreement under §29(a).

The other reason advanced by the McMahons for finding a waiver of their §10(b) rights is that arbitration does "weaken their ability to recover under the [Exchange] Act." *Ibid.* That is the heart of the Court's decision. *Wilko* listed several grounds why, in the Court's view, the "effectiveness [of the Act's provisions] in application is lessened in arbitration."

First, the *Wilko* Court believed that arbitration proceedings were not suited to cases requiring "subjective findings on the purpose and knowledge of an alleged violator." . . . at 435–436, . . . The *Wilko* Court also was concerned that arbitrators must make legal determinations "without judicial instruction on the law," and that an arbitration award may be made "without explanation of the arbitrator's reasons and without a complete record of their proceedings." . . . Finally, *Wilko* concluded that in view of these drawbacks to arbitration, §12(2) claims "require[d] the exercise of judicial direction to fairly assure their effectiveness."

. . . [M]ost of the reasons given in *Wilko* have been rejected subsequently by the Court as a basis for holding claims to be nonarbitrable . . . For example, we recognized that tribunals are readily capable of handling the factual and legal complexities of antitrust claims notwithstanding the absence of judicial instruction and supervision. . . . [W]e have concluded that the streamlined procedures of arbitration do not entail any consequential restriction on substantive rights. . . . Finally, we have indicated that there is no reason to assume at the outset that arbitrators will not follow the law; although judicial scrutiny of arbitration awards necessarily is limited, such review is sufficient to ensure that arbitrators comply with the requirements of the statute.

Thus, the mistrust of arbitration that formed the basis for the *Wilko* opinion in 1953 is difficult to square with the assessment of arbitration that has prevailed since that time. This is especially so in light of the intervening changes in the regulatory structure of the securities laws.

[6]We conclude, therefore, that Congress did not intend for §29(a) to bar enforcement of all predispute arbitration agreements. In this case, where the SEC has sufficient statutory authority to ensure that arbitration is adequate to vindicate Exchange Act rights, enforcement does not effect a waiver of "compliance with any provision" of the Exchange Act under §29(a). Accordingly, we hold the McMahons' agreements to arbitrate Exchange Act claims "enforce[able] . . . in accord with the explicit provisions of the Arbitration Act." *Scherk v. Alberto-Culver Co., supra* at 520, 94 S.Ct., at 2457

CHAPTER PROBLEM: A JURY OF ONE'S PEERS?

How can the courts ensure any jury comprises a representative cross section of the community so a defendant's constitutional right to a jury trial by one's peers is guaranteed? It is not as easy as one might think. The following selection from a scholarly examination of jury selection methods illustrates this point, and poses some difficult questions.

A Trilogy of Problems

Although many states adopted the federal model prescribed by the Jury Selection and Service Act of 1968, at times juries are still selected in rather casual fashion. Recently, for example, a judge in Laporte, Indiana, ran out of prospective jurors for the obscenity trial of a local bookstore owner. He solved the problem by sending sheriff's deputies into the streets to seize 10 unsuspecting passersby for jury duty.

Even among states that use the federal approach, a fair cross-section of the community is seldom achieved. In the many courts that rely exclusively on voter registration lists, the poor, the young, and racial minorities (e.g., people who do not register in large numbers) are substantially underrepresented. It is often argued that voters' lists should be supplemented by telephone directories and lists of licensed drivers, but this suggestion is seldom followed. A civil-rights case against Ku Klux Klan gunmen is a case in point. The Middle District of North Carolina, the site of that 1983 trial, relied exclusively on voter registration lists, which captured only

74 percent of the black population. Adding the drivers list would have increased that figure to 85 percent.

Turning to the second stage of selection, we find that the goal of impaneling a representative jury is compromised even further. To begin with, many courts fail to pursue those on their source list who do not return their jury questionnaires. As a result, certain segments of the population are missed in the process. And then there are the *exclusion policies.* In the federal courts, old age, child-care responsibilities, financial hardship, and certain occupational categories are automatic grounds for exemption upon request. Although there are reasonable arguments for and against granting these requests freely, this policy is often carried to extreme lengths, especially in the state courts. Until 1979, for example, Missouri automatically exempted all women, mothers and nonmothers alike. Even today, some courts extend these dispensations to veterinarians, pharmacists, and telephone operators. The result: Many courts receive more than their fair share of excuses, only some of which are based on valid need.

Finally, what we usually think of as jury selection—that is, actually choosing jurors from those who are physically present in the courtroom—is subject to its own share of abuse. Nobody questions the need to challenge for cause those people who exhibit clear signs of partiality. These are not granted freely. Unless a prospective juror has a concrete, verifiable interest in the trial's outcome or openly admits an inability to be fair and open-minded, a judge is unlikely to strike that person for cause.

Peremptory challenges, however, are another matter. On the one hand, it is widely believed that they are necessary to protect the right to an impartial jury. On the other hand, they often are used to eliminate certain segments of the community, eroding even further the ideal of a representative panel.

Source: Kassin and Wrightsman (1988, 24–25).

Questions

1. Evaluate the fairness of the exclusion policies mentioned in the excerpt. Should anyone be exempt from jury service? Explain.
2. Many lawyers believe they have a special instinct for choosing jury members. Do you think that choosing a jury is an art or a science?
3. Do you think that it would make sense to have specially trained jurors available to sit for complex legal cases—for example, panels of engineers available to hear product-liability cases?
4. What might be a good design for a system of jury selection that would enable a fair cross section of the community to be represented?

QUESTIONS FOR REVIEW

1. The text argues that it is reasonable to place certain restraints on what lawyers may introduce in evidence. Would it be better to let the judge and jury receive and evaluate any evidence that the participants might want to present?
2. What is the adversary system? What are its practical implications for courtroom procedure?
3. Lawyers are supposed to be advocates for their clients. Are there any clients for whom you would find it difficult to provide a defense? Can you think of any fair way of handling the defense of a client you disliked?
4. Discuss briefly some of the advantages and disadvantages of trial by jury.
5. As our society becomes more complex, the subjects that are litigated also become increasingly complex. Would you be in favor of a law that would allow a judge to appoint a blue-ribbon jury composed of experts in the subject matter of a particular case being litigated if such an appointment might speed the trial? Do you think such appointments would affect the quality of justice dispensed? In what way?
6. How do you feel about efforts to reform the judiciary by making judgeships appointive, rather than elective, offices?
7. Federal judges enjoy life tenure in their jobs. Do you think this benefit leads to better decision-making? Why or why not?
8. Contact a local court clerk and find out what the typical delay is for civil cases and for criminal cases. Ask if any reforms have been proposed to ease the backlog of cases in that particular court. What reforms?
9. Lawyers must pass a bar examination before being admitted to the practice of law. Would you be in favor of periodic reexamination of lawyers? Why or why not?

BIBLIOGRAPHY

Carson, Ralph M. 1966. "Jury Instructions in Criminal Antitrust Cases by the American Bar Association Section of Antitrust Law." *Michigan Law Review* 64 (January): 565–567.

Corsi, Jerome. 1984. *Introduction to Politics.* Englewood Cliffs, NJ: Prentice Hall.

Galenter, Marc. 1983. "Reading the Landscape of Disputes." *UCLA Law Review* 31 (October): 4–71.

Guinther, John. 1988. *The Jury in America.* New York: Facts On File.

Kassin, Saul M., and Lawrence S. Wrightsman. 1988. *The American Jury on Trial: Psychological Perspectives.* New York: Hemisphere.

CHAPTER 4

Judicial Lawmaking I
Law Built on Precedents

When do judges make law? They do so every time they decide a case that no existing rule quite fits. They also make law when they determine what rule applies to a case and when they interpret or construe a statute or a constitutional provision (discussed in Chapters 6 and 7.) They make law when, in the absence of either an applicable legislative rule or a directly controlling precedent, they have to create a rule by building on precedents established in analogous cases. This chapter is about judicial lawmaking by building on precedents.

Nowadays most major innovations in legal rules are introduced by legislatures, and much of the work of judges consists of interpreting legislative rules. But this has not always been so. In the early centuries of the legal tradition we share with England, legislative lawmaking was comparatively unimportant; most lawmaking was the work of judges building on precedents. Indeed, in some fields—contracts, for instance—the rules even to this day are primarily of judicial origin.

THE COMMON-LAW TRADITION

When the Normans conquered England in the eleventh century, they found a land with no nationwide, systematized body of law. Such law as existed was essentially a formalization of local custom. In an effort to unite the country under their rule, early Norman kings sent royal judges out into the land to adjudicate disputes and accusations brought before them by the people. Royal justice dispensed by these judges was firm but generally fair, inexpensive, and expeditious. By the beginning of the thirteenth century, it had wholly displaced the patchwork of Anglo-Saxon institutions that had prevailed before the Norman Conquest.

Since royal judges had no body of generally accepted rules on which to base their decisions, they had to create rules as they went along. Understandably, they drew heavily on the traditions, customs, business practice, and moral standards of the people. But they also relied on their own judgment, their sense of justice, and their notions of the community's needs. The body of rules that thus evolved came to be known as the *common law*—"common" because it was common to all of England.

The term *common law,* you will discover, is used in several slightly different senses.

Most broadly, the term is used to designate the Anglo-American legal tradition, which also prevails in most other English-speaking countries. This tradition is often contrasted with the civil-law tradition, which derives from Roman law and prevails today in the countries of continental Europe and some others. *Common law* is also generally used, as here, to distinguish a body of rules originally administered by the royal courts of law from the rules of equity administered by the Court of Chancery (discussed below). Sometimes the word *law* alone is also used in this sense.

The term *common law* is also often used to refer to all judge-made rules built on precedents, as distinguished from legislative enactments and decisions in which these enactments are interpreted. The phrase "At common law, the rule was that . . ." refers to a decisional rule that prevailed before passage of some statute. For well over a century, this process of judicial lawmaking provided England with virtually all its legal rules for channeling private conduct. It was not until the late thirteenth century that enacted law—first royal edicts and then acts of Parliament—became a significant element in English law. Lastly, the term *common law* occasionally refers to the body of English rules that was transplanted to the American colonies and was in force in 1776 when the colonies claimed their independence.

Emergence of Equity

By the fourteenth century, certain deficiencies had begun to appear in the justice being dispensed by royal courts. Would-be plaintiffs found themselves increasingly baffled and thwarted by rigid, highly technical procedural requirements. Moreover, the royal courts tended to confine themselves to redressing wrongs by awarding money damages to the person wronged. Money was not always an adequate remedy. Little by little, plaintiffs dissatisfied with the treatment they received from the royal courts began to petition the king for some other form of redress. The king adopted the practice of turning these petitions over to the Lord Chancellor, a high official in the king's court. By the latter part of the fifteenth century, this practice had become institutionalized, and the chancellor (now presiding over a new Court of Chancery) was issuing decrees on his own authority. The body of principles and remedies developed by the Court of Chancery came to be known as *equity* (from the Latin meaning "justice" or "fairness," not to be confused with equality).

In effect, England now had two bodies of judge-made law—the traditional common law of the older courts and the newer equity. Equity brought to English law some important new principles. One such principle, for example, held that a plaintiff must come to equity "with clean hands"—meaning that the plaintiff's own role in the affair at issue must have been wholly without fault (Zelermyer 1977, 228–285). Perhaps even more important were equity's new remedies. If a plaintiff could show that the common-law remedy of money damages would not be adequate in his case, he might persuade the Court of Chancery to grant him an *injunction* or a *decree of specific performance.* These are two kinds of court orders addressed to the defendant. On pain of a fine or imprisonment for contempt of court, the decree of specific performance requires a defendant to do, and the injunction requires a defendant *not* to do, specified acts.

The English Legal Tradition in North America

When English colonists settled in North America, they established a legal system modeled on what they had known in England. Although the demands of a new society in a new environment called for some changes in the old system, many English legal principles and institutions had become firmly rooted in the colonies by 1776. Despite strong anti-British revulsion that followed the Revolution, the states of the new nation preserved intact a large part of their legal heritage.

Furthermore, new states that were admitted to the Union as years passed borrowed heavily from the same tradition. A number of states have constitutional provisions or statutes specifically incorporating English common law into their legal systems. Only Louisiana had a legal system that was not based on the common-law traditions; its legal institutions were inherited from France and Spain, both of which belonged to the civil-law tradition.

Fusion of Law Courts and Equity Courts

Among legal institutions transplanted to the American colonies were rules and procedures of equity. In some colonies (and later in some of the states), separate courts of equity were established; in others, equity was administered by regular courts of law. In the nineteenth century, however, movements to reform court systems and to simplify judicial procedures led to elimination of most separate equity courts. Today only three states have such courts; in the others, original jurisdiction over equity cases is in trial courts of general jurisdiction, and appeals go to regular appellate courts.

Although the two court systems have been fused, there is still a significant distinction between a *law* case and an *equity* case. In some states, for instance, a plaintiff must indicate at the outset whether she is bringing an action at law or a suit in equity. Even when no such designation is required, the judge may have to classify the case if one of the parties asks for a trial by jury. This is because the constitutional guarantees of a jury trial extend only to those cases that are essentially legal in character. Thus, a plaintiff seeking an injunction or a decree of divorce cannot claim the right to a jury trial because those are *equity* cases. The procedures in the two kinds of cases are essentially the same, but some of the terms used are different: A complaint at law is sometimes still called a bill in equity, and a judgment is known as a decree.

The fusion of these courts has had some important consequences for litigants. It is now possible, for instance, for a litigant in an action at law to introduce arguments based on equity principles, and vice versa. Over the centuries, equitable principles and remedies have undergone gradual change as judges have had to decide new cases involving novel situations. In addition, legislatures from time to time have broadened the scope and flexibility of equitable remedies and have even created some new remedies modeled on the traditional ones.

THE ROLE OF PRECEDENTS: THE DOCTRINE OF
STARE DECISIS AND ITS RATIONALE

The power of judges to formulate legal rules in dealing with cases brought before them is limited by the duty, imposed on them by our legal tradition, to seek guidance by looking back at past decisions in similar cases. The principle that judges should build on precedents established by past decisions is known as the doctrine of *stare decisis,* from the Latin phrase *stare decisis et non quieta movere*, which means "to adhere to precedents and not unsettle things that are settled."

Observance of *stare decisis* is more than a deeply rooted tradition, however; it is a logical way for judges to act. Following precedents is often much easier and less time-consuming than working out all over again solutions to problems that have already been faced. It enables judges to take advantage of the accumulated wisdom of successive generations. It conforms to the community's instinctive belief that *like wrongs deserve like remedies* and to the desire for *equal justice under law.*

But above all, the practice of following precedents enables citizens (with expert assistance of lawyers) to plan their conduct in the expectation that past decisions will be honored in the future. Certainty, predictability, and continuity are not the only objectives of law, but they are important ones. Many disputes are avoided, and others settled without litigation, simply because people have a good idea about how the courts will respond to certain types of behavior.

Precedents: The Range of Their Influence

In Chapter 2, we examined the case of *Boyle v. Vista Eyewear*, which was decided in 1985 by the Missouri Court of Appeals. The court held that "an at-will employee who has been discharged by an employer in violation of a clear mandate of public policy has a cause of action against the employer for wrongful discharge."

Let us assume that the *Boyle* decision has not been overturned by the courts or superseded by statute. What precisely is its influence in determining the outcome of a later case involving closely similar facts?

First, suppose that such a case were to come before a Missouri trial court any time after 1985. The answer here is clear. A Missouri trial judge would be obliged under the *stare decisis* principle to apply the rule laid down in *Boyle*, no matter what she thought of that rule. Within each jurisdiction, lower courts must follow precedents established by higher courts.

But suppose the unsuccessful plaintiff in this case was dissatisfied with the trial-court judgment against her and decided to take an appeal to the highest court in Missouri. Under the *stare decisis* principle, the appellate judges would normally feel obliged to follow the court's own earlier decision, even though they might have doubts concerning its correctness and wisdom. From time to time, however, appellate courts do overrule their past decisions, as we shall discuss later in this chapter.

Finally, suppose a case very similar to *Boyle* came before a trial or appellate court in another jurisdiction—in Illinois, let us say. An Illinois court would be under no obligation to follow the rule laid down in *Boyle*. Properly speaking, *Boyle* is only an interpretation of the decisional and statutory law of Missouri and has no controlling effect on courts in other states. But judges normally do give consideration to decisions from other jurisdictions. If Missouri judges found no Missouri decisions covering the point at issue, they would almost certainly look at cases decided elsewhere for ideas and guidance. In fact, in *Boyle* Judge Nugent did precisely that: he noted that twenty-eight states "have to one degree or another recognized a new public policy exception to the at-will employment doctrine." After all, the American states—and, for that matter, Great Britain and the British Commonwealth—share a common legal tradition; moreover, their institutions and the problems they face are often similar. So it can be said that decisions from other jurisdictions, though not binding, are persuasive. The persuasiveness of a given decision depends on such factors as the cogency of a supporting opinion, the prestige of a deciding court, and the degree of unanimity among the judges. And any given decision will obviously have greater weight as a precedent if it coincides with decisions in other jurisdictions.

Building on Precedents

By simply describing our fictitious case in the preceding section as "closely similar" to *Boyle v. Vista Eyewear,* we put off answering some difficult questions. How similar must earlier Case A be to later Case B before it is considered a precedent? After all, no two cases are precisely identical. And once the requisite similarity has been established, how do judges go about determining precisely what rule Case A stands for and just how that rule applies to Case B?

If a Missouri court were faced with a case that was exactly like *Boyle v. Vista Eyewear* except that the parties' names, the date, and the locale of events were different, the *Boyle* decision would certainly be controlling. Any competent and scrupulous Missouri lawyer would tell a would-be plaintiff in such a controversy that his chances of winning were good enough to justify his bringing suit.

Litigation occurs because either the facts or the applicable legal rule is in dispute. When a court finds itself faced with a case in which *Boyle* is cited by one of the parties as a precedent, it is likely to be a case resembling *Boyle* in only some respects, so that while one party is insisting on the similarities, the other party is emphasizing the dissimilarities. Imagine, for instance, a case arising in Missouri in which a physician employer asks a nursing assistant to perform a medical procedure for which the nursing assistant is not licensed. Further, assume the nursing assistant is fired for failure to perform the procedure. The nursing assistant might argue the case is analogous to *Boyle v. Vista Eyewear.* How does a court decide whether the precedent established by *Boyle* must be followed?

Actually, the court has three questions to answer. First, is the earlier case essentially similar in its significant facts to the later one? Second, if it is found to be similar, what legal rule is inherent in the earlier case? Third, how does that rule apply to the later case?

Shortly, in the famous case of *MacPherson v. Buick Motor Co.,* we shall see how a new rule is built on old decisions. But a few preliminary observations will help you understand what the judges who wrote the opinions in that case were doing.

First of all, as we said in Chapter 3 about the role of lawyers under the adversary system, judges depend heavily on lawyers not only to identify relevant prior cases but also to present arguments demonstrating the similarity or dissimilarity of those earlier cases to the current one. In a very real sense, therefore, the skill (or lack of skill) of opposing lawyers plays a role in shaping the law. Of course, the litigants themselves also help shape the law. People who bring lawsuits are not always well thought of in our society, but if there had not been plaintiffs in the past ready to assert their rights, and defendants ready to resist those assertions, many decisional rules that today protect us would not exist.

Next, the judges who decided each earlier case now being cited as a precedent were preoccupied with disposing of the case before them; they were only secondarily concerned with the future influence of their decision. Appellate judges are aware that their decisions may become precedents, but they can foresee only to a limited extent what sorts of cases their decisions will influence. Knowing their opinions will probably be read by judges and lawyers for years to come, they still must concern themselves primarily with justifying their court's decisions to the litigants and their attorneys.

The most important implication of the foregoing observation is that what the judges' said in their decision in Case A did not crystallize for eternity the significance of that case. They could not have foreseen all the problems that would later arise in somewhat similar cases, such as Case B; hence the judges who must decide Case B should feel free to reevaluate the facts in Case A when they review it as a possible precedent. A fact to which the earlier judges attached little importance may very well strike the later judges as crucially significant. Their reevaluation of Case A may lead them, for instance, to conclude that the rule inherent in it is much narrower in scope than the earlier judges seemed to think, and therefore it would not apply to Case B. On the other hand, they may see similarities between Cases A and B that earlier judges would never have acknowledged; in other words, they may find a broader rule in Case A than the earlier judges had in mind. Nor does this reevaluation occur only once: each time Case A is reexamined in the course of deciding a later case, its significance as a precedent is likely to undergo some modifications.

The point here is not that judicial opinions are of no importance. On the contrary, they are enormously valuable. An opinion is essentially a brief essay—or sometimes several brief essays—in which judges discuss the relevance of principles and doctrines gleaned from earlier opinions and from scholarly treatises and other writings. What the judges say in their opinions is extremely useful to other judges and to lawyers; words reveal the thinking of decision-makers. But these opinions are not in themselves final or binding interpretations of the decisions they accompany. Later judges are likely to rely heavily on what earlier judges have written, but nonetheless they are free to find new meanings in old cases—meanings not envisaged by the earlier judges. The doctrine of precedent, after all, is known as *stare decisis*, not *stare opinionibus*. It is what the earlier court *decided,* not what it *opined* or said, that is precedent for a later court.

Clearly the act of an appellate judge in building on precedents involves much more than following rules of logic. Indeed, whenever we speak (as we repeatedly do in this book) of applying rules to cases, the phrase does not mean that the rules are all fixed and ready to be applied. The truth is that rules emerge during the process of deciding a case, and judges have a considerable range of discretion in determining which rules emerge. They can find that Case A contains either a rule broad enough to cover Case B or a rule narrow enough to exclude it. The Missouri judges would probably hold either that the rule did or did not cover the case before them. And their decision would probably be influenced less by the reasoning that produced the *Boyle* rule than by their own views on whether applying that rule in the later case would produce a just result.

Often an appellate court must fit cases into classifications whose boundaries are ill defined. Here the exercise of discretion—the creative act of lawmaking—is unavoidable. Consider, for instance, this problem in the law of agency: under what circumstances should an employer be held liable for harm caused by an employee who has an accident while driving a vehicle belonging to the employer? Is the employer relieved of liability if the employee has departed from the route he or she was ordered to take? Broadly stated, the applicable principle is that if an employee is on a mere "detour," the employer is probably liable for any harm caused, but if the employee is on a "frolic," the employer is not liable. So far, so good. But the real problem lies in deciding whether a particular employee in a particular case is on a detour or on a frolic. There are no rules of thumb for classifying a borderline case. Judges have to reexamine past decisions and decide whether a case before them is on the whole more like the detour cases or the frolic cases. If a case is close to the line, however, they must also redefine a portion of the line itself. If they do a good job of explaining their decision, they may make the distinction between detours and frolics a little clearer. But chances are slight they will arrive at a formulation so durable that the task of classification will be easy for all future judges.

This brings us to our last point. There are two reasons why few formulations of legal rules are ever final. The first is that the number of possible fact-combinations that may occur is infinite. The formulator of rules, whether judge or scholar, is forever being surprised by unforeseen cases. The second reason is that our society is constantly producing new problems, new needs, and new community attitudes and values. Not only are truck drivers continually becoming involved in slightly different kinds of accidents, but community attitudes on the proper legal relationships between employers, employees, and injured third parties are continually changing.

Many of the major changes that must take place in the law are made by legislatures. Most minor adjustments, though, are made by judges as they decide cases over the years. Judges owe a duty to the concept of certainty in the law, a duty they fulfill by relating each new decision to what has gone before and by providing in their opinions a justification of each new decision based on established principles. But that duty does not oblige them to maintain fixed and unchanging rules. Rather, it obliges them to preserve continuity—to see to it that change takes place by gradual steps, with each step rationally related to preceding steps, so no single decision will ever come as a total surprise to lawyers who have studied the pattern of the judges' decisions. Incremental decision-making is therefore enshrined in judicial decision-making for sound reasons related to the usefulness of stability and continuity in the law governing human behavior over time.

AN ILLUSTRATIVE CASE: *MacPHERSON V. BUICK MOTOR CO.*

Now let us look at a notable example of judicial lawmaking in action. The case that follows is a classic among judicial decisions, partly because the rule that emerged from it was important, and also because superb craftsmanship was exhibited by a great judge who wrote the majority opinion, Benjamin Nathan Cardozo (1870–1938). Cardozo was named to the U.S. Supreme Court in 1932, after serving for eighteen years on the Court of Appeals of New York, the highest court of that state, which decided the case given here.

MacPherson v. Buick Motor Co., decided in 1916 shortly after automobiles began appearing on the nation's roads, involved injuries suffered by an automobile owner when his car broke down because of a defective wheel. The trial jury, in awarding the plaintiff $5,000 in damages, had determined that the accident was caused by the defective wheel. It had also determined that the defendant, Buick Motor Co., had been negligent in failing to test sufficiently the wheel it put on the car. But a major issue of law remained: *to whom did Buick owe a duty to test the wheel?* It was reasonably clear that Buick had violated a duty of care that it owed to the dealer to whom it sold the car. It was also probable that the dealer was liable to MacPherson for a breach of warranty. But had Buick violated any duty of care owed to MacPherson? There had been no dealings between them; indeed, Buick had never heard of MacPherson until he brought the suit. Throughout the nineteenth century, the courts had held, with only a few exceptions, that manufacturers were liable solely to those with whom they had contractual relations. The decisions involving vehicles seemed wholly unfavorable to MacPherson, from the leading case of *Winterbottom v. Wright* in 1842 right down to a 1915 case decided in a federal court the year before *MacPherson* came before the New York Court of Appeals.

The MacPherson case is particularly useful for our purposes because the majority opinion and the dissenting opinion review the same group of cases but interpret them quite differently. The writer of each opinion is thus able to establish a reasoned justification for his conclusions by basing them on established precedents and principles. But the majority opinion in this case seeks to justify a new rule, a step forward in response to new needs, while the dissent argues that the new rule favored by the majority entails an unwarranted break with the past.

Both opinions are quite long, and each has been abridged here. If you attend law school, it is highly probable you will read the entire case and discuss it in class. To point up the techniques of analysis used by the two opinion-writers, we have interpolated a few explanatory notes and italicized certain key passages.

MacPherson v. Buick Motor Co.

Court of Appeals of New York
217 N.Y. 382, 111 N.E. 1050 (1916)

CARDOZO, J.: The defendant is a manufacturer of automobiles. It sold an automobile to a retail dealer. The retail dealer resold to the plaintiff. While the plaintiff was in the car, it suddenly collapsed. He was thrown out and injured. One of the wheels was made of defective wood, and its spokes crumbled into fragments. The wheel was not made by the defendant; it was bought from another manufacturer. There is evidence, however, that its defects could have been discovered by reasonable inspection, and that inspection was omitted. There is no claim that the defendant knew of the defect and willfully concealed it. The case, in other words, is not brought within the rule of *Kuelling v. Lean Mfg. Co.*, 183 N.Y. 78. The charge is one, not of fraud, but of negligence. The question to be determined is whether the defendant owed a duty of care and vigilance to any one but the immediate purchaser.

[Here Judge Cardozo introduces the leading case in New York on the manufacturer's liability to persons other than the immediate purchaser.]

The foundations of this branch of the law, at least in this state, were laid in *Thomas v. Winchester*, 6 N.Y. 397 [1853]. A poison was falsely labeled. The sale was made to a druggist, who in turn sold to a customer. The customer recovered damages from the seller who affixed the label. "The defendant's negligence," it was said, "put human life in imminent danger." A poison falsely labeled is likely to injure anyone who gets it. Because the danger is to be foreseen, there is a duty to avoid the injury. Cases were cited by way of illustration in which manufacturers were not subject to any duty irrespective of contract. The distinction was said to be that their conduct, though negligent, was not likely to result in injury to any one except the purchaser. We are not required to say whether the chance of injury was always as remote as the distinction assumes. Some of the illustrations might be rejected today. The principle of the distinction is for present purposes the important thing.

[Cardozo now goes on to discuss some later New York cases. The first two seemed to set narrow limits to manufacturers' liability, but two later decisions extended the scope of what might be called the *Thomas* rule. The opinion points out certain factors that might account for the different results in the two groups of cases.]

Thomas v. Winchester became quickly a landmark of the law. *In the application of its principle there may at times have been uncertainty or even error. There has never in this state been doubt or disavowal of the principle itself.* The chief cases are well known, yet to recall some of them will be helpful. *Loop v. Litchfield*, 42 N.Y. 351 [1870] is the earliest. It was the case of a defect in a small balance wheel used on a circular saw. The manufacturer pointed out the defect to the buyer, who wished a cheap article and was ready to assume the risk. The risk can hardly have been an imminent one, for the wheel lasted five years before it broke. In the meanwhile the buyer had made a lease of the machinery. It was held that the manufacturer was not answerable to the lessee. *Loop v. Litchfield* was followed in *Losee v. Clute*, 51 N.Y. 494 [1873], the case of the explosion of a steam boiler. That decision has been criticized (Thompson on Negligence, 233; Shearman & Redfield on Negligence, 117); but *it must be to its special facts. It was put upon the ground* that the risk of injury was too remote. The buyer in that case had not only accepted the boiler, but also had tested it. The manufacturer knew that his own test was not the final one. The finality of the test has a bearing on the measure of diligence owing to persons other than the purchaser.

These early cases suggest a construction of the rule. Later cases, however, evince a more liberal spirit. First in importance is *Devlin v. Smith*, 89 N.Y. 470 [1882]. The defendant, a contractor, built a scaffold for a painter. The painter's servants were injured. The contractor was held liable. He knew that the scaffold, if improperly constructed, was a most dangerous trap. He knew that it was to be used by the workmen. He was building it for that very purpose. Building it for their use, he owed them a duty, irrespective of his contract with their master, to build it with care.

From *Devlin v. Smith* we pass over intermediate cases and turn to the latest case in this court in which *Thomas v. Winchester* was followed. That case is *Statler v. Ray Mfg. Co.*, 195 N.Y. 478 [1909]. The defendant manufactured a large coffee urn. It was installed in a restaurant. When heated the urn exploded and injured the plaintiff. We held that the manufacturer was liable. We said that the urn "was of such a character inherently that, when applied to the purposes for which it was designed, it was liable to become a source of great danger to many people if not carefully and properly constructed."

It may be that *Devlin v. Smith* and *Statler v. Ray Mfg. Co.* have *extended the rule of Winchester. If so, this court is committed to the extension.* The defendant argues that things imminently dangerous to life are poisons, explosives, deadly weapons—things whose normal function it is to injure or destroy. *But whatever the rule in* Thomas v. Winchester *may once have been, it has no longer that restricted meaning.* A scaffold is not inherently a destructive instrument. It becomes destructive only if imperfectly constructed. A large coffee urn may have within itself, if negligently made, the potency of danger, yet no one thinks of it as an implement whose normal function is destruction. What is true of the coffee urn is equally true of bottles of aerated water, *Torgeson v. Schultz*, 192 N.Y. 156 [1908]. . . .

[Judge Cardozo then quotes with approval the opinion of an English judge in a case similar to *Devlin* decided by the Court of Appeals of England in 1883. He sums up:]

What was said by Lord Esher in that case did not command the full assent of his associates. It may not be an accurate exposition of the law of England. Perhaps it may need some qualification even in our own state. *Like most attempts at comprehensive definition, it may involve errors of inclusion and of exclusion. But its tests and standards, at least in their underlying principles, with whatever may be called for as they are applied to varying conditions, are the tests and standards of our law.*

[The *Thomas v. Winchester* "principle" is now reformulated:]

We hold, then, that *the principle of* Thomas v. Winchester *is not limited to poisons, explosives, and things of like nature, to things which in their operation are implements of destruction. If the nature of a thing is such that it is reasonably certain to place life and limb in peril when negligently made, it is then a thing of danger.* Its nature gives warning of the consequences to be expected. If to the element of danger there is added knowledge that the thing will be used by persons other than the purchaser, and used without new tests, then, irrespective of contract, the manufacturer of this thing of danger is under a duty to make it carefully. That is as far as we are required to go for the decision of this case. There must be knowledge of a danger, not merely possible, but probable. It is *possible* to use almost anything in a way that will make it dangerous if defective. That is not enough to charge the manufacturer with a duty independent of his contract. Whether a given thing is dangerous may be sometimes a question for the court and sometimes a question for the jury. There must also be knowledge that in the usual course of events the danger will be shared by others than the buyer. . . . We are not required at this time to say that it is legitimate to go back of the manufacturer of the finished product and hold the manufacturer of the component parts liable. . . . *We leave that question open. We shall have to deal with it when it arises.* The difficulty which it suggests is not present in this case. . . .

[The rule as reformulated is now applied to automobiles:]

From this survey of the decisions, *there thus emerges a definition of the duty of a manufacturer which enables us to measure this defendant's liability.* Beyond all question, the nature of an automobile gives warning of probable danger if its construction is defective. This automobile was designed to go fifty miles an hour. Unless its wheels were sound and strong, injury was almost certain. It was as much a thing of danger as a defective engine for a railroad. The defendant knew the danger. It knew also that the car would be used by persons other than the buyer. This was apparent from its size; there were seats for three persons. It was apparent also from the fact that the buyer was a dealer in cars who bought to resell. The maker of this car supplied it for the use of purchasers from the dealer just as plainly as the contractor in *Devlin v. Smith* supplied the scaffold for use by the servant of the owner. The dealer was indeed the one person of whom it might be said with some approach to certainty that by him the car would *not* be used. Yet the defendant would have us say that he was the one person whom it was under a legal duty to protect. The law does not lead us to so inconsequent a conclusion. *Precedents drawn from the days of travel by stagecoach do not fit the conditions of travel today. The principle that the danger must be imminent does not change, but the things subject to the principle do change. They are whatever the needs of life in a developing civilization require them to be.*

[Contrary decisions from other jurisdictions are noted:]

In reaching this conclusion, *we do not ignore the decisions to the contrary in other jurisdictions.* It was held in *Cadillac M. C. v. Johnson*, 221 F. 801 [1915] that an automobile is not within the rule of *Thomas v. Winchester.* There was, however, a vigorous dissent. Opposed to that decision is one of the Court of Appeals of Kentucky. *Olds Motor Works v. Shaffer*, 145 Ky. 616 [1911]. The earlier cases are summarized by Judge Sanborn in *Huset v. J.I. Case Threshing Machine Co.*, 120 F. 865 [1903]. Some of them, at first sight inconsistent with our conclusion, may be reconciled upon the ground that the negligence was too remote, and that another cause had intervened. *But even when they cannot be reconciled, the difference is rather in the application of the principle than in the principle itself.* Judge Sanborn says, for example, that the contractor who builds a bridge, or the manufacturer who builds a car, cannot ordinarily foresee injury to other persons than the owner as a probable result. We take a different view. We think that injury to others is to be foreseen not merely as a possible, but as an almost inevitable result. Indeed, Judge Sanborn concedes that his view is not to be reconciled with our decision in *Devlin v. Smith. The doctrine of that decision has now become the settled law of this state, and we have no desire to depart from it.*

[Judge Cardozo goes on to discuss the principal English cases. Some of these he finds "distinguishable" (meaning the facts are not similar); in others, he finds statements of principle that he views as supporting his formulation of the rule. In the final paragraphs of his opinion, he notes an analogous rule in the law governing the duties of landlords to tenants, discusses the issues raised by the trial judge's instructions to the jury, and rules that the defendant was not absolved from its duty to inspect merely because it had bought the defective wheel from a reputable wheel manufacturer].

[One judge dissented. In his dissenting opinion, Chief Judge Willard Bartlett reviews most of the cases already discussed by Cardozo. But he finds no justification in them for Cardozo's view that "the *Thomas* rule" had been broadened so that it covered articles not "inherently" dangerous, such as automobiles.]

[Bartlett's opinion, excerpts from which follow, leans heavily on *Winterbottom v. Wright*, the English case decided in 1842, which Cardozo mentions only briefly. The relevance of *Winterbottom* lies partly in the fact that it involved an injury occurring in a defectively constructed stagecoach. (The defendant was not, however, the maker of the coach, as Cardozo's opinion points out.) Wrote Bartlett:]

The *doctrine of that decision [Winterbottom]* was recognized as the *law of this state by the leading New York case* of *Thomas v. Winchester,* which, however, involved an exception to the general rule. . . .

The case of *Devlin v. Smith* is cited as an *authority in conflict with the view* that the liability of the manufacturer and vendor extends to third parties only when the article manufactured and sold is inherently dangerous. . . . It is said that the scaffold, if properly constructed, was not inherently dangerous, and hence that this decision affirms the existence of liability in the case of an article not dangerous in itself, but made so only in consequence of negligent construction. Whatever logical force there may be in this view it seems to me clear from the language of Judge Rapallo, who wrote the opinion of the court, that the scaffold was deemed to be an inherently dangerous structure, and that the case was decided as it was because the court entertained that view. Otherwise he would hardly have said, as he did, that the circumstances *seemed to bring the case fairly within the principle of Thomas v. Winchester.*

I do not see how we can uphold the judgment in the present case *without overruling what has been so often said by this court and other courts of like authority* in reference to the absence of any liability for negligence on the part of the original vendor of an ordinary carriage to any one except his immediate vendee. The absence of such liability was the very point decided in the English case of *Winterbottom v. Wright.* . . . In the case at bar, the defective wheel on an automobile, moving only eight miles an hour, was not any more dangerous to the occupants of the car than a similarly defective wheel would be to the occupants of a carriage drawn by a horse at the same speed, and yet, unless the courts have been all wrong on this question up to the present time, there would be no liability to strangers to the original sale in the case of the horse-drawn carriage.

The rule upon which, in my judgment, the determination of this case depends, and the recognized exceptions thereto, were discussed by Circuit Judge Sanborn, of the United States Circuit Court of Appeals in the Eighth Circuit, in *Huset v. J.I. Case Threshing Machine Co.,* in an opinion which reviews all the leading American and English decisions on the subject up to the time when it was rendered (1903). I have already discussed the leading New York cases, but as to the rest I feel that I can add nothing to the learning of that opinion or the cogency of its reasoning. I have examined the cases to which Judge Sanborn refers, but if I were to discuss them at length, I should be forced merely to paraphrase his language, as a study of the authorities he cites has led me to the same conclusions; and the *repetition of what has already been so well said would contribute nothing to the advantage of the bench, the bar, or the individual litigants whose case is before us.*

A few cases decided since his opinion was written, however, may be noticed. In *Earl v. Lubbock,* the Court of Appeal [of England] in 1904 considered and approved the *propositions of law* laid down by the

Court of Exchequer in *Winterbottom v. Wright*, declaring that the decision in that case, since the year 1842, *had stood the test of repeated discussion.* The Master of the Rolls approved the principles laid down by Lord Abinger as based upon sound reasoning; and all the members of the court agreed that his decision was a *controlling authority which must be followed.* That the federal courts still adhere to the general rule, as I have stated it, appears by the decision of the Circuit Court of Appeal in the Second Circuit, in March, 1915, in the case of *Cadillac Motor Car Co. v. Johnson.* That case, like this, was an action by a subvendee against a manufacturer of automobiles for negligence in failing to discover that one of its wheels was defective, the court holding that such an action could not be maintained. It is true there was a dissenting opinion in that case, *but it was based chiefly upon the proposition that rules applicable to stagecoaches are archaic when applied to automobiles, and that if the law did not afford a remedy to strangers to the contract, the law should be changed. If this be true, the change should be effected by the Legislature and not by the courts.* A perusal of the opinion in that case and in the *Huset* case will disclose *how uniformly the courts throughout this country have adhered to the rule and how consistently they have refused to broaden the scope of the exceptions.* I think we should *adhere to it in the case at bar,* and therefore, I vote for a reversal of this judgment.

HISCOCK, CHASE, and CUDDEBACK, J.J., concur with CARDOZO, J., and HOGAN, J., concurs in result. WILLARD BARTLETT, C.J. reads dissenting opinion. POUND, J., not voting.
Judgment affirmed.

It has been suggested that legal standards—such as the "inherently dangerous" test for manufacturer's liability discussed in *MacPherson*—have a life span marked by three stages. In the first stage, the courts are groping toward a new verbal formula that will aid them in their task of drawing fine distinctions. Eventually they arrive at a standard that seems to do the job. In the second stage, the standard is fairly well accepted, though it is still being tested and refined. In the third stage, cases are arising that show that the standard is no longer satisfactory. Eventually it crumbles, whereupon the search begins for a new standard. *MacPherson* marked the decline and fall of the "inherently dangerous" standard. As a result of the decision, what had once been an exception to the general rule that manufacturers were liable only to those who purchased from them swallowed the rule itself. Today manufacturers are normally held liable for foreseeable harm resulting from defects in their products.

Deciding Truly Novel Cases

What happens, you may wonder, when a case arises for which there simply are no precedents, a case that is in no way similar to anything that can be found in the court reports?

During the centuries after the Norman Conquest of England, when the common-law tradition was being established, courts frequently had to cope with just this problem. As we have seen, judges of those days drew heavily for their rules on prevailing customs, traditions, business usages, and moral standards, as well as on their own sense of justice. These extralegal sources of social rules continue to influence the growth of law today. But as more and more cases are decided over the years and as more and more laws are enacted, the network of legal rules becomes ever more closely woven. An increasing number of fact-situations have been directly ruled upon by the courts, and many other situations are sufficiently similar to decided cases to make it possible to predict a probable rule with some assurance. Moreover, legal scholars are continually publishing treatises, articles, and *restatements* of the law full of speculative generalizations about the probable rules governing situations not yet ruled upon. These writings do not have the authority of judicial opinions, but they are nonetheless of great value to judges and lawyers dealing with difficult cases.

In short, the truly novel case is harder to find than you might think. Indeed, it is impossible to imagine a case for which no precedents or established principles would have any relevance whatever. However, cases do arise for which there are no close and obvious analogies in previous decisions.

Consider, for example, a problem that judges first had to face during the 1920s, when farmers began to complain that airplanes flying over their land were disturbing the peace and frightening livestock. For a while, there were no statutes concerning the respective rights and duties of landowners and of persons who flew over their land, nor were there any precedents. Yet the courts could not simply tell plaintiffs to come back later; some decisions on their complaints had to be reached. What the judge in our illustrative case did, essentially, was to reach back to some of the fundamental concepts that underlie the particular subjects of law. He attempted to see whether any logical inferences could be drawn from conceptual underpinnings.

Hinman v. Pacific Air
Hinman v. United Air Lines Transport

Circuit Court of Appeals, Ninth Circuit
84 F.2d 755 (1936)

HANEY, CIRCUIT JUDGE: From decrees sustaining motions to dismiss filed by defendants in two suits, appellants appeal and bring for review by this court the rights of a landowner in connection with the flight of aircraft above his land. . . .

It is . . . alleged that defendants are engaged in the business of operating a commercial air line, and that at all times "after the month of May, 1929, defendants daily, repeatedly, and upon numerous occasions have disturbed, invaded and trespassed upon the ownership and possession of plaintiff's tract"; that at said times defendants have operated aircraft in, across, and through said airspace at altitudes less than 100 feet above the surface; that plaintiffs notified defendants to desist from trespassing on said airspace; and that defendants have disregarded said notice, unlawfully and against the will of plaintiffs, and continue and threaten to continue such trespasses. . . .

The prayer asks an injunction restraining the operation of the aircraft through the airspace over plaintiff's property and for $90,000 damages in each of the cases.

Appellees contend that it is settled law in California that the owner of land has no property rights in superjacent airspace, either by code enactments or by judicial decrees and that the ad coelum [up to the sky] doctrine does not apply in California. We have examined the statutes of California . . . , but we find nothing therein to negate the ad coelum formula. Furthermore, if we should adopt this formula as being the law, there might be serious doubt as to whether a state statute could change it without running counter to the Fourteenth Amendment to the Constitution of the United States. If we could accept and literally construe the ad coelum doctrine, it would simplify the solution of this case; however, we reject that doctrine. We think it is not the law, and that it never was the law.

This formula "from the center of the earth to the sky" was invented at some remote time in the past when the use of space above land actual or conceivable was confined to narrow limits, and simply meant that the owner of the land could use the overlying space to such an extent as he was able, and that no one could ever interfere with that use.

This formula was never taken literally, but was a figurative phrase to express the full and complete ownership of land and the right to whatever superjacent airspace was necessary or convenient to the enjoyment of the land.

In applying a rule of law, or construing a statute or constitutional provision, we cannot shut our eyes to common knowledge, the progress of civilization, or the experience of mankind. A literal construction of this formula will bring about an absurdity. The sky has no definite location. It is that which presents itself to the eye when looking upward; as we approach it, it recedes. There can be no ownership of infinity, nor can equity prevent a supposed violation of an abstract conception.

The appellants' case, then, rests upon the assumption that as owners of the soil they have an absolute and present title to all the space above the earth's surface, owned by them, to such a height as is, or may become, useful to the enjoyment of their land. This height, the appellants assert in the bill, is of indefinite distance, but not less than 150 feet.

If the appellants are correct in this premise, it would seem that they would have such a title to the airspace claimed, as an incident to their ownership of the land, that they could protect such a title as if it were an ordinary interest in real property. Let us then examine the appellants' premise. They do not seek to maintain that the ownership of the land actually extends by absolute and exclusive title upward to the sky and downward to the center of the earth. They recognize that the space claimed must have some use, either present or contemplated, and connected with the enjoyment of the land itself.

Title to the airspace unconnected with the use of land is inconceivable. Such a right has never been asserted. It is a thing not known to the law. [Emphasis added.]

Since, therefore, appellants must confine their claim to 150 feet of the airspace above the land, to the use of the space as related to the enjoyment of their land, to what extent, then, is this use necessary to perfect their title to the airspace? Must the use be actual, as when the owner claims the space above the earth occupied by a building constructed thereon; or does it suffice if appellants establish merely that they may reasonably expect to use the airspace now or at some future time?

This, then, is appellants' premise, and upon this proposition they rest their case. Such an inquiry was never pursued in the history of jurisprudence until the occasion is furnished by the common use of vehicles of the air. . .

We believe, and hold, that appellant's premise is unsound. The question presented is applied to a new status and little aid can be found in actual precedent. The solution is found in the application of elementary legal principles. The first and foremost of these principles is that the very essence and origin of the legal right of property is dominion over it. Property must have been reclaimed from the general mass of the earth, and it must be capable by its nature of exclusive possession. Without possession, no right in it can be maintained.

The air, like the sea, is by its nature incapable of private ownership, except in so far as one may actually use it. This principle was announced long ago by Justinian. It is in fact the basis upon which practically all of our so-called water codes are based. . . .

When it is said that man owns, or may own, to the heavens, that merely means that no one can acquire a right to the space above him that will limit him in whatever use he can make of it as a part of his enjoyment of the land. To this extent his title to the air is paramount. No other person can acquire any title or exclusive right to any space above him.

Any use of such air or space by others which is injurious to his land, or which constitutes an actual interference with his possession or his beneficial use thereof, would be a trespass for which he would have remedy. But any claim of the landowner beyond this cannot find a precedent in law, nor support in reason.

It would be, and is, utterly impracticable and would lead to endless confusion, if the law should uphold attempts of landowners to stake out, or assert claims to definite, unused spaces in the air in order to protect some contemplated future use of it. . . .

We cannot shut our eyes to the practical result of legal recognition of the asserted claims of appellants herein, for it leads to a legal implication to the effect that any use of airspace above the surface owned on land, without his consent, would be a trespass either by the operator of an airplane or a radio operator. We will not foist any such chimerical property rights upon the jurisprudence of this country. . . .

The decree of the District Court is affirmed. MATTHEWS, CIRCUIT JUDGE, dissents.

There are other ways of approaching such situations. Judges have often searched through property-law cases for any analogies that seemed suggestive. For example, were a landowner's rights with respect to overflying planes similar to rights that enabled her to prohibit people from shooting bullets or stringing wires over her land? Or were they more like rights of the beach owner who objects to boats passing in front of her property? Since a landowner can do much more about wires and bullets passing over her property than she can about boats sailing past her beach, the judges' choice of an analogy would have a great deal to do with how much relief the landowners would get from the airplane nuisance.

This power to choose between competing analogies, neither of which is very close to the case at hand, is obviously an instance of judicial discretion (freedom of choice), which was discussed in the preceding section. The question before the judges is not really "Which of these analogies is the closer?" but rather "Which analogy will lead to the more desirable result?" Judge Cardozo's opinion in *MacPherson* makes it clear he believed the public interest would best be served by holding automobile manufacturers liable to final purchasers who were injured because of defects in cars they bought. Nor is there any doubt the judges who decided that farmers had no legal right to forbid all plane flights over their land recognized that to grant such a right would probably strangle the infant aviation industry. Although judges traditionally stress in their opinions the foundations of precedent and principle more heavily than they stress considerations of public policy, the latter unquestionably play an important part in their thinking.

On *Hinman v. United,* the court had no real precedents on which to build. In *Escola v. Coca-Cola,* which follows, public-policy considerations are given a good deal of attention. Recall that Judge Benjamin Cardozo used his skill as a judicial craftsperson to extend liability for products to any reasonably foreseeable person who is injured as a proximate result of another's failure to experience reasonable care in manufacture. This is the basis of negligence actions against manufacturers. In 1944 Justice Roger Traynor, another skilled legal scholar, wrote an opinion that was among the very first to call for *strict liability in tort* as a basis for product liability. Under negligence theory, it was often very difficult for a plaintiff to prove that a particular defendant was at fault for causing a defect. Strict liability holds the manufacturer responsible irrespective of fault.

Escola v. Coca-Cola

Supreme Court of California
150 P.2d 436 (1944)

GIBSON, CHIEF JUSTICE: Plaintiff, a waitress in a restaurant, was injured when a bottle of Coca-Cola broke in her hand. She alleged that defendant company, which had bottled and delivered the alleged defective bottle to her employer, was negligent in selling "bottles containing said beverage which on account of excessive pressure of gas or by reason of some defect in the bottle was dangerous . . . and likely to explode." This appeal is from a judgment upon a jury verdict in favor of plaintiff.

[Chief Justice Gibson, speaking for the majority, affirmed the judgment of the trial court. He stated that under the rule of *res ipsa loquitur* (the facts speak for themselves) there was enough evidence of negligence for a jury to find for the plaintiff.]

TRAYNOR, JUSTICE: I concur in the judgment, but I believe the manufacturer's negligence should no longer be singled out as the basis of a plaintiff's right to recover in cases like the present one. *In my opinion it should now be recognized that a manufacturer incurs an absolute liability when an article that he has placed on the market, knowing that it is to be used without inspection, proves to have a defect that causes injury to human beings. MacPherson v. Buick Motor Co.*, 217 N.Y. 382, established the principle, recognized by this court, that irrespective of privity of contract, the manufacturer is responsible for an injury caused by such an article to any person who comes in lawful contact with it. In these cases the source of the manufacturer's liability was his negligence in the manufacturing process or in the inspection of component parts supplied by others. Even if there is no negligence, however, public policy demands that responsibility be fixed wherever it will most effectively reduce the hazards to life and health inherent in defective products that reach the market. It is evident that the manufacturer can anticipate some hazards and guard against the recurrence of others, as the public cannot. Those who suffer injury from defective products are unprepared to meet its consequences. The cost of an injury and the loss of time or health may be an overwhelming misfortune to the person injured, and a needless one, for the risk of injury can be insured by the manufacturer and distributed among the public as a cost of doing business. It is to the public interest to discourage the marketing of products having defects that are a menace to the public. If such products nevertheless find their way into the market it is to the public interest to place the responsibility for whatever injury they may cause upon the manufacturer, who, even if he is not negligent in the manufacture of the product, is responsible for its reaching the market. However intermittently such injuries may occur and however haphazardly they may strike, the risk of their occurrence is a constant risk and a general one. Against such a risk there should be general and constant protection and the manufacturer is best situated to afford such protection. . . .

The inference of negligence may be dispelled by an affirmative showing of proper care. If the evidence against the fact inferred is "clear, positive, uncontradicted, and of such a nature that it can not rationally be disbelieved, the court must instruct the jury that the nonexistence of the fact has been established as a matter of law." *Blank v. Coffin*, 126 P.2d 868, 870. An injured person, however, is not ordinarily in a position to refute such evidence or identify the cause of the defect, for he can hardly be familiar with the manufacturing process as the manufacturer himself is. In leaving it to the jury to decide whether the inference has been dispelled, regardless of the evidence against it, the negligence rule approaches the rule of strict liability. It is needlessly circuitous to make negligence the basis of recovery and impose what is in reality liability with negligence. If public policy demands that a manufacturer of goods be responsible for their quality regardless of negligence there is no reason not to fix that responsibility openly. . . .

The liability of the manufacturer to an immediate buyer injured by a defective product follows without proof of negligence from the implied warranty of safety attending the sale. Ordinarily, however, the immediate buyer is a dealer who does not intend to use the product himself, and if the warranty of safety is to serve the purpose of protecting health and safety it must give rights to others than the dealer. In the words of Judge Cardozo in the *MacPherson* case: "The dealer was indeed the one person of whom it might be said with some approach to certainty that by him the car would *not* be used. Yet the defendant would have us say that he was the one person whom it was under a legal duty to protect. The law does not lead us to so inconsequent a conclusion." While defendant's negligence in the *MacPherson* case made it unnecessary for the court to base liability on warranty, Judge Cardozo's reasoning recognized the injured person as the real party in interest and effectively disposed of the theory that the liability of the manufacturer incurred by his warranty should apply only to the immediate purchaser. It thus paves the way for a standard of liability that would make the manufacturer guarantee the safety of his product even when there is no negligence. . . .

As handicrafts have been replaced by mass production with its great markets and transportation facilities, the close relationship between the producer and consumer of a product has been altered. Manufacturing processes, frequently valuable secrets, are ordinarily either inaccessible to or beyond the ken of the general public. The consumer no longer has means or skill enough to investigate for himself the soundness of a product, even when it is not contained in a sealed package, and his erstwhile vigilance has been lulled by the steady efforts of manufacturers to build up confidence by advertising and marketing devices such as trademarks. See *Thomas v. Winchester,* 6 N.Y. 397, *Baxter v. Ford Motor Co.,* 168 Wash. 456. Consumers no longer approach products warily but accept them on faith, relying on the reputation of the manufacturer or the trade mark. . . . Manufacturers have sought to justify that faith by increasingly high standards of inspection and a readiness to make good on defective products by way of replacements and refunds. . . . The manufacturer's obligation to the consumer must keep pace with the changing relationship between them; it cannot be escaped because the marketing of a product has become so complicated as to require one or more intermediaries. Certainly there is greater reason to impose liability on the manufacturer than on the retailer who is but a conduit of a product that he is not himself able to test.

The manufacturer's liability should, of course, be defined in terms of the safety of the product in normal and proper use, and should not extend to injuries that cannot be traced to the product as it reached the market.

Refusal to Follow Precedents

Some decisions withstand the test of time better than others. Some become valuable precedents on which judges can build; others become barriers to progress.

Let us suppose that the highest court of State X, in trying to decide a case, comes upon its own decision in an earlier case entitled *Smith v. Jones.* Although *Smith v. Jones* appears to be a controlling precedent, the court is reluctant to follow it. Perhaps the court perceives that the reasoning in the opinion is faulty. Perhaps it realizes that the facts in the case were peculiar—not really typical of the fact-combinations usually found in such cases. But the judges who decided it did not recognize this peculiarity and therefore stated the rule of the case in too broad a form, giving it a scope that made it appear to cover future situations for which it was ill suited. Or perhaps the present court realizes that since the time when *Smith v. Jones* was decided, changes in social arrangements or in community attitudes have undermined the appropriateness of the rule of this case for cases with apparently similar facts.

Cardozo's opinion has shown us a number of ways in which the inconvenient precedent can be dealt with. It is often possible, for instance, to emphasize dissimilarities between the previous case and the present one, sometimes relying on facts in the earlier case to which earlier judges attached little importance. This is known as *distinguishing* the earlier case or *reconciling* two decisions.

But this technique has its limits. Some precedents are so obviously relevant it would be intellectually dishonest to distinguish or ignore them. In such a situation, judges usually feel obliged to follow precedent. They may justify doing so with words like these: "The decision in *Smith v. Jones* is at variance with what now seems to be the more reasonable view. If the question that the present case raises were now before us for the first time, we might well answer it differently. But *Smith v. Jones* has long been a part of our law, and under the principle of *stare decisis* we have no alternative but to follow it." The judges may go on to point out that, after all, primary responsibility for making changes in the law belongs to the legislature.

As we have seen, there are excellent reasons for following precedents. Occasionally, though, courts find themselves faced with cases in which the value of continuity is clearly outweighed by the injustice, or the plain absurdity, of blindly following an old rule. In such cases, the possibility that a legislature may someday take note of the undesirable effects of a rule does not seem to justify doing a present injustice, and a court concludes that the precedent must be swept out of the way once and for all. Such overrulings must be exceptional, of course, or *stare decisis* would become meaningless. In some fields of law in which continuity and predictability are particularly important—in property law, for instance—precedents are almost never overruled. But in other fields, decisional rules can be changed by new decisions with less danger of defeating legitimate expectations.

In some states, for instance, judge-made rules once held that the driver of a vehicle had a duty to dismount and look up and down railroad tracks before proceeding over a grade crossing. If he failed to do so and was hit by a train, his contributory negligence prevented him from recovering damages. As the normal speeds of trains and automobiles increased, the obligation to dismount became absurd. In states where the rule had not already been changed by statute, the courts usually felt free to overrule earlier cases.

Let us now examine another New York case in which Judge Cardozo spoke for the majority. In *Hynes v. New York Central Railroad*, the court's problem was not whether it had to follow a particular precedent, but whether it had to apply literally the traditional definition of a legal concept. In four lower-court decisions in this case (two by trial judges, each of which was appealed to an intermediate appellate court), judges had ruled that since plaintiff's son was a "trespasser" when defendant's negligence caused his death, the mother could not recover damages. But the result was a harsh one. The Hynes boy had trespassed only in a technical sense; his act did not fall within the reason for the rule holding that no duty of care is owed by a property owner to a trespasser on his or her property. Could the highest court arrive at a result that would be just and yet would not create doubt and confusion about the continuing validity of established principles? Though his own vote decided the final majority, Judge Cardozo was able to persuade only three of the six other judges who heard the case to join in his bold—and superbly written—opinion.

Hynes v. New York Central Railroad

Court of Appeals of New York
231 N.Y. 229, 131 N.E. 898 (1921)

CARDOZO, J.: On July 8, 1916, Harvey Hynes, a lad of sixteen, swam with two companions from the Manhattan to the Bronx side of the Harlem River or United States Ship Canal, a navigable stream. Along the Bronx side of the river was the right of way of the defendant, the New York Central Railroad, which operated its trains at that point by high-tension wires, strung on poles and crossarms. Projecting from the defendant's bulkhead above the waters of the river was a plank or springboard from which boys of the neighborhood used to dive. One end of the board had been placed under a rock on the defendant's land, and nails had been driven at its point of contact with the bulkhead. Measured from this point of contact the length behind was five feet; the length in front eleven. The bulkhead itself was about three and a half feet back of the pier line as located by the government. From this it follows that for seven and a half feet the springboard was beyond the line of the defendant's property, and above the public waterway. Its height measured from the stream was three feet at the bulkhead, and five feet at its outermost extremity. For more than five years swimmers had used it as a diving board without protest or obstruction.

On this day Hynes and his companions climbed on top of the bulkhead intending to leap into the water. One of them made the plunge in safety. Hynes followed to the front of the springboard, and stood poised for his dive. At that moment a crossarm with electric wires fell from the defendant's pole. The wires struck the diver, flung him from the shattered board, and plunged him to his death below. His mother, suing as administratrix, brings this action for her damages. Thus far the courts have held that Hynes at the end of the springboard above the public waters was a trespasser on the defendant's land. They have thought it immaterial that the board itself was a trespass, an encroachment on the public ways. They have thought it of no significance that Hynes would have met the same fate if he had been below the board and not above it. The board, they have said, was annexed to the defendant's bulkhead. By force of such annexation, it was to be reckoned as a fixture, and thus constructively, if not actually, an extension of the land. The defendant was under a duty to use reasonable care that bathers swimming or standing in the water should not be electrocuted by wires falling from its right of way. But to bathers diving from the springboard, there was no duty, we are told, unless the injury was the product of mere willfulness or wantonness, no duty of active vigilance to safeguard the impending structure. Without wrong to them, crossarms might be left to rot; wires highly charged with electricity might sweep them from their stand, and bury them in the subjacent waters. In climbing on the board, they became trespassers and outlaws. The conclusion is defended with much subtlety of reasoning, with much insistence upon its inevitableness as a merely logical deduction. A majority of the court are unable to accept it as the conclusion of the law.

We assume, without deciding, that the springboard was a fixture, a permanent improvement of the defendant's right of way. Much might be said in favor of another view. We do not press the inquiry, for we are persuaded that the rights of bathers do not depend upon these nice distinctions. Liability would not be doubtful, we are told, had the boy been diving from a pole, if the pole had been vertical. The diver in such a situation would have been separated from the defendant's freehold. Liability, it is said, has been escaped because the pole was horizontal. The plank when projected lengthwise was an extension of the soil. We are to concentrate our gaze on the private ownership of the board. We are to ignore the public ownership of the circumambient spaces of water and of air. Jumping from a boat or a barrel, the boy would have been a bather in the river. Jumping from the end of a springboard, he was no longer, it is said, a bather, but a trespasser on a right of way.

Rights and duties in systems of living law are not built upon such quicksands.

Bathers in the Harlem River on the day of this disaster were in the enjoyment of a public highway, entitled to reasonable protection against destruction by the defendant's wires. They did not cease to be bathers entitled to the same protection while they were diving from encroaching objects or engaging in the sports that are common among swimmers. Such acts were not equivalent to an abandonment of the highway, a departure from its proper uses, a withdrawal from the waters, and an entry upon land. A plane of private right had been interposed between the river and the air, but public ownership was unchanged in the space below it and above. The defendant does not deny that it would have owed a duty to this boy if he had been leaning against the springboard with his feet upon the ground. He is said to have forfeited protection as he put his feet upon the plank. Presumably the same result would follow if the plank had been a few inches above the surface of the water instead of a few feet. Duties are thus supposed to arise and to be extinguished in alternate zones or strata. Two boys walking in the country or swimming in a river stop to rest for a moment along the side of the road or the margin of the stream. One of them throws himself beneath the overhanging branches of a tree. The other perches himself on a bough a foot or so above the ground. Both are killed by falling wires. The defendant would have us say that there is a remedy for the representatives of one, and none for the representatives of the other. We may be permitted to distrust the logic that leads to such conditions.

The truth is that every act of Hynes, from his first plunge into the river until the moment of his death, was in the enjoyment of public waters, and under cover of the protection which his presence in those waters gave him. The use of the springboard was not an abandonment of his rights as a bather. It was a mere by-play, an incident, subordinate and ancillary to the execution of his primary purpose, the enjoyment of the highway. The by-play, the incident, was not the cause of the disaster. Hynes would have gone to his death if he had been below the springboard or beside it. The wires were not stayed by the presence of the plank. They followed the boy in his fall, and overwhelmed him in the waters. The defendant assumes that the identification of ownership of a fixture with ownership of land is complete in every incident. But there are important elements of difference. Title to the fixture, unlike title to the land, does not carry with it rights of ownership *usque ad coelum* [up to the sky]. There will hardly be denial that a cause of action would have arisen if the wires had fallen on an aeroplane proceeding above the river, though the location of the impact could be identified as the space above the springboard. The most that the defendant can fairly ask is exemption from liability where the use of the fixture is itself the efficient peril. That would be the situation, for example, if the weight of the boy upon the board had caused it to break and thereby throw him into the river. There was no such causal connection here between his position and his injuries. We think there was no moment when he was beyond the pale of the defendant's duty—the duty of care and in the storage of destructive forces.

This case is a striking instance of the dangers of "a jurisprudence of conceptions" (Pound, Mechanical Jurisprudence, 8 *Columbia Law Review* 605, 608, 610), the extension of a maxim or a definition with relentless disregard of consequences to a "dryly logical extreme." The approximate and relative become the definite and absolute. Landowners *are* bound to regulate their conduct in contemplation of the presence of trespassers intruding upon private structures. Landowners *are* bound to regulate their conduct in contemplation of the presence of trouble in marking off the field of exemption and immunity from that of liability and duty. Here structures and ways are so united and commingled, super-imposed upon each other, that the fields are brought together. In such circumstances, there is little help in pursuing general maxims to ultimate conclusions. They have been framed *alio intuitu* [from another point of view]. They must be reformulated and readapted to meet exceptional conditions. Rules appropriate to spheres which are conceived of as separate and distinct cannot, both, be enforced when the spheres become concentric. There must then be readjustment or collision. In one sense, and that a highly technical and artificial one, the diver at the end of the springboard is an intruder on the adjoining lands. In another sense, and one that realists will accept more readily, he is still on public waters in the exercise of public rights. The law must say whether it will subject him to the rule of the one field or of the other, of this sphere or of that. We think that considerations of analogy, of convenience, of policy, and of justice, exclude him from the field of the defendant's immunity and exemption, and place him in the field of liability and duty.

The judgment of the Appellate Division and that of the Trial Term should be reversed, and a new trial granted, with costs to abide the event.

HOGAN, POUND and CRANE, JJ., concur; HISCOCK, C.J., CHASE and MCLAUGHLIN, JJ., dissent [without opinion].
Judgments reversed, etc.

Questions

1. If you had been one of the judges hearing this case, would you have joined in the majority opinion?
2. Do you think Cardozo avoided creating doubt and confusion about established legal principles?

RESTRAINTS ON JUDICIAL LAWMAKING

Whenever appellate judges make a choice among alternative rules in deciding a case, they are making law. They are also making a decision about public policy. In every case we have studied in this chapter, the judges took into account not only legal precedents and principles but the community's changing needs, desires, and notions of what is fair.

Students of the law used to be reluctant to acknowledge the influence of such considerations on judicial decisions. The writings of Oliver Wendell Holmes, onetime law teacher, state appellate judge, and finally justice of the Supreme Court of the United States from 1902 to 1932, helped bring about a more realistic understanding of the things judges consider when they decide cases. At the beginning of his book *The Common Law*, Holmes stated, "The life of the law has not been logic: it has been experience. The felt necessities of the time, the prevalent moral and political theories, intuitions of public policy, avowed or unconscious, even the prejudices which judges share with their fellowmen, have had a good deal more to do than the syllogism in determining the rules by which men should be governed" (1881, 1). Some years later, he noted that "logical method and form flatter that longing for certainty and for repose which is in every human mind. But certainty generally is illusion, and repose is not the destiny of man. Behind the logical form lies a judgment as to the relative worth and importance of competing legislative grounds. . . . I think that the judges themselves have failed adequately to recognize their duty of weighing considerations of social advantage" (2006, 181).

The notion that judges weigh "considerations of social advantage" inevitably raises a question: what is to prevent them from simply deciding cases in accordance with, for example, their political (or religious or social) predilections? In fact, it is quite common to hear that particular judges generally do write decisions that have a politically conservative or politically liberal cast to them.

It would be naive to assume that judges never exercise their power to effect public policy. It is much more useful, however, to examine the question of the proper role of the court in this regard. In Chapter 7 we explore the difference between judicial activism and judicial conservatism and its impact on policy. We will also look briefly at the politics and process of appointing justices to the Supreme Court.

Regardless of judges' prejudices and political party affiliations, there are still a number of reasons why judges by and large exercise judicial discretion in decision-making. First, appellate judges do not sit singly; three or more judges hear each appeal. Thus each judge's peculiar biases are to some extent canceled out by those of his or her colleagues. Second, appellate judges have no power to create situations in which they make law; they must decide cases brought before them. Nor can they ignore legal contentions presented by the lawyers for each party. Third, they must explain their decisions in carefully reasoned opinions, which are subsequently published. These obligations—to convince their colleagues on the bench, to decide each case on the basis of the facts and contentions in the lawyers' briefs and oral arguments, and finally to explain to the world in a published opinion how they arrived at their decision—impose important constraints on judges.

But the most important constraint on the freedom of judges is subtler. Judges are heirs to a judicial tradition of individual self-restraint and objectivity that goes back to the twelfth century, a tradition that stresses continuity of the law and requires that each new decision be related to established principles and precedents. However prone to bias, however ardent a partisan a person may have been before becoming a judge, he or she is likely to find it well nigh impossible to violate this tradition.

In *Southern Pacific Company v. Jensen* (244 U.S. 205, 221, 1917), Justice Holmes made this comment on the limits of judicial thinking: "Judges do and must legislate, but they do so only interstitially. . . . A common-law judge could not say, 'I think the doctrine of consideration a bit of historical nonsense and shall not enforce it in my court.'"

Here is how Canon 20 of the Canons of Judicial Ethics drawn up by the American Bar Association states the argument against unrestricted judicial lawmaking: "[O]urs is a government of laws and not of men, and [the judge] violates his duty as a minister of justice under such a system if he seeks to do what he may personally consider substantial justice in a particular case and disregards the general law as he knows it to be binding on him. Such action may become a precedent unsettling accepted principles and may have detrimental results beyond the immediate controversy" (American Bar Association, 1971, 46).

The evidence is plentiful that judges, with rare exceptions, accept restraints imposed by the judicial tradition. If anything, they are perhaps too cautious at times. Deciding where justice and the public interest lie is difficult. Criteria are likely to be few and uncertain. Moreover, cases rarely present whole problems; they tend rather to present fragments of problems. Judges are therefore hesitant to build bold new rules on the inadequate base provided by a single case; they tend rather to stick pretty close to rules indicated by established precedents and principles whenever these can be found. Judges make choices between what Holmes candidly called "competing legislative grounds" only when precedents and clearly relevant analogies are absent. Moreover, when they do make such choices, they do their best to maintain continuity with the past and to articulate not their own views but Holmes's "felt necessities of the time"—the shared purposes of the community.

COMMON LAW AND EQUITY THEORIES IN STATUTORY LAW

Well before the British legal system was transplanted to the American colonies, regulation of the human environment was accomplished in England on a piecemeal basis through both criminal prosecutions and civil suits at common law and equity, under legal theories of nuisance, trespass, and negligence.

Nuisance

Three categories of nuisance developed over time: public, private, and mixed. The legal theory of public or common nuisance had developed in England by the 1200s as a kind of low-grade common-law crime consisting of an act or omission that interferes with rights of the community at large by obstructing or causing inconvenience or damage to the public in the exercise of rights common to all persons. In cases decided as early as

1725, the crime included interference with the public health, such as keeping a malarial pond; with the public safety, as in storing explosives; with the public peace, as by loud and disturbing noises; with the public comfort, as by emission of bad odors, smoke, dust, and vibration; and with the public convenience, as by obstructing a highway or navigable stream or by polluting a stream, killing its fish (Prosser 1971, 572–585, references to cases omitted).

The legal theory of private nuisance had other origins in civil law, based on interference with the use and enjoyment of land, and was commonly expressed in the form of a Latin maxim: *sic utere tuo ut alienum non laedas,* meaning "use your own property so as not to injure another." In cases decided by U.S. courts as early as 1832, the civil wrong of private nuisance included interference with the enjoyment of private land by pollution of a stream or an underground water supply or by unpleasant odors, smoke, dust, or loud noises (Prosser 1971, 592–593, references to cases omitted).

The familiar saying "a man's home is his castle" suggests that he may do whatever he wishes within the confines of his own property, but this is no more than a somewhat gender-biased popular myth that was probably never embraced at common law. A property owner does have a right to undisturbed possession of his property, but that right is not absolute. When that right comes in conflict with similar rights of others, it was determined long ago to be preferable, as a matter of public policy, that a single individual refrain from use of his land for special purposes injurious to others, rather than that others should be deprived of the use of their property altogether or be subjected to great danger, loss, or injury that might result if the rights of the former were without any restriction or restraint. This is roughly the equivalent of the common-sense maxim that one person's right to swing her arms stops at the end of another person's nose.

Thus, the right of a property owner to use one's land as one pleases was probably never an absolute right at common law, but was limited to uses that did no injury to one's neighbors. To say this a bit differently, the community has always had some rights superior to the individual's right to undisturbed possession of private land.

Legal theories of nuisance were applied in the United States to abate environmental disruption in the form of air pollution from cement manufacturing plants (e.g., see *Hulbert v. California Portland Cement Co.,* 161 Cal. 239, 118 P. 928, 1911) and water pollution from sulfate pulp and paper manufacturing plants (e.g., see *Weston Paper Co. v. Pope,* 155 Ind. 394, 57 N.E. 719, 1900; *Hampton v. North Carolina Pulp Co.,* 223 N.C. 535, 27 S.E.2d 538) prior to enactment of statutory environmental controls. Note that economically beneficial activities may nonetheless be considered nuisances. Protection of the general public from unreasonable actions of individuals was broadly construed across a wide range of activities in many decisions that substantially predated development of local zoning controls in the early 1900s and air, water, and noise pollution control statutes of the 1970s.

The distinction between a public nuisance and a private nuisance is based on the difference between injury to the community at large and injury to a single individual. Yet the same thing or act may constitute at one time both a public nuisance and a private nuisance, if special harm done to an individual is different in kind or severity from that done to the community: this has been called a *mixed nuisance.* Neither public nor private nor mixed nuisance requires physical entry on the property of another, though any nuisance might involve such an intrusion.

Trespass

As it emerged during the 1200s in English common law, the legal theory of trespass was broad, concerning all conduct of a forcible, direct, and injurious nature—whether to person or property—likely to lead to a breach of the peace by provoking retaliation. Originally a common-law crime against the community, later trespass cases awarded damages to injured plaintiffs in civil law proceedings (Prosser 1971, 28).

Thus, an act of uninvited or unwanted physical contact is considered one of violence at common law, whether violence is actual or implied, and the courts will infer violence though none is actually used when the injury is of a direct and immediate kind and committed on the person or personal property of a plaintiff. Battery, unwelcome physical touching, and assault involving a verbal or physical threat—even in the absence of touching—are examples of trespass involving actual violence. A peaceable but wrongful entry upon a person's land is an example of implied violence.

In a limited sense, then, trespass concerns a wrongful physical entry on land owned or possessed by another. The common-law action for damages for an unlawful entry or trespass on another's land was called *trespass quare clausum fregit,* meaning roughly "entry where one broke the close." The term *close* signified a real or imaginary fence or boundary enclosing land, across which the trespasser moved without invitation or permission from the rightful occupant.

This concept was extended by the Oregon Supreme Court and accepted by the U.S. Court of Appeals for the Ninth Circuit when it defined trespass as: "any intrusion which invades the possessor's protected interest in exclusive possession, whether that intrusion is by visible or invisible pieces of matter or by energy which can be measured only by the mathematical language of the physicist" (*Reynolds Metals Co. v. Martin,* 337 F.2d 780, 9th Cir. 1964). In this case, fluoride fumes and particulates from an aluminum reduction plant had invaded a nearby cattle ranch, poisoning the cattle. This decision, which illustrates a situation in which the same act may constitute both a nuisance and a trespass, constitutes a precursor to statutory regulation of toxic air pollutants.

Negligence

In the early 1800s, the legal theory of negligence developed, thinly disguised, in trespass and nuisance cases to describe a mental state, usually one of inattention or indifference during breach of a legal obligation or commission of some wrongful act. Negligence may be defined as omitting to do something a reasonable person, guided by those considerations that ordinarily regulate the conduct of human affairs, would do or as doing something a prudent and reasonable person would not do (Prosser 1971, 139–143, references to cases omitted). Injuries resulting from exposure to fluorides emitted from an aluminum reduction plant with air pollution control equipment inadequate to control health-impairing levels of emissions were redressed under negligence theory (*Reynolds Metals Co. v. Martin*, 337 F.2d 780, 9th Cir. 1964), as well as under trespass and nuisance, as discussed above.

Restatement

To summarize the foregoing discussion, the common-law legacy that the United States acquired from England included several important attributes. First, we inherited a process of binding judicial interpretation and application of social values. During the early development of English common law, courts were the most prevalent source of law and public policy, but over time the British executive and the American legislature displaced the court's role in their respective countries.

Second, we inherited the practice of building on decisions made in the past, known as *stare decisis* (following precedent) or incremental decision-making. Sticking close to the familiar—whether extending a line of case precedents in the courtroom, using standard operating procedures in administration, or amending existing statutes in Congress—provides some predictability, if not certainty, in the law, permitting change, but slower change than might be the case in the absence of such practice. Most environmental statutes, for example, have now been through several iterations of amendment since their initial enactment.

The third important attribute that the United States inherited from English common law is the use of criminal sanctions to enforce some regulatory measures, such as public health and pollution-control standards. For example, several federal statutory environmental programs provide for such sanctions under specified circumstances. Reliance upon private action initiating a claim for relief against persons doing harm to the community, in addition to criminal sanctions, is a fourth attribute of our common-law heritage. This deliberate redundancy is reflected in statutory provisions allowing citizen lawsuits to enforce contemporary pollution-control measures and other environmental policies. Some observers believe that such provisions have proven indispensable in securing federal agency implementation of environmental policy in the United States.

And finally, common law provided in substance both legal theories and precedents for later legislative enactment of environmental policies and land-use control mechanisms. For example, the notion that ownership of land does not confer an absolute right to use of the land is fundamental to zoning, building codes, and subdivision controls. Thus, activities previously determined to constitute nuisances, trespass, or negligence at common law provided ample (if nonbinding) precedents for development of more recent air, water, and hazardous waste control statutes.

In addition, we also inherited suits in equity, with their special forms of nonmonetary relief—the decree of specific performance and the injunction—requiring a person to do or to refrain from doing specified acts in situations where money damages would not provide an adequate remedy for a wrongful act. The injunction, in specifying what a person could not do, contained the seed of preventive action, as distinct from remedying a wrongful act after the fact. The decree of specific performance, in specifying what a person must do, is most commonly used to require the reluctant performance of obligations specified in contracts. Yet it also implied an ability to specify when and how that action should be done, and thus it perhaps contained the germinal beginnings of the notion that industrial performance standards for air and water pollution could and should be set in policy.

Many states today have statutes or constitutional provisions explicitly incorporating English common law into their legal systems, although common law is generally superseded by subsequent statutory enactments in a particular subject area. Congress has gone further, incorporating and adapting legal theories from the common law and equity into legislation now codified in the *U.S. Code*, discussed in Chapter 5.

CHAPTER PROBLEM: THE LIMITS OF JUDICIAL CREATIVITY

Justice Roger Traynor, who wrote the *Escola v. Coca-Cola* decision excerpted above, offered the following comments on the judicial process:

> The very caution of the judicial process offers the best of reasons for confidence in the recurring reformation of judicial rules. A decision that has not suffered premature birth has a reduced risk of premature death. Insofar as a court remains uncommitted to unduly wide implications of a decision, it gains time to inform itself further through succeeding cases. It is then better situated to retreat or advance with little disturbance to the evolutionary course of the law and to those who act in reliance upon judicial decisions.
>
> After a generation of experience, I believe that the primary obligation of a judge, at once conservative and creative, is to keep the inevitable evolution of the law on a rational course. Twenty years ago I wrote that the danger was not that judges would exceed their power, but that they would fall short of their obligation. Better the active pilot, sensitive to the currents of the river, than an armchair captain hidebound to a dated rulebook. The pilot who knows the river, however, must above all know the moorings well. If he disengages his bark from one, he must be certain he can reach another.
>
> So constant a responsibility, involving such active thought, resists inclusion within so befuddled a term as activism. Given reason and not merely the rulebook as the soul of law, I would also voice a cautionary note that the reasoning judge, the pilot on the *qui vive* [keeping a sharp lookout], is not one indifferent to rulebooks. He takes care to keep them up-to-date, reading more than ever to do so, with a critical eye for words that wear poorly and a discriminating sense for those that wear well. If he is on guard against mechanical incantations of obsolescent rules in the name of ancestral loyalty, he is also on guard against mechanical rejections of sturdy rules in the name of social justice. The complacent captain in the armchair is not more of a danger than the pilot who would navigate with a clenched fist in the air instead of at the helm.
>
> In sum, the thinking judge might reexamine the rules that had been preserving the status quo of Marie Antoinette, but he would not join those who would repudiate the spirit of the law so that they could proceed to behead her.

Source: Traynor (1978, 7–8).

Questions

1. Justice Traynor states elsewhere in his article that some lawyers would argue, "that it is for a judge to state, restate, occasionally expand or even contort established precedents, but that he cannot properly create new ones." Would you agree with that argument? Explain.
2. Continuing his argument, Traynor then states that "innovation today rests with the legislators by virtue of their unique sensitivity to public moods, or what is sometimes called an ear to the ground." What assumptions are involved in using the "ear to the ground" method to create law? Do you agree that legislators are the best lawmakers?
3. Based on your reading of *Escola v. Coca-Cola,* how faithful has Justice Traynor been to the spirit of his own article?

QUESTIONS FOR REVIEW

1. Based upon what you now know of the judge's role in lawmaking, how do you think judges should gain their positions (election or political appointment)?
2. How can personal bias in a judge's decision be detected? What recourse, if any, should the public have against judges whose decisions seem to reflect personal bias rather than precedent?
3. Do you believe that a judge should first research the law on a case and then come to a decision? Or do you believe that she should first decide what is right and then find cases to support her view? Defend your position.
4. Are there a sufficient number of restraints on judicial lawmaking?
5. If equity is such an important part of the law, why do you think there has been a merger of most courts of equity and law?
6. Using the concepts developed in this chapter, especially the role of precedent, how might a case be decided concerning possession of land on the moon?

BIBLIOGRAPHY

American Bar Association. 1971. *Canons of Professional Ethics, Canons of Judicial Ethics.* Chicago: American Bar Association.
Holmes, Oliver Wendell. 1881. *The Common Law.* Boston: Little, Brown.
———. 2006. *Collected Legal Papers.* Clark, NJ: Lawbook Exchange.
Prosser, William L. 1971. *The Law of Torts*, 4th ed. St. Paul, MN: West.
Traynor, Roger J. 1978. "The Limits of Judicial Creativity." *Iowa Law Review* 63 (1977): 1–16. Also in *Hastings Law Journal* 29 (1978): 1025–1040.
Zelermyer, William. 1977. *The Legal System in Operation: A Case Study from Procedural Beginning to Judicial Conclusion.* San Francisco: West.

CHAPTER 5

Lawmaking by Legislatures

We described in the last chapter how courts create new legal rules by building on judge-made precedents and principles. This was once the only type of lawmaking, and it remains extremely important. In the last 150 years or so, however, legislatures have become the primary makers of new law. And in many areas, including the field of business law, even long-standing rules that were originally established by courts have now been embodied in *statutes*: acts of Congress, state legislatures, and ordinances of local governments. The common characteristic of statutes is that all are enacted by elected legislative bodies.

In this discussion of legislative lawmaking, we first describe how statutes are enacted. Then we examine some differences between statute law and decisional law. Finally, we consider some problems that legislators must face in deciding what to put into statutes.

THE LEGISLATIVE PROCESS

Before a draft proposal for legislation can be enacted into law, it must clear a series of hurdles. Some have been erected by federal or state constitutions, others by legislatures, either by rule or tradition. Although the legislative process is not the same in every legislature, the following brief description of how a bill moves through the U.S. Congress will give a good idea of the procedures followed in most state legislatures as well. Figure 5.1 provides a simplified diagram of how a bill becomes a law.

Preparation and Introduction of the Bill

A *draft proposal*, or *bill*, must first be introduced in one house or the other of the legislature. A bill is a proposal for legislative action, but it has no legally binding significance until finally enacted into a law. Let us assume that our bill is introduced first in the House of Representatives. Although the bill must be introduced by a member of Congress, it may have been conceived and drafted by someone else: by a legislator's staff, by staff of a House committee, by the House's Office of Legislative Counsel, by a bureau in the executive branch, or by a private interest group outside government. Ideas and proposals can come from almost anywhere, but a bill can be introduced only by a member of the legislative body.

102

Figure 5.1   **A Bill Becomes a Law**

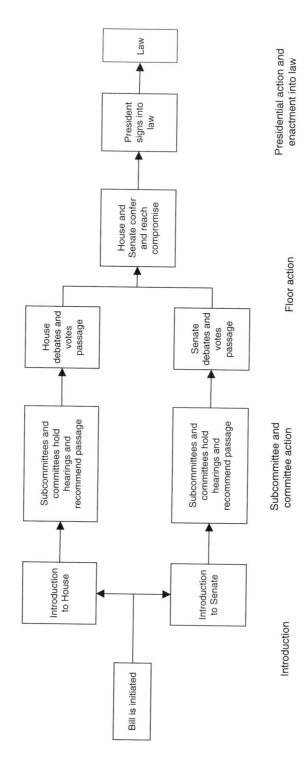

Bill is initiated

Introduction to House

Introduction to Senate

Subcommittees and committees hold hearings and recommend passage

Subcommittees and committees hold hearings and recommend passage

House debates and votes passage

Senate debates and votes passage

House and Senate confer and reach compromise

President signs into law

Law

Introduction

Subcommittee and committee action

Floor action

Presidential action and enactment into law

The Committee Stage

Once a bill has been introduced, it is referred to one of the standing (i.e., permanent) committees of the House. Most bills never get any further. It is almost impossible to compel a committee to send a bill back to the floor of the full House, and most proposals simply die in committee. If a committee or subcommittee chair, whose power is great, decides a bill is worthy of consideration, he or she usually schedules a public hearing at which interested groups and individuals have an opportunity to testify about it. The committee may end up by approving a bill as originally written, amending it, completely redrafting it, or declining to act favorably on it.

Modern legislative bodies are faced with such enormous workloads that they are obliged to rely heavily on their committees and, in the U.S. Congress, their subcommittees. No legislator can hope to become familiar with more than a fraction of the legislative proposals that are introduced. Each legislator has only general knowledge of most subjects and can become expert in only a few policy areas, so he or she must trust the judgment of other committee and subcommittee members in most areas—many of whom have become intimately familiar with a particular subject and have studied hundreds of bills related to it. So when a majority of a committee refuses to act favorably on a bill, other lawmakers can rarely be induced to override the committee's decision. Nor are they likely to oppose revisions the committee has suggested or to propose further amendments of their own.

In a very real sense, then, the committees and subcommittees determine what bills become laws and what the content of those bills will be. This is why special-interest groups, in their efforts to push a bill, try so hard to influence committee members, especially chairs. It is also why the committee's report on a bill, and the committee chair's remarks on a bill when it comes up for debate, are taken as the most authoritative interpretation of what the final enactment is intended to accomplish. We shall see in Chapter 6 that when judges attempt to interpret a statute, they often rely on these items of legislative history in their search for *legislative intent* (i.e., what the legislature intended the law to do); the assumption is that the purposes that motivated the legislature as a whole to enact a law are likely to be the same as those that prompted the committee to recommend passage. For the great majority of bills, then, the House does little more than review and ratify decisions of its committees.

Action by the Whole House

Responsibility for deciding when each of the bills reported out of committee should be brought before the House of Representatives rests with the House Rules Committee. This practice gives the Rules Committee almost a life-or-death power over the fate of each bill, making it probably the most influential committee of the House.

Some House members usually want to speak on the floor about a newly introduced bill. In the House (unlike the Senate), the total time allowed for discussion on any bill is severely restricted, and members who wish to speak must arrange speaking time with the leaders of their party. Often the purpose of these speeches is to impress a member's constituents at home rather than to influence other legislators.

While most bills that pass the House are little changed from the versions recommended by its committees, amendments are sometimes offered. Supporters of a bill must then decide whether to resist each proposed amendment. If opposition to a bill is strong, they may decide to accept certain amendments in the hope of ensuring the bill's adoption.

Passage Through the Other House

After a bill has been passed by the House of Representatives, it must clear a similar set of hurdles in the Senate. If the Senate fails to approve a bill before the current two-year term of Congress comes to an end, the bill is dead. Then the process must start all over again with reintroduction of a new bill in the next Congress, if supporters are determined to enact it.

Reconciliation of Differences

If the Senate passes a bill whose text is identical to that passed by the House, the bill goes at once to the President for signature. If the House and Senate versions of a bill are different, however, further action is necessary to secure agreement on a single version acceptable to both houses, because, for the law to be knowable, there can be only one set of words describing its rule; two versions of the same law would admit continuing confusion and debate about its meaning after enactment. Sometimes the house that first passed a bill will accept changes later made by the other house. At other times, a temporary *conference committee* made up of representatives of each house will try to work out a compromise version, which each house must then approve before it becomes law. Bills that have cleared all the earlier stages have failed to be enacted even at this late stage.

Action by the President

Before a bill can become law, it must be brought before the chief executive, the President of the United States, who has the choice of signing the bill into law, letting it become law without signing it, or vetoing it. A veto can be overridden by a two-thirds vote in each house, but vetoes are seldom overridden.

The decision to sign a bill is not always an easy decision for the President. For example, it is a common practice for Congress to attach additions, called *riders*, to bills that it forwards to the White House. These riders may be controversial, but the President cannot veto specific items within a bill; he must accept or reject the whole package. This makes it possible for Congress to obtain passage of certain items—often of interest to particular groups—that might otherwise never have been enacted into law.

When a bill has passed through all these stages, it becomes a law of the United States and an Act of Congress, and in due course it is published in several compilations of federal statutes.

DIFFERENCES BETWEEN DECISIONAL AND LEGISLATIVE LAWMAKING

The two lawmaking processes, and the two forms of law that they produce, are obviously quite different. Let us consider exactly what are some of the differences.

Big Steps and Little Ones

We said in the last chapter that judicial tradition sharply restricts the freedom of courts to create new legal rules. Judges do make law, but since they must build on principles and precedents, they are essentially limited to *interstitial* lawmaking—that is, to filling gaps and making small adjustments in the rules. Rarely do they take bold strides. When they do, it is usually because a truly novel case has come before them for decision, though occasionally they bring about an abrupt shift in legal rules by overruling (either explicitly or implicitly) a well-established but outmoded precedent.

Legislators are much less restrained. They are quite free, for instance, to repeal tomorrow a law that they passed today. They can, and quite often do, pass laws that annul long-established decisional rules. They and they alone can establish those arbitrary dividing lines so essential to any system of laws. For example, a legislature can pass a law stating that contracts to sell personal property for a price exceeding $500 are enforceable only if certain formal prerequisites can be shown to have been met. Judges can apply such a rule, of course, but they could not have originated it. The rules that judges make must be reasoned extensions of established principles, and an arbitrary dividing line like $500, however useful, cannot be justified in terms of principle. Finally, legislators have the power to establish new government agencies and to alter the authority of existing ones. This makes possible the adoption of far-reaching legal solutions that no court could attempt, since judges have no comparable power to create and alter institutional arrangements.

This is not to say, of course, that legislatures can do anything they choose. For one thing, constitutions impose various real limitations on legislative action, some of which we discuss in Chapter 7. More important, the need to reconcile change with continuity, progress with tradition, limits legislatures just as it does the courts. It is true that legislators have no formal obligation to relate what they do to what has gone before. Nonetheless, considerations of what is politically prudent and administratively feasible effectively prevent bold innovations most of the time. More often than not, legislation is a belated and insufficient response to needs that have finally become too urgent to ignore. And when legislators do take action, even when they are dealing with a new problem (such as that raised by our need to protect the environment), they are likely to build on existing rules, to adapt old and tested models to new uses, or to copy effective solutions worked out in other jurisdictions. Legislators are like judges, then, in preferring small, incremental steps to large ones.

The electorate may believe, at times, that a legislature is acting too slowly or is not adequately reflecting public sentiment. Two tools available to voters in these circumstances are *referenda* and *initiatives*. Referenda are policy issues proposed by the legislature and placed on a ballot, while initiatives are proposed by the electorate and placed on a ballot. In either case, the electorate is offered or demands a direct say in establishing public policy. It should be noted that not all states have a system for instituting referenda or initiatives.

Yet the difference remains: Legislatures have much more freedom to make major changes and innovations in the law than do courts. Most people would agree, moreover, that this is both inevitable and desirable. The accumulation of precedents and the growth of an ever more complex body of principles have inevitably narrowed the scope of judicial innovation. Meanwhile, with the strengthening of democratic traditions and institutions, legislatures have become the governmental bodies most immediately responsive to the popular will and hence the most appropriate makers of major changes in the law. Finally, and perhaps most important, the swift social, economic, and technological changes of the last hundred years have necessitated creation of new rules and new techniques of regulation at a rate that the slow judicial process of case-by-case accretion simply could not achieve.

General Problems and Particular Instances

One reason for limiting the freedom of judges to make bold policy innovations is that they do not encounter problems whole but in fragments. The first responsibility of a court is to decide the case before it. A court is well equipped intellectually to fit rules to cases, to fill in gaps, and to adjust existing rules; opposing lawyers can normally be counted on to supply needed information. A court, of course, cannot ignore the significance of its decision for future cases, but its perception of future situations that its decision will affect must always be imperfect. A court has limited means of investigating the broader problem area of which a case before it is but a part. It has neither a mandate nor the apparatus for conducting general investigations.

Appellate judges are not, of course, wholly unable to inform themselves concerning legislative facts (i.e., the background facts needed for lawmaking, as distinguished from adjudicative facts concerning events in a particular case). Opposing lawyers may include legislative facts—statistical data, for instance—in their briefs and oral arguments, and judges (or their clerical staff) may do a certain amount of research on their own. Before deciding the famous school desegregation cases culminating in *Brown v. Board of Education of Topeka, Kansas* in 1954, for example, the Supreme Court of the United States received an enormous amount of evidence on the social and psychological consequences of school segregation. Still, nobody would seriously contend that a court is as well equipped as a legislature to undertake extensive investigations.

A legislature, on the other hand, spends far more time dealing with problem areas, with whole classes of related situations, than with particular instances. Sometimes the legislature's attention is drawn to a problem by a particular incident, but the law it eventually passes is designed for general applicability. Thus, when Congress passed the federal kidnapping law of 1932, the Lindbergh case (the kidnapping and death of the baby son of famed aviator Charles Lindbergh, which had been much in the news) was fresh in the legislators' minds; however, the law they enacted was designed to deal with a whole class of possible occurrences. Although legislatures often base their efforts on what proves to be a distorted and fragmentary picture of a problem area, at least their attention is focused on the general problem rather than on a single case. And their traditionally broad investigatory powers enable them to make a much more thorough study of the problem than can the courts.

The Opportunity and the Obligation to Act

What we have been saying suggests a relatively simple division of functions. Legislators, we might conclude, are solely responsible for formulating broad new rules and for creating and revising the institutions necessary to put them into effect. Judges, limited to the function of disposing of cases that others have brought before them, decide how the rules apply to the cases, and in the course of doing so, they make such interstitial adjustments in the rules as are needed to meet new situations.

In practice, the division of functions is not so sharp. For while legislatures are certainly in a better position than judges to take major steps to deal with whole problems, it does not follow that they always assume responsibility for doing so. Legislatures may choose between broad and restricted action, but they have a third alternative: they may refrain from acting at all. With few exceptions, when a court is presented with a case that falls within its jurisdiction, it must make some decision. That decision may be bold and creative or it may be narrowly confined. Only the U.S. Supreme Court and a few other top appellate courts have the power to choose which cases they will hear; when these courts refuse to hear a case, the decision of the lower court of appeals is final.

The statute books are full of outmoded laws that are no longer appropriate to the situations they were designed to cover, but are still in force because legislatures have not amended or repealed them. And all states have numerous outmoded decisional rules that their courts feel compelled to apply because legislatures have not got around to passing laws superseding them.

Nearly all legislatures have more work than they can handle during their regular sessions. Only a small fraction of their time is spent on enacting laws affecting private transactions and relationships. Legislators spend much more time, for instance, on discharging their responsibility for the operation and financing of government and on keeping in touch with their constituents. If they are to be induced to revise an existing rule, strong, persuasive, and articulate pressure must be exerted on them. If those who favor change are unable to organize and give voice to their views or if any strong opposition to the change is expressed, busy legislators are likely to avoid taking any action.

Some fifty years ago Judge Cardozo wrote an article proposing, as a means of counteracting this inertia, that each state should establish a commission for law revision. These commissions, staffed by experts, would have no power of their own. They would simply carry on a continuing study of the state's legal rules, both decisional and statutory, and from time to time submit to the state legislature draft proposals embodying needed changes in the law. New York adopted this proposal, and its commission has done valuable work.

The need for revision and modernization in most states is too great, however, for any commission, even if it works with the most conscientious and energetic of legislatures, to do much more than scratch the surface of this problem.

Under the *stare decisis* principle, primary responsibility for changing established but unsatisfactory decisional rules may be said to lie with legislatures, not with courts. However, persistent failure of legislatures to meet this responsibility puts the courts under pressure to change unsatisfactory rules themselves by overruling offending precedents. Some critics believe the courts have not been sufficiently willing to take this responsibility for keeping decisional rules up-to-date.

Influencing Lawmakers

The Judiciary

The foregoing remarks about legislative inertia suggest that another difference between the two types of lawmaking lies in the methods by which private persons seek to influence judges and legislators, respectively.

Assume for a moment you are a member of a group in Illinois that is extremely dissatisfied with the 1973 Supreme Court decision in *Roe v. Wade*. The court ruled that no state may interfere with a woman's right to have an abortion during the first trimester (three months) of her pregnancy. Your group recognizes that over the years the court's guidelines have limited the state's powers to regulate abortions. Thus, you would like to see the court change the ruling. What can you do?

One possibility is to arrange for a lawsuit in the courts in which the issue will be raised again. Arranging for such a test case can be costly and difficult, but let us assume that it can be done. Presumably the lower courts will feel obliged to follow the *Roe v. Wade* precedent and thus will decide against the party your group is backing.

Knowing how reluctant courts are to overrule their earlier decisions, your group may ask itself whether it could supplement the briefs and oral arguments of the appellant's lawyer by bringing other pressures to bear on the judges. For instance, could it send a delegation to explain to the judges why the *Roe* rule is so bad? Could it persuade as many citizens as possible to write letters to the judges urging them to overrule *Roe?* If other pressures seemed insufficient, could it send pickets with placards to parade around the courthouse?

As you know, these are not proper ways to influence judges. Picketing a court is illegal in many places, and the other proposed methods, if tried, would certainly be ignored or rebuffed by the judges. The only permissible method for trying to influence a judicial decision is through formal presentation of evidence and arguments, with each party having an opportunity to refute the evidence and arguments of the other. This is the essence of the adversary system.

Judges are supposed to be immune to private pressures of the sort traditionally exerted on political leaders. Their decisions should not be affected by concern for their personal popularity and career advancement. Moreover, their religious beliefs, personal associations, and political affiliations should not determine their decisions. This is not to say, of course, that improper pressures, biases, and calculations of advantage have never been known to affect a judge's decision. Such influences, however, are repugnant to the whole judicial tradition. Certainly no competent attorney would even hint at such considerations in his or her argument.

Lobbying and Political Action Committees

Suppose now that, after your experience with the abortion issue in the courts, you decide to look for an alternative to the judiciary and turn to the legislature. Influencing a legislature is completely different from influencing a court. The freedom of choice of legislators, as we have seen, is relatively unconfined; no adversary principle limits the permissible methods of influencing them. Legislators are openly and avowedly makers of policy decisions, and consequently legislatures are the main arena of debate over policy.

In fact, the pressure of interest groups has always been a part of the legislative process. An *interest group* may be defined as a group of people with shared values or interests seeking to influence public policy. In this country there are thousands of interest groups, large and small, actively working on causes ranging from gun control (National Rifle Association) to Social Security (American Association of Retired Persons). Finding an interest group presenting a "pro-life" position (such as the National Right to Life Committee) would not be difficult at all. Incidentally, the choice of symbolic labels such as "pro-life" instead of "anti-abortion" reflects the public relations efforts of interest groups to win support for their positions. The use of labels is value-laden and sometimes volatile. Many people who will willingly associate with "pro" labels would be put off by "anti" labels.

Having found an appropriate interest group, the next logical step would be to present your arguments to legislators. Most legislators would, in fact, be willing and able to listen to points of view that could not be presented to a court. Legislators would want to know whether changes in the law would be popular, whether they would please more voters than they would displease. A citizens' group could quite openly argue that change would bring about social or ethical advantages for a community, a type of persuasion that would not be of primary importance in arguments presented to a court.

These arguments would most likely be presented by a lobbyist working on behalf of your interest group. Lobbying has not always had a good reputation. Nonetheless, given the number and complexity of issues that face legislators every session, lobbyists perform an important role. Many lobbyists have specialized knowledge they can share with members of a legislature. Moreover they are able to gather a good deal of additional information about particular pieces of legislation that they readily share with members of Congress and their staffs.

In addition to talking to legislators about the abortion issue, you may also wish to work with a political action committee (PAC). These groups are specifically established to contribute money to political candidates and to work toward particular policy goals. For example, a PAC might use its money to support candidates who avow an interest in "protecting the rights of the unborn." Some PACs currently at work in Washington, DC, have spent millions of dollars supporting candidates for federal positions. According to data released by the Federal Election Commission in October 2006, for example, the National Association of Realtors PAC spent more than $3 million and the National Beer Wholesalers Association almost $2.4 million on the 2006 congressional elections (Center for Responsive Politics 2006).

The number of PACs has grown dramatically in the United States. In 1976 there were fewer than 100 PACs. At the end of 2004 there were over 4,800, with an increase of about 1,000 in the months just before the 2004 elections (Federal Election Commission 2005). The reasons for this growth are numerous, one being the 1976 Supreme Court case *Buckley v. Valeo* (424 U.S. 1), which upheld the Federal Election Campaign Act of 1974 permitting unions and corporations to establish political groups and allowing up to $5,000 to be contributed to each candidate in an election. Another spur to the growth of PACs was an advisory opinion given to Sun Oil Company by the Federal Election Commission on the right to use corporate treasury funds to pay PAC operating expenses. The Election Commission upheld the corporate right to use funds, provided the corporations established a separate, segregated fund for such political contributions.

Lobbying and PACs are effective, legal means for influencing the direction of legislative action. Some critics advocate very strict control over such activities because they hold such great potential for abuse of power, given the large sums of money at the disposal of some PACs. Defenders of PACs think that fewer regulations are needed. They believe the variety of points of view represented by different PACs are part of what should be as open and free an exchange of ideas as possible in our pluralistic society.

Written versus Unwritten Law

Up to this point we have been discussing differences between two *processes* of lawmaking. There is also a difference between the *products.* Laws passed by legislatures are often referred to as "written" law, in contrast to the "unwritten" decisional law produced by courts. Actually, of course, decisions that embody decisional rules are reported and published. The distinction is that statutes and other enactments—constitutions, executive orders, and administrative regulations—are written in the sense that they have an exclusive, official text; decisional rules, on the other hand, are unwritten in the sense that, although they can be extracted from what happened in decided cases, they have no official text.

While the words of a statute often have to be interpreted, the words themselves may not be ignored. The words *are* the law. As we shall explain in Chapter 6, they set limits to the meanings that can be attributed to a statute. For instance, if a law provides that no male under the age of sixteen may marry, no amount of interpreting will make it permissible for a boy of fifteen to get married.

The language of the opinion that accompanies a judicial decision has no comparable force. As we explained in Chapter 4, the precedent is established by what the court *does*, not by what it *says.* An opinion is an authoritative discussion of rules relating to the problem at hand, but it is not the official text of a rule or rules. To put it differently, an opinion announcing an appellate decision could be phrased in a number of ways without changing the rule of the case.

Convenience, Codification, and Uniformity

A final basis of comparison concerns the relative convenience of decisional and statutory forms of law for lawyers and judges who have to work with them. On the whole, it is easier to determine the applicable rule in a particular case when the basic rules are statutory than when they are purely decisional. Even with all the modern aids to case research—treatises, digests, encyclopedias, and the like—finding controlling precedents is usually a much more arduous task than finding relevant statutory provisions.

In recent years there has been a development of great interest to legal researchers: the increasing capacity of computers to assist in searching for legal reference matter. Law libraries of courts, universities, and law firms now have computer terminals that will, among other things, provide a lawyer with many current statutes, case citations, and articles on particular topics in legal periodicals. Persons interested in computer-assisted research resources such as InfoTrac or Lexis/Nexis can obtain more information by contacting a law librarian or visiting www.gale.com or www.lexisnexis.com online.

The searcher's work is not always finished when a statute is found, however; looking up cases may still be necessary. This is because a statute is likely to include concepts and subordinate rules taken from decisional law. To understand these, it may be necessary to look up cases antedating the statute. Moreover, once a statute has been applied and interpreted by a court, the court's interpretation becomes in effect a part of the statute; in the future, lawyers and judges must look at the interpretation as well as the statute itself. This is why many statute books are *annotated*: following each provision is a brief summary of decisions interpreting it, with references to them. These books include annotated versions of the *U.S. Code* published commercially as *U.S. Code Annotated* (USCA) and *U.S. Code Service* (USCS). Title and section numbers are the same in all three versions of the code, but annotated versions also include references to court cases decided under each provision, and lists of relevant articles in legal periodicals.

The greater convenience of working with statutes is one of several reasons why, over the past century, our legislatures have enacted a considerable part of U.S. decisional law into statutory form. The process of assembling scattered decisional rules into an orderly statutory code is known as *codification.* Sometimes the transformation has taken place without change in the rules themselves; but sometimes codification has been in response to pressures for substantive change, and legislators have modified the rules in the course of codifying them.

Much of the stimulus for codification has arisen from the need for greater uniformity among the rules of the several states. This has been particularly true in the field of commercial law, where conflicting state decisional rules greatly complicated the conduct of interstate business. In 1890 the states set up a Conference of Commissioners on Uniform State Laws. The commissioners, appointed by their state governors, were to be specialists in the various fields of law under study. Over the years the conference has drafted a number of legislative proposals for submission to state legislatures. Some of these proposals—most notably the Uniform Commercial Code—have been adopted by all or most of the states; others have been less well received.

The extent to which decisional law has been codified differs from state to state. Many states have codified their criminal law and now have no purely common-law crimes (i.e., acts made criminal solely by judicial decision). There is, however, still a great deal of uncodified decisional law in every one of the states; nowhere do we find the comprehensive codification that characterizes the civil-law tradition.

The term *codification* is also used to describe a process whereby new statutes enacted each year by a legislative body are integrated with all enactments from previous years in the same jurisdiction. Although this is not done in all countries, in the United States, statutes and regulations of the national government are published as they are created and subsequently codified (Hamilton 2005, 24–25). Statutes first appear as paper *slip laws* in pamphlet form when enacted, then are published in chronological order at the end of each year in hardbound volumes of *Statutes at Large.* Thereafter, the text of each new statute is integrated and codified section by section with previously enacted statutes concerning similar subject matter in the *United States Code,* first by insertion of "paper part" supplements in the back of existing hardbound volumes and subsequently (about every five years) by publication of new hardbound volumes replacing earlier versions.

Provisions of law repealed by later enactments are deleted from the new volumes, language of amended provisions is changed, and new provisions are located with previous enactments on the same or similar subjects in the *U.S. Code*, providing a single, authoritative, relatively up-to-date text of current law. These volumes are extensively indexed, with tables of cross-references to related statutes, for ease of use. An attorney who purchases a complete set of volumes must also purchase a subscription to keep them up-to-date.

A similar process is applied to regulations, which are first published in the *Federal Register*, the official daily publication of the executive branch of the U.S. government. Each year these regulations are integrated and codified with the text of previous regulations of the same agency concerning similar subject matter in the *U.S. Code of Federal Regulations*, which is bound in a set of paperback volumes. After codification, the result is a single set of current regulations issued by each agency on particular subjects, also extensively indexed, with tables of cross-references to related statutes and regulations of other agencies.

Thus, codification makes it easier than it would otherwise be for lawyers, citizens, and judges to research statutes, regulations, and previous court decisions. With the development of computerized databases and search engines, a tedious and laborious task has been made somewhat less onerous, but it remains time consuming because of the ever-increasing volume of information available to be searched.

SOME PROBLEMS OF LEGISLATIVE DRAFTING

Some day you may be asked to collaborate with a lawyer in preparing a draft proposal for legislation in some field in which you are an expert. It is more likely, however, that your contacts with legislation will be confined to figuring out with a lawyer how some already enacted statute affects transactions that concern you. Thus, even if you never have anything to do with the actual drafting of legislation, you will find it useful to have some conception of the problems involved in this process. Before setting to work, the drafter of a statute must decide the answers to certain broad questions, relating them to the specific object at hand.

How Is Conduct Best Channeled?

As an example, imagine that the framer's object in drafting a statute is to limit the actions that a debt collector may take in collecting money from a debtor. Should the law be written to limit these actions sharply, no matter what form they take? Or should debt collectors be restrained only from acting outrageously? What penalties should be imposed on the erring debt collector? Should collectors treat consumers who routinely evade their bills differently than those who have failed to pay due to temporary financial difficulties? Should the consumer protection division of the state attorney general's office launch a major educational campaign to inform consumers of the pitfalls of failing to pay their bills?

Nowadays the drafter of legislation is likely to be not a legislator but a trained specialist. Although a given problem may lie outside the expertise of the specialist, he or she must be familiar with alternative techniques of channeling private conduct and with experiences that different jurisdictions have had in applying these techniques to similar problems in the past. Only then will the drafter be able to outline alternatives and suggest what their respective advantages and disadvantages are likely to be.

How Precise Should a Statute Be?

How far should the legislative drafter go in trying to devise specific provisions to cover future situations? The ideal statute would specify all the possible situations to which it should apply, and its words would convey precisely the same meaning to everyone who read them. Obviously, no statute writer could ever realize these goals. Since human foresight is limited, a drafter could never hope to anticipate all possible situations to which a statute might conceivably apply. And words are at best imperfect symbols for communicating intent.

Most people believe that perfect clarity and precision, although impossible to achieve, must always be the ideals toward which a statute writer should strive. There are circumstances, however, in which the framers of a statute are justified in being deliberately imprecise. Sometimes legislators realize that some sort of action must be taken to deal with a certain problem, but that the scope of the problem and of the remedies needed are not yet clear and will be revealed only as the future unfolds. The lawmakers may therefore decide to enact a statute that merely identifies the problem, outlines in relatively broad terms the primary and remedial rules to be applied, and leaves the details to be filled in through successive applications of the statute to particular cases.

This is, of course, the typical approach of framers of constitutional provisions, for they realize that constitutions must last a long time and usually are hard to amend. What phrase could be more deliberately imprecise, for instance, than "No State shall . . . deprive any person of life, liberty, or property, without due process of law?"

The key provision of the Sherman Antitrust Act of 1890 is embodied in a single sentence: "Every contract, combination in the form of trust or otherwise, or conspiracy, in restraint of trade or commerce among the several states or with foreign nations, is hereby declared to be illegal." Another sentence of about equal length and imprecision makes it illegal to "monopolize or attempt to monopolize." The rest of the brief statute consists of remedial provisions. No attempt is made to define the broad terms used in the key sentence, thereby leaving such attempts to administrators and judges. However, terms like *contract, combination, restraint of trade,* and *monopolize* are not quite so empty of specific content as they may seem to the layperson. They had taken on meaning from their use in judicial opinions and statutes before 1890. Even so, judges have had a large measure of freedom to create law when they apply the Sherman Act provisions to particular cases.

A statute is a sort of communication addressed to various categories of people who will be affected by its enactment. It requires (or forbids or permits or enables) private persons to do certain things, it tells enforcement officials what they must or may do, and it provides judges with a new set of rules to apply and interpret in disposing of cases. In effect, a broad, generally worded statute "passes the buck" to those it addresses, effectively delegating to them the task of elaborating its meaning, progressively, case by case. Ambiguous statutory language thus increases administrative discretion; more specific wording restricts official decisions.

A private person is likely to be the first to test a statute, by doing something that causes another private person or an official to react. Each of them is, in a sense, interpreting the statute. The ultimate and authoritative interpretation, however, must come from the courts, when controversies engendered by conduct with which the statute is concerned are brought before them.

A broad, general statute starts out, then, as a somewhat cryptic communication. It takes on greater precision as those to whom it is addressed test it out and arrive at successive interpretations. The uncertainty produced initially by an imprecise law is often preferable to the crippling certainty of a highly specific law that is ill adapted to situations that arise after its enactment. Premature, excessive precision may deny enforcement officials and judges all latitude of interpretation and may make it impossible for them to administer justice in an orderly and reasonable way: Should a case arise of a sort not foreseen by the lawmakers, a judge who must decide it may be left with no choice but to apply a rule that he or she knows will produce an inappropriate result.

We must not make too strong a case for vagueness and imprecision in statute writing, however. More often than not, imprecision is inappropriate and troublesome. Statute writers usually fall into vague language not because they decide to do so, but because their thinking is fuzzy or because they are in a hurry. However, sometimes vague words are used deliberately with the hope of lulling potentially antagonistic legislators into voting for what seems to be a harmless bill, to secure the requisite majority vote.

What Vocabulary Is Appropriate?

The legislative drafter must first try to identify the sort of people who will probably read the statute and then choose a vocabulary that speaks most directly to them. Such questions as these are appropriate: Are the private addressees members of the general public, or are they a restricted group familiar with a technical vocabulary (for example, the vocabulary of pharmacology)? Are the officials who must read the statute likely to be familiar with a technical vocabulary? Must the statute be made understandable to persons without legal training?

Anyone who reads statutes should be aware that the typical drafter assumes the principal readers will be lawyers, experienced administrative officials, and judges. Little effort is made to use language intelligible to persons outside the legal profession. The usual aim is to avoid ambiguity at all costs, so a drafter tends to choose words and phrases with sharply delimited meanings familiar to persons trained in the law. This accounts for the unlovely style sometimes known as *legalese* or legal English, which many people assume is designed to confuse and mystify them. Among its characteristics are repetition of the same words or phrases, strings of near synonyms, and awkward words like *aforesaid* and *heretofore*. Inelegant though they may seem, such words and phrases often have a relatively precise scope and content established by judicial interpretation. Under most circumstances, drafters are justified in their decision to concentrate on speaking clearly and unambiguously to the reader trained in law.

CHAPTER PROBLEM: DRAFTING A STATUTE

Imagine you have been elected to the U.S. Senate from your state. Suppose that a group of citizens from your state wants to draft a statute to reduce the amount of unethical behavior, such as bribes and illegal payments, that big business practices overseas. The citizens ask you to prepare a short draft statute for them, together with notes explaining your inclusions and exclusions. You are aware that many so-called large corporations do business in your state and that executives at some of these firms might argue that standards of morality should not be imposed throughout the world.

Please prepare a brief draft for your constituents. As a starting point, consider the following section of a hypothetical statute (based on the Foreign Corrupt Practices Act of 1977, slightly modified and renumbered to make sense in this context):

Foreign Corrupt Practices by Domestic Concerns

Sec. 104. [A] It shall be unlawful for any domestic concern . . . to make use of the mails or any means or instrumentality of interstate commerce corruptly in furtherance of an offer, payment, promise to pay, or authorization of the payment of any money, or offer, gift, promise to give, or authorization of the giving of anything of value to . . . any person, while knowing or having reason to know that all or a portion of such money or thing of value will be offered, given or promised, directly or indirectly, to any foreign official, to any foreign political party or official thereof, or to any candidate for foreign political office, for purposes of—

[1] influencing any act or decision of such foreign official, political party, party official, or candidate in his or its official capacity, including a decision to fail to perform his or its official functions; or

[2] inducing such foreign official, political party, party official, or candidate to use his or its influence with a foreign government or instrumentality thereof to affect or influence any act or decision of such government or instrumentality, in order to assist such domestic concern in obtaining or retaining business for or with, or directing business to, any person.

[B] Except as provided in subsection [C], any domestic concern that violates subsection [A] shall, upon conviction, be fined not more than $1,000,000.

[C] Any individual who is a domestic concern and who willfully violates subsection [A] shall, upon conviction, be fined not more than $10,000, or imprisoned not more than five years, or both.

Questions

1. What would seem to be the goals of the Foreign Corrupt Practices Act?
2. How would you respond to an argument made by a corporate representative that the Foreign Corrupt Practices Act places U.S. businesses at a competitive disadvantage because other countries are not burdened by such a law?

QUESTIONS FOR REVIEW

1. How does a draft proposal become law?
2. Judging from the description of the process by which legislation is enacted, what do you think would be the most appropriate stage at which an interest group might seek to influence the shaping of a particular legislative proposal? Why?
3. The pressure of interest groups has always been an intrinsic part of the legislative process in the United States. But if a legislature responds only to the interest groups that apply the most pressure, will the laws that it makes be unjust? Explain your answer.
4. Explain how the House Rules Committee has life-or-death power over the fate of each bill. Do you feel it is right for the committee to have this power? Why or why not?
5. What are some of the differences between the lawmaking role of a judge (decisional lawmaking) and that of a committee member of a house of the legislature (legislative lawmaking)?
6. Explain the statement made earlier in this chapter: "An opinion announcing an appellate decision could be phrased in a number of ways without changing the rule of the case."
7. What is the purpose of codification?

8. What are some important points that a legislator must consider before writing a draft proposal for legislation?
9. Many new statutes are enacted by Congress every year. How are statutes organized to relate a new law to all previous laws that are still in effect?

BIBLIOGRAPHY

Center for Responsive Politics. 2006. www.opensecrets.org.
Federal Election Commission. 2005. "PAC Activity Increases for 2004 Elections." Press release, April 13. www.fec.gov/press/press2005/2005041pac/PACFINAL2004.html.
Hamilton, Michael S. 2005. *Mining Environmental Policy: Comparing Indonesia and the USA*. London: Ashgate.

CHAPTER 6

Judicial Lawmaking II
Interpretation of Statutes

The meaning of a statutory provision and the types of situations it does or does not cover are matters ultimately determined by the courts. Citizens who wish to understand their legal environment should know something about this process of interpretation and application, which is called *statutory construction.* They do not, of course, need detailed knowledge of the many rules of statutory construction that judges have developed, but they should have some idea of the main problems that judges encounter.

In the vast majority of cases, courts have no trouble determining how a statute applies. But problems in application do arise in a significant minority of cases. Some statutes contain unintentional errors and ambiguities because they were poorly drafted. Other statutes are unclear because those who pushed them through a legislature sought to avoid opposition by being vague or silent on potentially controversial matters. The most important reason for the lack of absolute clarity and preciseness in statutes is that their framers were not able to foresee and provide for all possible future situations. Realizing their inability to foretell the future, the wisest legislators usually prefer to be deliberately imprecise, by the generality of their language necessarily delegating to others the task of filling in the details. The principal recipients of this task are administrative officials and judges. The more imprecise a statute is, the greater the delegated authority must be. With a very broad and general statute like the Sherman Antitrust Act, the "interpreter" becomes, in effect, the true lawmaker.

Problems of statutory interpretation typically fall into one of the following categories:

1. A legislature passes a statute that applies to a designated class of persons or objects, but fails to specify precise boundaries of the class. For example, if a statute applies to "vehicles," does the class of "vehicles" include an airplane, a tricycle, or an ancient carriage mounted on a pedestal? Or a statute may refer to "persons," and a case arises involving a corporation: is a corporation a "person"?

2. From its language alone, a statute seems to apply to a particular situation, but common sense suggests that it really should not. For example, a federal statute makes it a crime to detain a postal employee while on duty. Does this statute apply to a local sheriff who serves an arrest warrant on a mail carrier charged with murder?

3. From its language alone, a statute does *not* seem to apply to a particular situation, but common sense suggests that it really should. For example, an old act of Congress providing for the sale of public land at a low price to settlers specified the amount of land that single men and married men might buy. A widow sought to buy some land. Was she a "single man" or a "married man," or was she not qualified under the law to buy land?

4. An old statute remains on the books long after the immediate problems it was designed to deal with have changed. For example, a statute passed in 1880 refers to "vehicles." A case arising in 1962 involves an automobile. Since automobiles were unknown in 1880, does the statute apply? Is it reasonable to assume that any vehicle unknown to the statute writers in 1880 should be excluded from its coverage? Or should any object to which the designation "vehicle" could reasonably be applied at any later date automatically be covered? Or is some intermediate interpretation preferable?

THE INTENTION OF THE LEGISLATURE

When writing an opinion in a case requiring statutory construction, a judge usually says at the outset that the court's object is to carry out as best it can the intention of the legislature. There is no disagreement over this objective, but difficulties arise in trying to achieve it. Some of these difficulties are discussed in the following sections.

Finding a Collective Intention

Determining what a group of legislators intended when they voted for a bill is not easy. Although they all voted for the same set of words, it does not follow that they all did so with the same intention. What they thought is largely unrecorded, but we can be sure they did not all favor the law for precisely the same reasons or with the same expectations as to what it would accomplish. Many of them unquestionably voted for it merely because they trusted or were beholden to its sponsors. Others voted for it because they expected those sponsors to reciprocate on some later occasion, and still others were pressed to vote for it by leaders of their party. Some legislators, particularly the bill's sponsors and members of the committees that worked on it, certainly had definite views on what the bill was designed to accomplish.

As we suggested in Chapter 5, it is usually assumed that, in voting for a bill, legislative majorities are in effect ratifying policies enunciated by their committees. Although this assumption is usually justified, one of the reasons for adopting it is the difficulty of making any better generalization about collective legislative intentions.

Finding an Intention with Respect to Specific Situations

Hard as it is to identify a general legislative intention, it is harder still to surmise what the legislature intended with respect to particular situations not explicitly provided for.

Few legislators give much thought to the detailed application of a statute. Even those who are most concerned with its passage inevitably fail to foresee some situations that later arise; consequently, its applicability to these situations is uncertain. In short, talking about the legislative intent with reference to specific fact-situations is likely to be largely unrealistic and speculative.

Finding an Underlying Purpose

Judges have tended to conclude that the only sensible solution to this problem is to identify not a specific intent shared by all the legislators who voted for the law but to search instead for broad purposes and policies that probably motivated those who actively favored the bill. The judges ask themselves such questions as these: What were the legal rules channeling conduct in this area of activity before this statute was enacted? How does the statute seem to have changed those rules? What seem to have been the ills that a statute was designed to cure? Then, having identified as best they can the general purposes underlying the statute, the judges ask themselves one final question: What interpretation of the specific statutory provisions that are apparently applicable to the fact-situation before us will best serve the purposes of the statute as a whole?

Not only is this somewhat speculative use of logic the only realistic way to use legislative intent, but it is also the way in which legislators almost certainly expect judges to behave. Having done their best to embody their collective objectives in a final enactment, legislators do not expect judges to figure out precisely what their thoughts were with respect to particular fact-situations or what their thoughts *would have been* if the situations had occurred to them. Legislators are aware that the applicability of their statute to particular cases will not always be clear. They expect judges to decide cases by accepting the authority delegated to them to elaborate the statute's meanings—that is, to work out sensible applications of a statute's identified purposes. And by accepting this authority, judges exercise a limited power to make law that our legal system bestows upon them.

The case of *Temple v. City of Petersburg* provides an excellent illustration of the difficulties faced by judges in interpreting ambiguous statutes.

Temple v. City of Petersburg

Supreme Court of Appeals of Virginia
182 Va. 418, 29 S.E. 2d 357 (1944)

GREGORY, JUSTICE: The appellants, who were the complainants in the court below, filed their bill in equity against the city of Petersburg, praying that it be restrained and enjoined from using a tract of 1.01 acres of land acquired by it in 1942 for cemetery purposes. This plot of land adjoined Peoples Memorial Cemetery, which had been established and used as a cemetery for more than one hundred years. [It was acquired by the city with the intention of re-interring in it bodies that had to be exhumed in order that a road on another side of the cemetery could be widened. The tract lies directly across St. Andrews Street from the front of appellants' residence.]

The court below temporarily restrained the city from using the 1.01-acre tract as an addition to the cemetery. Later the city filed its answer to the bill and, by consent, the cause was set for hearing upon the bill, the answer, and a stipulation of counsel. The court dissolved the injunction and refused the prayer for relief.

Code, sec. 56 (Michie 1942) provides in part as follows:

> No cemetery shall be hereafter established within the corporate limits of any city or town; nor shall any cemetery be *established* [emphasis added] within two hundred and fifty yards of any residence without the consent of the owner of the legal and equitable title of such residence. . . .

We are called upon to ascertain the proper meaning of the statute, and to decide whether or not it has been violated by the city. Specifically the controversy concerns the meaning to be given to the word, "established," used therein. The appellants maintain that under the statute the enlargement of an existing cemetery, such as is sought here, in reality is the establishment of a cemetery, while the appellee contends that to enlarge an existing cemetery is not the establishment of a cemetery and, therefore, constitutes no violation of the statute. . . .

The principal and determinative issue to be determined in this case is whether or not the proposed enlargement of Peoples Memorial Cemetery, by the additional 1.01-acre tract, is prohibited by section 56 of the Code.

The appellants most strongly contend that the word "established," as used in the statute, means "located," and that the evil intended to be inhibited is the location of a cemetery in a city or town upon ground not previously dedicated for cemetery purposes, or the location of a cemetery within 250 yards of a residence, whether by enlargement or otherwise. They contend that the purpose of the statute is to protect residences and lands from the ill effects growing out of close proximity to a cemetery. They further contend that it is unreasonable to say that residences and lands are to be protected against the "establishment" of cemeteries, but are not to be protected against the encroachment or enlargement of existing cemeteries; that the evil created by one is equally as real as that created by the other.

The position of the appellee is that the word "established" has such a clear and precise meaning that no question of statutory construction arises. That the statute provides that no cemetery shall be "hereafter established" in a city or town, and that this language does not mean that a cemetery already established shall not be hereafter enlarged. To hold otherwise would be not to construe the statute, but in effect to amend it.

It is elementary that the ultimate aim of rules of interpretation is to ascertain the intention of the legislature in the enactment of a statute, and that intention, when discovered, must prevail. If, however, the intention of the legislature is perfectly clear from the language used, rules of construction are not to be applied. We are not allowed to construe that which has no need of construction. If the language of a statute is plain and unambiguous, and its meaning perfectly clear and definite, effect must be given to it regardless of what courts think of its wisdom or policy. In such cases courts must find the meaning within the statute itself.

In *Commonwealth v. Sanderson,* 170 Va. 33, we quoted with approval from *Saville v. Virginia Ry. and Power Co.,* 114 Va. 444, this statement of the rule:

> It is contended that the construction insisted upon by the plaintiff in error is violative of the spirit or reason of the law. The argument would seem to concede that the contention is within the letter of the law. We hear a great deal about the spirit of the law, but the duty of this court is not to make law, but to construe it; not to wrest its letter from its plain meaning in order to conform to what is conceived to be its spirit, in order to subserve and promote some principle of justice and equality which it is claimed the letter of the law has violated. It is our duty to take the words which the legislature has seen fit to employ and give to them their usual and ordinary signification, and, having thus ascertained the legislative intent, to give effect to it, unless it transcends the legislative power as limited by the Constitution.

The word "established" is defined in Webster's New International Dictionary, 2d Ed., 1936, thus: "To originate and secure the permanent existence of; to found; to institute; to create and regulate;—said of a colony, a State or other institutions."

Just why the Legislature, in its wisdom, saw fit to prohibit establishment of cemeteries in cities and towns, and did not see fit to prohibit enlargements or additions, is no concern of ours. Certain it is that language could not be plainer than that employed to express the legislative will. From it we can see with certainty that while a cemetery may not be established in a city or town, it may be added to or enlarged without running counter to the inhibition found in section 56. We are not permitted to read into the statute an inhibition which the Legislature, perhaps advisedly, omitted. Our duty is to construe the statue as written.

If construction of the statute were necessary and proper in this case, we would be forced to the same conclusion. Even if it be assumed that there is ambiguity in the language in section 56, the legislative history of its enactment and a consideration of Code, sec. 53, a related statute, would remove all doubt as to what the legislature intended by its language in section 56.

Code, sec. 53, affords a complete answer to the question of legislative intent in the use of the word "established" in section 56, for the former section makes a distinction between "establish" and "enlarge" in these words: "If it be desired at any time to establish a cemetery, for the use of a city, town, county, or magisterial district, or to enlarge any such already established, and the title to land needed cannot be otherwise acquired, land sufficient for the purpose may be condemned . . ."

The foregoing language, taken from section 53, completely demonstrates that the Legislature did not intend the words "establish" and "enlarge" to be used interchangeably, but that the use of one excluded any idea that it embraced or meant the other. As used, they are mutually exclusive. To enlarge or add to a cemetery is not to establish one within the meaning of section 56.

The language of the statute being so plain and unambiguous, and the intention and meaning of the Legislature so clear, we hold that the city of Petersburg has not violated Code, sec. 56, and the decree accordingly should be affirmed.

Affirmed.

The Meaning and Context of a Statute's Words

Justice Gregory has two arguments to support his conclusion that the restrictions on cemeteries "hereafter established" do not apply to enlargements of existing cemeteries. The first concerns the "plain meaning" of the words of section 56 of the Virginia Code; the second involves an interpretation of section 56 in the light of the wording of section 53, a related statute. Let us confine ourselves for the present to the first argument.

The justice starts out with the familiar statement that the court's aim must be to discover and carry out the intention of the legislature and that that intention must be looked for first in the statutory language. He appears to apply the usual approach to statutory interpretation, that in the absence of ambiguity or conflicting passages, the words mean what they say on their face, in the ordinary meaning of plain language. But he makes it clear that he has *not* looked for the *purpose* of the statute. Perhaps if he had considered the language ambiguous, he would have looked for an underlying purpose. But "rules of construction," he says, become relevant only when language is ambiguous. When it is unambiguous, no interpretation is necessary. Since the court finds the meaning of *established* perfectly plain, its only task is to apply the plain meaning, with no regard to the policy behind it.

At first this seems to be a sensible argument. If words are plain, why waste time applying rules of construction to them? A traditional argument for literalism in statutory interpretation is that, since the legislature presumably chose its words carefully, the best way to carry out its intention is to give those words their natural meaning. The argument clearly has merit. After all, if judges are allowed to interpret plain words, what is to prevent them from nullifying or distorting statutes to suit their own predilections? This plain-meaning rule would seem to be a useful curb on judicial usurpations of the legislative function, of which there have been some notorious examples. The case reports are full of instances in which judges resorted to literal, strict, narrow interpretations not because of a scrupulous desire to carry out the legislative intent but as a means to avoid carrying out legislative policies of which they disapproved. In short, judges bent on usurping the legislative function may resort to either a too liberal or a too literal policy of interpretation. A similar argument may be advanced concerning liberal or strict construction of the U.S. Constitution, discussed below in Chapter 7.

What are the criteria for deciding whether or not a word or phrase is "plain and unambiguous"? And what should a judge do when she realizes that to give effect to an apparently clear meaning of a statutory provision would produce a result that seems absurd, or harsh and unreasonable, or at least surprising? The perils of interpreting words too literally are illustrated by a simple story. The mistress of the house calls to a nursemaid, "Drop what you're doing and come here as fast as you can!" The nurse is giving a baby a bath. Should she obey? If she is reasonably intelligent, she will realize that her mistress does not want the baby dropped into the bath, plain though her words are.

Should the judge say, as Justice Gregory does, that "effect must be given to [the language] regardless of what courts think of its wisdom or policy" and let it go at that? Or should the judge perhaps take a second look at the statute to see whether it cannot be interpreted in another way? When, as sometimes happens, a statute is passed that obviously contains a clerical error—the omission of the word *not*, for instance—judges are always willing to give the provision its corrected meaning in order to arrive at the obviously intended result. A statutory clause reading "Unfair competitive practices are hereby declared to be lawful" makes sense of a sort; it is not gibberish. But we must assume that legislators are reasonable people, pursuing reasonable objectives by reasonable methods, and that they could not have meant to legalize at one stroke all unfair competitive practices. If one reads the phrase in the context of surrounding provisions, moreover, it will doubtless become clear that the final word in the clause should have been *unlawful*, and judges will so assume in applying the statute.

But when giving a phrase its literal meaning would produce a result that is not downright absurd but merely surprising and seemingly unreasonable, the court's problem is more difficult. After all, judges have no general mandate to rewrite legislative enactments to make them more fair and reasonable.

The U.S. Supreme Court once interpreted an immigration law in such a way as to deny to the alien wife of a native-born American citizen a privilege that, it held, the law granted only to alien wives of naturalized citizens. "The words of the statute being clear," the Court concluded, "if it unjustly discriminates against the native-born citizen, or is cruel and inhuman in its results, as is forcefully contended, the remedy lies with Congress and not with the courts. Their duty is simply to enforce the law as it is written." But if the result reached was obviously "cruel and inhuman," should not the Court have asked itself whether the meaning of the words was really as plain as it appeared to be?

Justice Gregory's interpretation of *established* raises a similar question. The result reached is not, to be sure, cruel or inhuman, but it is certainly hard to explain. Why should the Virginia legislature have wished to protect property owners against the establishment of new cemeteries but not against the expansion of old ones? Maybe the legislators had a reason for making such a distinction, but surely some effort should have been made to find it.

Justice Gregory's opinion suggests he may have lost sight of two important truths about words: Words may have a range of meanings, and words must be understood in their contexts.

Words Rarely Have Only a Single Meaning

A few words have perfectly specific referents, but most words have a range of meanings. Indeed, they have a slightly different meaning each time they are used in a new sentence. The proper question to ask about a word, then, is not just "What *does* it mean?" but "What *can* it mean?" What are the limits of permissible meaning that can be attributed to it?

"A word," Justice Holmes once wrote, "is not a crystal, transparent and unchanged; it is the skin of a living thought, and may vary greatly in color and context according to the circumstances and the time in which it is used" (*Towne v. Eisner*, 245 U.S. 418, 425, 1918).

To support his position, Justice Gregory cites a dictionary definition of *establish*. His implication seems to be that, since the dictionary does not list *enlarge* or *extend* as a synonym of *establish*, *established* may not be interpreted as including *enlarged*. But the function of dictionaries is simply to report the usual meanings of words at a particular point in time. Two dictionaries published by different authors or publishers, or at different times, may list identical or different meanings of a single word. The failure to report a particular meaning is not proof that the word can never have that meaning in any context. True, the rules of etymology (the science of word meanings) prevent *black* from being used to mean *white*, which is beyond the limits of permissible meaning of *black*. But no such etymological limitation prevents *establish* from including the notion of enlarging something that already exists.

Words Cannot Be Understood Apart from Their Contexts

Context first of all means *textual* context. Textual context includes not only the sentence in which a word or phrase appears but also the successively larger units of the paragraph, section, chapter or article, and the entire statute. The word *established* in a statute dealing with cemeteries obviously means something different from what it means in statutes dealing with the founding of colonies or banks.

In the final portion of the *Temple* opinion, Justice Gregory turns to his second argument, which is based on textual context. Here he considers the word *established* in the broad context of the Virginia Code, which includes a section (described as "a related statute") because it also concerns cemeteries but was apparently not part of the same piece of legislation as section 56. In section 53 a clear distinction is drawn between the establishment and enlargement of cemeteries. Justice Gregory argues that the legislature could not have intended that *established* in section 56 should have a broader meaning than it had in section 53. This argument is much more persuasive than that based on "plain meaning," but perhaps less conclusive than Justice Gregory suggests. After all, the framers of Section 56 may have ascribed to the term *established* in that section a meaning broad enough to include enlargements, without remembering that the same word had been used in a more restricted sense in section 53. Consistency is not always an attribute of human thinking.

Much broader than textual context is what is sometimes called *circumstantial context*. The circumstantial context of a statutory provision embraces such relevant matters as the sources of dissatisfaction that gave rise to the new act (e.g., the decline of land values in the vicinity of cemeteries) and the legal rules in effect prior to the new enactment (e.g., rules on the use of urban land for burials). Circumstantial context may also include relevant social, economic, and technological circumstances that prevailed at the time the statute was passed.

A consideration of a statute's circumstantial context is indispensable to a search for its purpose. To discover what legislators intended to include under the term *vehicle* in a statute passed in 1880, for instance, a judge will probably want to know what types of vehicle existed in 1880 and will also want to identify the particular problem to which the legislators were addressing themselves. Whether the term *vehicles* in a statute enacted in 1880 should be construed today as covering automobiles and airplanes will depend on what the statute is trying to accomplish. If it concerns safety on the roads, for instance, it presumably covers automobiles (even though they did not exist in 1880) but not airplanes. If, on the other hand, it is a tax statute designed to offset local government expenditures in aid of transportation, perhaps airplanes are also covered. Similarly, whether a statute referring to "persons" covers corporations again depends on the reasons that led to its enactment. If it was designed to regulate marriages, obviously corporations are not persons, but if its purpose was to regulate the use of property, perhaps they are.

It is important to understand what we are *not* saying. We are *not* saying that judges are free to give to statutory words a meaning outside their range of etymologically permissible meanings just to produce a more reasonable result in a particular case. Judges have no authority to rewrite statutes merely because they think that the indicated meaning of language would lead to an undesirable result or because they suspect that legislators have overlooked some important policy consideration. The words used *do* limit the judges' freedom of interpretation; judges may not assign a wholly unnatural meaning to words in order to carry out some surmised purpose.

Here we have stressed the importance of carrying out the legislature's purpose. Another reason for limiting the freedom of judges to interpret words is that private persons to whom a statute is addressed may have assumed that the statutory words mean what they appear to mean. If a judge is too free to interpret, he may defeat the legitimate expectations of these persons. The courts are particularly careful in construing criminal statutes to make sure that those who are subject to them have had fair warning about what behaviors constitute crimes. Such statutes are construed strictly: courts try not to attribute to their words any but the clearest and most obvious meanings, lest the charge be made that a defendant was not given fair warning and has therefore been denied due process of law.

What we *are* saying is that, whenever an apparently clear meaning would produce a surprising result, a judge should look again to see whether the meaning is really as clear as it seems. The judge should make sure that he has read the provision in relation to its underlying purpose as indicated by the textual and circumstantial contexts, both of which are important. If, after doing this, the judge remains convinced that no other meaning can reasonably be attributed to the words, then he must give effect to that meaning and leave to the legislature the responsibility for amending the statute if it so desires.

Suppose, for instance, that a legislature has passed a law saying that certain occupational categories are subject to a special tax, but has inadvertently omitted one category from the list. That category could not be made subject to the tax by a judge no matter how overwhelming the evidence that it should have been included.

But "perfectly clear" statutory words are much rarer than many judges have intimated. *Established* in section 56 of the Virginia Code did not have a single, perfectly plain meaning. The principal trouble with Justice Gregory's opinion in *Temple* is not that it leads him to a result that is necessarily wrong, but that it represents an inadequate and incomplete approach to interpreting the meaning of words. Further examination of the statute—and perhaps of its legislative history, if necessary—might or might not have revealed whether the Virginia legislature meant to distinguish between establishing new urban cemeteries and extending old ones. But Justice Gregory undertook no such examination.

THE USE OF LEGISLATIVE HISTORY

Since the text of a statute is the final, official embodiment of the legislature's efforts, it is obviously the first place that judges must look in their search for purpose. More often than not, they can find the purpose or policy behind a statute by reading it, bearing in mind what they know of its context. But sometimes the most careful reading of language reveals no underlying purpose that is readily applicable to the problem before a court. Faced with this situation, judges may turn to other sources of evidence of legislative purpose. Of these, the most important is the statute's *legislative history*—the proceedings in the legislature that led to its enactment.

As we suggested in Chapter 5, the most significant items of evidence in a legislative history are reports of committees that worked on a bill and statements made for the record by heads of those committees, who are usually sponsors of legislation reported by committees for votes of the full house. This occurs because legislatures ordinarily accept the work of their committees (and committees ordinarily accept the work of their subcommittees) on matters of detail and merely vote to ratify the purposes that the committees have announced.

When different bills have been voted by the two houses and have had to be reconciled, conference committee reports are valuable, too. Committee and conference reports now usually include a section-by-section analysis of legislation reported, describing which bill each provision came from and briefly explaining any changes made to them. The fact that a committee kept one version of a provision rather than an alternative may provide indications of legislative purpose. Also consulted, though less reliable, are speeches made during debate on a bill (especially by sponsors of the bill, who presumably know more about what it was intended to do than opponents), testimony received in committee hearings, and recorded votes on amendments.

Judges have not always been willing to hear evidence about a statute's legislative history. Their reluctance is not just a sign of judicial conservatism. The evidence provided by legislative history is often meager, contradictory, and hard to appraise. Much of what legislators say and do while they are acting on a bill cannot be trusted as an indication of the collective intention. Moreover, legislators who know that future courts may look at the legislative record are occasionally tempted to manufacture bits of legislative history, perhaps by placing their own interpretations of key clauses in speeches or scripted exchanges between members during debate on a bill.

Take the hypothetical case of Senator Mugwump, who represents a widget-manufacturing community. He rises during debate on a tax bill to remark, "Naturally the excise tax that this bill establishes does not fall on widgets." Nobody contradicts him—possibly because nobody is listening. Later, when the widget manufacturers claim exemption from the tax, they point to Senator Mugwump's uncontradicted statement as evidence of legislative purpose. However, competent judges would presumably not accept this assertion by a single legislator as conclusive proof of a collective intention to exempt widgets.

We are not suggesting that statements inserted into the record for the purpose of creating evidence of legislative intention are always unreliable. Normally, committee reports and statements by committee members are prompted, at least in part, by a desire to help citizens interpret legislation. For this purpose, copies of congressional documents—bills, staff reports, hearings testimony, committee reports, congressional debates and recorded votes, and statements made by presidents upon signing bills into law—are commonly available to the general public in law school libraries, regional repository government document libraries, and court libraries throughout the United States. Yet the practice of reviewing evidence of legislative history may be burdensome for litigants. Knowing the courts may look at this kind of evidence, lawyers may feel that in all cases involving problems of statutory interpretation, they must pore over legislative records for evidence to put in their briefs. But often these records are not readily accessible in local libraries. In many states, especially less populated states that try to keep legislative expenditures low, the use of legislative history is effectively prevented by the absence or inadequacy of records of legislative proceedings. Some small states do not keep records of testimony received at legislative hearings or require detailed committee reports; other states merely tape-record testimony or archive written documents in a legislative library without preparing an index for them. Searching through such materials is a time-consuming job that may prove a waste of time in the end.

For many years the Supreme Court of the United States was reluctant to consider evidence of legislative history. The Court would only consider such evidence if the language of a statute before it was "of doubtful meaning and susceptible on its face of two constructions" (to quote one of its opinions). If the language was plain, the Court would look no further, even though the result produced by applying the plain meaning might seem questionable. In 1940, however, a majority of the Court joined in expressing a much more receptive view: whenever there could be any doubt about the legislature's purpose—even though the literal meaning of a statute's language was clear—a consideration of legislative history might be appropriate. Today, the justices' law clerks are adept at researching legislative history—a skill that law school students learn in courses on legal research. The 1940 opinion is worth quoting at some length, since it probably represents the present position of members of the Supreme Court and of many other judges.

> There is, of course, no more persuasive evidence of the purpose of a statute than the words by which the legislature undertook to give expression to its wishes. Often these words are sufficient in and of themselves to determine the purpose of the legislation. In such cases we have followed their plain meaning. When that meaning has led to absurd or futile results, however, this Court has looked beyond the words to the purpose of the act. Frequently, however, even when the plain meaning did not produce absurd results but merely an unreasonable one "plainly at variance with the policy of the legislation as a whole" this Court has followed that purpose, rather than the literal words. When aid to construction of the meaning of words, as used in the statute, is available, there certainly can be no "rule of law" which forbids its use, however clear the words may appear on "superficial examination." The interpretation of the meaning of statutes, as applied to justiciable controversies, is exclusively a judicial function. This duty requires one body of public servants, the judges, to construe the meaning of what another body, the legislators, has said. Obviously there is danger that the courts' conclusion as to legislative purpose will be unconsciously influenced by the judges' own views or by factors not considered by the enacting body. A lively appreciation of the danger is the best assurance of escape from its threat but hardly justifies an acceptance of a literal interpretation dogma, which withholds from the courts available information for reaching a correct conclusion. *United States v. American Trucking Associations,* 310 U.S. 534 [1940].

To illustrate the courts' use of legislative history, we have chosen the case of *United Steelworkers of America v. Weber,* decided by the Supreme Court of the United States in 1979. The issue of interpretation in this case was relatively complex, so a few background facts are necessary.

The Civil Rights Act of 1964 is one of the most significant pieces of legislation passed in the last fifty years. Title VII of the act specifically forbids employers from discriminating in employment practices on the basis of color, religion, race, sex, or national origin. This rather broad statement is qualified by allowing discrimination when religion, sex, or national origin could be considered a "bona fide occupational qualification."

Personnel managers and labor relations executives have made significant attempts to improve their hiring, training, and promotion strategies in line with the mandate of Title VII. In fact, many major employers have instituted affirmative action plans to help them find, hire, train, and reward individuals who were previously targets of discrimination. But not all employees are pleased with the results of affirmative action: some workers think the plans do not create equal employment opportunities for all, but rather discriminate against those who are not specifically targets of affirmative action. Kaiser Aluminum and Chemical Corporation had its affirmative action plan tested for precisely that reason. Brian Weber, a white male, brought a class-action suit against Kaiser, complaining he had been discriminated against in violation of his own Title VII rights when Kaiser implemented its affirmative action plan, which reserved 50 percent of training openings for black employees.

When Weber's case came before the Supreme Court, the justices were faced with a difficult problem: the Court wanted to make sure that *all people* were treated equally, yet it also wanted to help groups that had been hurt in the past. The Court also wanted to be certain, by acquainting itself with the history of the legislation, that it did not contradict the purpose of the Civil Rights Act.

United Steelworkers of America v. Weber

Supreme Court of the United States
443 U.S. 193 (1979)

MR. JUSTICE BRENNAN delivered the opinion of the Court.

Challenged here is the legality of an affirmative action plan—collectively bargained by an employer and a union—that reserves for black employees 50% of the openings in an in-plant craft training program until the percentage of black craft workers in the plant is commensurate with the percentage of blacks in the local labor force. The question for decision is whether Congress, in Title VII of the Civil Rights Act of 1964 as amended, left employers and unions in the private sector free to take such race-conscious steps to eliminate manifest racial imbalances in traditionally segregated job categories. We hold that Title VII does not prohibit such race-conscious action plans. . . .

In 1974 petitioner United Steelworkers of America (USWA) and petitioner Kaiser Aluminum & Chemical Corporation (Kaiser) entered into a master collective-bargaining agreement covering terms and conditions of employment at 15 Kaiser plants. The agreement contained, inter alia, an action plan designed to eliminate conspicuous racial imbalances in Kaiser's then almost exclusively white craft work forces. Black craft hiring goals were set for each Kaiser plant equal to the percentage of blacks in the respective local labor forces. To enable plants to meet these goals, on-the-job training programs were established to teach unskilled production workers—black and white—the skills necessary to become craft workers. The plan reserved for black employees 50% of the openings in these newly created in-plant training programs. . . .

This case arose from the operation of the plan at Kaiser's plant in Gramercy, La. Until 1974 Kaiser hired as craft workers for that plant only persons who had had prior experience. Because blacks had long been excluded from craft unions, few were able to present such credentials. As a consequence, prior to 1974 only 1.83% (five out of 273) of the skilled craft workers at the Gramercy plant were black, even though the work force in the Gramercy area was approximately 39% black.

Pursuant to the national agreement Kaiser altered its craft hiring practice in the Gramercy plant. Rather than hiring already trained outsiders, Kaiser established a training program to train its production workers to fill craft openings. Selection of craft trainees was made on the basis of seniority, with the proviso that at least 50% of the new trainees were to be black until the percentage of black skilled craft workers in the Gramercy plant approximated the percentage of blacks in the local labor force. . . .

During 1974, the first year of the operation of the Kaiser-USWA affirmative action plan, 13 craft trainees were selected from Gramercy's production work force. Of these, 7 were black and 6 white. The most junior black selected into the program had less seniority than several white production workers whose bids for admission were rejected. Thereafter one of those white production workers, respondent Brian Weber, instituted this class action in the United States District Court for the Eastern District of Louisiana.

The complaint alleged that the filling of craft trainee positions at the Gramercy plant pursuant to the affirmative action program had resulted in junior black employees receiving training in preference to more senior white employees, thus discriminating against respondent and other similarly situated white employees in violation of §§703(a) and (d) of Title VII. The District Court held that the plan violated Title VII, entered a judgment in favor of the class, and granted a permanent injunction prohibiting Kaiser and the USWA "from denying plaintiffs, Brian F. Weber and all other members of the class, access to on-the-job training programs on the basis of race." 415 F. Supp. 761 (1976). A divided panel of the Court of Appeals for the Fifth Circuit affirmed, holding that all employment preferences based upon race, including those preferences incidental to bona fide affirmative action plans, violated Title VII's prohibition against racial discrimination in employment. . . .

We emphasize at the outset the narrowness of our inquiry. Since the Kaiser-USWA plan does not involve state action, this case does not present an alleged violation of the Equal Protection Clause of the Constitution. Further, since the Kaiser-USWA plan was adopted voluntarily, we are not concerned with what Title VII requires or with what a court might order to remedy a past proven violation of the Act. The only question before us is the narrow statutory issue of whether Title VII forbids private employers and unions from voluntarily agreeing upon bona fide affirmative action plans that accord racial preferences in the manner and for the purpose provided in the Kaiser-USWA plan. That question was expressly left open in *McDonald v. Santa Fe Trail Trans. Co.*, 427 US 273 (1976) which held, in a case not involving affirmative action, that Title VII protects whites as well as blacks from certain forms of racial discrimination.

Respondent argues that Congress intended in Title VII to prohibit all race-conscious affirmative action plans. Respondent's argument rests upon a literal interpretation of §§703(a) and (d) of the Act. Those sections make it unlawful to "discriminate . . . because of . . . race" in hiring and in the selection of apprentices for training programs. Since, the argument runs, *McDonald v. Santa Fe Trans. Co., supra,* settled that Title VII *forbids* discrimination against whites as well as blacks, and since the Kaiser-USWA affirmative action plan operates to discriminate against white employees solely because they are white, it follows that the Kaiser-USWA plan violates Title VII.

Respondent's argument is not without force. But it overlooks the significance of the fact that the Kaiser-USWA plan is an affirmative action plan voluntarily adopted by private parties to eliminate traditional patterns of racial segregation. In this context respondent's reliance upon a literal construction of §§703(a) and (d) and upon *McDonald* is misplaced. The prohibition against racial discrimination . . . *must therefore be read against the background of the legislative history of Title VII and the historical context from which the Act arose.* [Emphasis added.] . . .

Congress's primary concern in enacting the prohibition against racial discrimination in Title VII of the Civil Rights Act of 1964 was with "the plight of the Negro in our economy" 110 *Cong Rec,* 6548 (remarks of Sen. Humphrey). Before 1964, blacks were largely relegated to "unskilled and semi-skilled jobs." Id., at 6548 (remarks of Sen. Humphrey) . . . Because of automation the number of such jobs was rapidly decreasing. See 110 *Cong Rec,* at 6548 (remarks of Sen. Humphrey); id., at 7204 (remarks of Sen. Clark). As a consequence "the relative position of the Negro worker (was) steadily worsening. In 1947 the non-white unemployment rate was only 64 percent higher than the white rate; in 1962 it was 124 percent higher." Id., at 6547 (remarks of Sen. Humphrey). . . . Congress considered this a serious social problem. . . .

Congress feared that the goals of the Civil Rights Act—the integration of blacks into the mainstream of American society—could not be achieved unless this trend was reversed. And Congress recognized that that would not be possible unless blacks were able to secure jobs "which have a future." Id., at 7204 (remarks to Sen. Clark). . . . As Senator Humphrey explained to the Senate: "What good does it do a Negro to be able to eat in a fine restaurant if he cannot afford to pay the bill? What good does it do him to be accepted in a hotel that is too expensive for his modest income? How can a Negro child be motivated to take full advantage of integrated educational facilities if he has no hope of getting a job where he can use that education?" Id., at 6547. . . .

[I]t was clear to Congress that "the crux of the problem (was) to open employment opportunities for Negroes in occupations which have been traditionally closed to them," id., at 6548 (remarks of Sen. Humphrey), and it was to this problem that Title VII's prohibition against racial discrimination in employment was primarily addressed. . . .

Given this legislative history, we cannot agree with respondent that Congress intended to prohibit the private sector from taking effective steps to accomplish the goal that Congress designed Title VII to achieve. [Emphasis added.] . . . It would be ironic indeed if a law triggered by a Nation's concern over centuries of racial injustice and intended to improve the lot of those who had "been excluded from the American dream for so long," 110 *Cong Rec*, at 6552 (remarks of Sen. Humphrey), constituted the first legislative prohibition of all voluntary, private, race-conscious efforts to abolish traditional patterns of racial segregation and hierarchy.

Our conclusion is further reinforced by examination of the language and legislative history of §703(j) of Title VII. Opponents of Title VII raised two related arguments against the bill. First, they argued that the Act would be interpreted to *require* employers with racially imbalanced work forces to grant preferential treatment to racial minorities in order to integrate. Second, they argued that employers with racially imbalanced work forces would grant preferential treatment to racial minorities, even if not required to do so by the Act. See 110 Cong Rec (remarks of Sen. Sparkman). Had Congress meant to prohibit all conscious affirmative action, as respondent urges, it easily could have answered both objections by providing that Title VII would not require or *permit* racially preferential integration efforts. But Congress did not choose such a course. Rather Congress added §703(j) which addresses only the first objection. The second provides that nothing contained in Title VII "shall be interpreted to require any employer . . . to grant preferential treatment . . . to any group because of the race . . . of such . . . group on account of" a de facto racial imbalance in the employer's work force. The section does *not* state that "nothing in Title VII shall be interpreted to *permit*" voluntary affirmative efforts to correct racial imbalances. The natural inference is that Congress chose not to forbid all voluntary race-conscious affirmative action.

The reasons for this choice are evident from the legislative record. [emphasis added] Title VII could not have been enacted into law without substantial support from legislators in both Houses who traditionally resisted federal regulation of private business. Those legislators demanded as a price for their support that "management prerogatives and union freedoms . . . be left undisturbed to the greatest extent possible." HR Re No. 914, 88th Cong, 1st sess, Pt 2 (1963), at 29. Section 703(j) was proposed by Senator Dirkson to allay any fears that the Act might be interpreted in such a way as to upset this compromise. The section was designed to prevent §703 of Title VII from being interpreted in such a way as to lead to undue "Federal Government interference with private businesses because of some Federal employee's ideas about racial balance or imbalance." 110 *Cong Rec*, at 14314 . . . In view of this legislative history and in view of Congress' desire to avoid undue federal regulation of private businesses, use of the word "require" rather than the phrase "require or permit" in §703(j) fortifies the conclusion that Congress did not intend to limit traditional business freedom to such a degree as to prohibit all voluntary, race-conscious affirmative action.

We therefore hold that Title VII's prohibition in §703(a) and (d) against racial discrimination does not condemn all private, voluntary, race-conscious affirmative action plans. . . .

We need not today define in detail the line of demarcation between permissible and impermissible affirmative action plans. It suffices to hold that the challenged Kaiser-USWA affirmative action plan falls on the permissible side of the line. The purposes of the plan mirror those of the statute. . . .

At the same time the plan does not unnecessarily trammel the interests of the white employees. The plan does not require the discharge of white workers and their replacement with new black hires. . . . Nor does the plan create an absolute bar to the advancement of white employees; half of those trained in the program will be white. Moreover, the plan is a temporary measure; it is not intended to maintain racial balance, but simply to eliminate a manifest racial imbalance. . . .

We conclude, therefore, that the adoption of the Kaiser-USWA plan for the Gramercy plant falls within the area of discretion left by Title VII to the private sector voluntarily to adopt action plans designed to eliminate conspicuous racial imbalance in traditionally segregated job categories. Accordingly, the judgment of the Court of Appeals for the Fifth Circuit is reversed.

MR. JUSTICE POWELL and MR. JUSTICE STEVENS took no part in the consideration or decision of this case.

MR. JUSTICE REHNQUIST, with whom THE CHIEF JUSTICE joins, dissenting.

In a very real sense, the Court's opinion is ahead of its time: it could more appropriately have been handed down five years from now, in 1984, a year coinciding with the title of a book from which the Court's opinion borrows, perhaps subconsciously, at least one idea.

Orwell describes in his book a governmental official of Oceania, one of the three great world powers, denouncing the current enemy, Eurasia, to an assembled crowd:

> It was almost impossible to listen to him without being first convinced and then maddened. . . . The speech had been proceeding for perhaps twenty minutes when a messenger hurried onto the platform and a scrap of paper was slipped into the speaker's hand. He unrolled and read it without pausing in his speech. Nothing altered in his voice or manner, or in the content of what he was saying, but suddenly the names were different. Without words said, a wave of understanding rippled through the crowd. Oceania was at war with Eastasia! . . . The banners and posters with which the square was decorated were all wrong! . . .
>
> [T]he speaker had switched from one line to the other actually in mid-sentence, not only without a pause, but without even breaking the syntax. G. Orwell, *Nineteen Eighty-Four* 181–182 (1949).

Today's decision represents an equally dramatic and equally unremarked switch in this Court's interpretation of Title VII.

The operative sections of Title VII prohibit racial discrimination in employment *simpliciter*. Taken in its normal meaning and as understood by Members of Congress who spoke to the issue during the legislative debates, see *infra* at 2741–2751, this language prohibits a covered employer from considering race when making an employment decision, whether the race be black or white. Several years ago, however, a United States District Court held that "the dismissal of white employees charged with misappropriating company property while not dismissing a similarly charged Negro employee does not raise a claim upon which Title VII relief may be granted." *McDonald v. Santa Fe Trail Transp. Co.*, 427 U.S. 273, 278, 96 S.Ct. 2574, 2578, 49 L.Ed.2d 493 (1976). This Court unanimously reversed, concluding from the "uncontradicted legislative history" that "[T]itle VII prohibits racial discrimination against the white petitioners in this case upon the same standards as would be applicable were they Negroes . . ." Id., at 280, 96 S.Ct., at 2579.

We have never wavered in our understanding that Title VII "prohibits *all* racial discrimination in employment, without exception for any group of particular employees." Id., at 283, 96 S.Ct., at 2580 (emphasis in original). In *Griggs v. Duke Power Co.*, 401 U.S. 424, 431, 91 S.Ct. 849, 853, 28 L.Ed.2d 158 (1979), our first occasion to interpret Title VII, a unanimous Court observed that ["d]iscriminatory preference, for any group, minority or majority, is precisely and only what Congress has proscribed." And in our most recent discussion of the issue, we uttered words seemingly dispositive of this case: "It is clear beyond cavil that the obligation imposed by Title VII is to provide an equal opportunity for each applicant regardless of race, without regard to whether members of the applicant's race are already proportionately represented in the work force." *Furnco Construction Corp. v. Waters*, 438 U.S. 567, 579, 98 S.Ct. 2943, 57 L.Ed.2d 957 (1978) (emphasis in original).

Today, however, the Court behaves much like the speaker earlier described, as if it had been handed a note indicating that Title VII would lead to a result unacceptable to the Court if interpreted here as it was in our prior decisions. Accordingly, without even a break in syntax, the Court rejects "a literal construction of §703(a)" in favor of newly discovered "legislative history," which leads it to a conclusion directly contrary to that compelled by the "uncontradicted legislative history" unearthed in McDonald and our other prior decisions. Now we are told that the legislative history of Title VII shows that employers are free to discriminate on the basis of race: an employer may, in the Court's words, "trammel the interests of the white employees" in favor of black employees in order to eliminate "racial imbalance." *Ante,* at 2730. Our earlier interpretations of Title VII, like the banners and posters decorating the square in Oceania, were all wrong.

As if this were not enough to make a reasonable observer question this Court's adherence to the oft-stated principle that our duty is to construe rather than rewrite legislation, *United States v. Rutherford,* 442 U.S. 544, 555, 99 S.Ct. 2470, 2477, 61 L.Ed.2d 68 (1979), the Court also seizes upon §703(j) of Title VII as an independent, or at least partially independent, basis for its holding. Totally ignoring the wording of that section, which is obviously addressed to those charged with the responsibility of interpreting the law rather than those who are subject to its proscriptions, and totally ignoring the months of legislative debates preceding the section's introduction and passage, which demonstrate clearly that it was enacted to prevent precisely what occurred in this case, the Court infers from §703(j) that "Congress chose not to forbid all voluntary race-conscious affirmative action." *Ante,* at 2729.

Thus, by a *tour de force* reminiscent not of jurists such as Hale, Holmes, and Hughes, but of escape artists such as Houdini, the Court eludes clear statutory language, "uncontradicted" legislative history and uniform precedent in concluding that employers are, after all, permitted to consider race in making employment decisions. It may be that one or more of the principal sponsors of Title VII would have preferred to see a provision allowing preferential treatment of minorities written into the bill. Such a provision, however, would have to have been expressly or impliedly excepted from Title VII's explicit prohibition on all racial discrimination in employment. There is no such exception in the Act. And a reading of the legislative debates concerning Title VII, in which proponents and opponents alike uniformly denounced discrimination in favor of, as well as discrimination against, Negroes, demonstrates clearly that any legislator harboring an unspoken desire for such a provision could not possibly have succeeded in enacting it into law.

Questions

1. How did the Supreme Court use legislative history to support its decision? Was its examination of circumstantial context important ("Congress's primary concern in enacting the prohibition . . .")?
2. Would it have been possible for the Supreme Court to arrive at its decision without the use of legislative history? Why or why not?
3. Did the author of the dissenting opinion quote the majority opinion out of context (". . . trammel the interests of the white employees . . .")?

OTHER AIDS TO STATUTORY INTERPRETATION

Private and Administrative Interpretations

We have said that when the courts cannot discover the purpose underlying a statutory provision by examining the statute itself, they may turn to other sources of evidence. Since it is the legislature's purpose they are seeking, the most important of these sources is the legislative history of the statute. Judges are aware, however, that legislatures often count on the primary addressees of a statute, both private and official, to fill in some of the gaps themselves. Hence they may sometimes be influenced by interpretations that these addressees adopt.

Private persons and organizations have to work out their own tentative interpretations of a new statute long before any case arising under it comes before the courts. If their interpretations seem to be relatively uniform and motivated by a desire to comply with the law rather than by a search for loopholes in it, they may influence interpretations adopted by the courts. Likewise, interpretations that administrative officials adopt in the course of administering a statute may be taken into account by judges who later must work out a definitive interpretation. Administrators usually have specialized experience in the area regulated, and their interpretations are likely to be molded to fit the practical problems of administration. Judges often hesitate to adopt an interpretation at variance with a well-established administrative interpretation, displaying some deference to the presumed superior expertise of administrators.

Prior Judicial Interpretations

When a court must apply a statutory provision in a case, what weight should it give to earlier judicial interpretations of the provision? Does the *stare decisis* principle oblige a court to follow prior interpretations even if they seem wrong? Or is the court free to return to the language and legislative history of the statute in search of a better interpretation?

One view is that when a court is convinced an earlier interpretation is wrong, it should adopt a new interpretation in order to give proper effect to the legislative purpose. This is particularly necessary, it is argued, because legislatures so often fail to exercise their power to pass new laws correcting erroneous interpretations. If courts are unwilling to get rid of bad judicial interpretations, those interpretations are likely to remain in effect indefinitely.

The prevailing view, probably, is that decisions interpreting statutes should exert approximately the same control over the future as do decisions interpreting common-law rules, and for essentially the same reason. People should be able to plan their conduct on the assumption that once an appellate court has interpreted a statutory provision, it will normally adhere to that interpretation in later cases. Most judges refuse to accept the view that the inability of legislatures to review and revise decisional rules is sufficient reason for courts to ignore precedents they have established.

Occasional Need for Creative Judicial Lawmaking

In a large majority of cases involving application of statutory provisions, the meaning of a statute is so clear that no real problems of interpretation arise. In a smaller number of cases, interpretation is more difficult. Even in most of these, though, judges can reach a satisfactory solution by examining the language of a statutory provision in its textual and circumstantial context. Occasionally they find it useful to look also at legislative history or private or administrative interpretations. Sometimes a provision has already been interpreted by a court.

Once in a while, however, judges' efforts to discover the legislative purpose of a statute are all in vain. It simply is not clear how a statute applies to the case before them. In those cases the judges must do just what they do when faced with a case for which there are no precedents: they must perform a creative act of lawmaking. In all likelihood this is exactly what the legislature, unwilling to prescribe details for an unknown future, counted on them to do. It is the duty of judges to infer a purpose that is applicable to a particular case from what they know of the legislature's broader purposes and of the shared purposes and aims of the community. As long as they advance these broad purposes and not private purposes of their own, judges are acting within the limits of the judicial function.

CHAPTER PROBLEM: A TAXING PROBLEM FOR PHYSICIANS

Suppose a state legislature has recently enacted a statute to prohibit price-fixing agreements among sellers of goods and services. The provisions of the new law cover business firms and "all self-employed persons engaged in business or trade."

Now suppose that somebody brings a lawsuit under the new act against several physicians who, he says, have caused him injury by their price-fixing activities. The defendants demur: regardless of whether the facts alleged are true, the law does not apply to them, they say, because they are not "engaged in business or trade." The trial judge's decision overruling this demurrer has been appealed to the state supreme court.

Several years earlier, the state legislature had adopted a statute imposing a special tax on certain classes of persons and organizations, but specifically exempting (presumably because they were thought to be sufficiently taxed under existing levies) "all self-employed persons engaged in business or trade." Thus, the phrasing of the two statutes was identical. For understandable reasons, physicians were eager to be classified as persons "engaged in business or trade" under this earlier statute, and they rejoiced when the state supreme court so classified them in a case in which it interpreted the provision.

The state supreme court must now deal with the apparent conflict between the two statutes and the resulting impact on physicians. In particular, the court must determine whether its decision that physicians were "engaged in business or trade" under the earlier tax statute obliges it to classify them similarly under the price-fixing law.

Questions

1. Sketch the arguments for both sides of the question: Is the court now obliged to apply its earlier classification of physicians to the price-fixing statute, or is it not? What are the premises of each argument?
2. What is your opinion as to the proper resolution? Explain your reasoning.

QUESTIONS FOR REVIEW

1. What are the major categories of problems in interpreting statutes?
2. "When judges must apply a statutory provision to a particular case, the best way for them to understand the statute is to look up the key words in the dictionary. Having done that, they will usually have no further difficulty." Comment on this statement.
3. To what sources might a judge turn when trying to interpret an imprecise statute?
4. What is the difference between legislative intent and legislative purpose?
5. If you were a judge, how much weight would you give to materials other than the statute itself in interpreting a statute? Would you give the same weight to committee reports as to materials that appear in the *Congressional Record*, which serves as the daily record of proceedings in the U.S. Congress? Would you take into consideration private interpretations? Explain your answer.
6. It has been suggested that a statement of general purpose should be appended to each future law. Would such a statement be useful? Would it be workable from a political point of view? Why or why not?
7. Comment on the following statement by Justice Felix Frankfurter: "The Court no doubt must listen to the voice of Congress. But often Congress cannot be heard clearly because its voice is muffled" (Frankfurter 1947).

BIBLIOGRAPHY

Frankfurter, Felix. 1947. "Some Reflections on the Reading of Statutes," 2 *Record of New York City Bar Association:* 234.

CHAPTER 7

Judicial Lawmaking III
Interpreting the Constitution

We have discussed in the last five chapters how the courts and legislatures make and apply rules that channel private conduct. We have taken for granted the authority of those bodies to make and apply legal rules. But think for a moment of citizens who find their activities thwarted by statutes, decisions, or administrative rulings they consider outrageous. These citizens might well wonder about the authority exercised by those whose actions have proved so annoying. If they explore the matter, they would learn that the ultimate sources of all official authority in the U.S. legal system are the state and federal constitutions and that rules about official authority stated in those constitutions or developed through judicial interpretation are known collectively as *constitutional law.*

This chapter describes how constitutional rules are created and how they evolve as new cases involving constitutional issues are decided. Although each state has its own constitution, we shall speak only about the U.S. Constitution, since it is far more important in the lives of most of us than any of the fifty state constitutions. Much of what we have to say about the federal Constitution, however, applies to the state constitutions as well.

EXAMPLES OF CONSTITUTIONAL ISSUES

Here are five examples of constitutional controversies, based on actual cases brought before the Supreme Court of the United States by parties challenging as unconstitutional the action of governmental officials or bodies:

1. Seeking to avert a threatened strike, the President of the United States orders federal officials to seize and operate the nation's steel mills. The steel companies challenge his power to do so under Article II of the Constitution, which deals with the powers and duties of the President.
2. Congress enacts a heavy tax on the sale of colored margarine and a much lighter tax on uncolored oleomargarine, with the avowed goal of restricting the sale of margarine that has been colored to resemble butter. A dealer refuses to pay the tax, claiming that Congress's power to tax under Article I cannot be used to achieve a regulatory objective unrelated to the raising of revenue.

137

3. An overzealous sheriff in a small town breaks into the offices of a business firm and searches for evidence of illegal sales, even though he has no search warrant. When the firm's owners are brought to trial for unlawful operations, they challenge the admission of the evidence offered against them on the grounds that it has been illegally obtained and that admitting it would violate the due-process clause of the Fourteenth Amendment, which is supposed to protect individuals from irregular official procedures.

4. A state legislature enacts a privilege tax on all persons or corporations not regularly doing business in the state who display samples in hotel rooms for the purpose of securing retail orders. An out-of-state firm pays the tax under protest and then sues for a refund, contending that the tax, by discriminating in favor of intrastate firms, places an unconstitutional burden on interstate commerce.

5. A group of homeowners sign an agreement that none of them will sell a home to persons "not of the Caucasian race." When one of the signers later sells his home to a black citizen, another signer asks a court for an injunction restraining the buyer from taking possession and divesting him of his title. The buyer resists on the ground that for a court to lend its coercive power to the enforcement of a restrictive agreement based on race would be a denial of the "equal protection of the laws" guaranteed by the Fourteenth Amendment.

U.S. CONSTITUTIONS

When Americans think of a constitution, they think of a written document adopted by a representative body. The fifty states and the federal Union each have such a document. In contrast, when the British speak of the basis for their government, they often refer to an "unwritten constitution" because they have no single document in mind; they are referring to the sum of the basic laws and traditions that determine the form and functioning of their government.

The difference, however, is more apparent than real, since U.S. constitutional law is by no means limited to the rules explicitly enunciated in constitutional documents. Constitutions typically perform three functions:

1. They prescribe the structure, organization, and major duties of the legislative, executive, and judicial branches of government.
2. They allocate power between the respective levels of government—that is, between the central and local authorities.
3. Having established and allocated power, constitutions place restrictions on the exercise of that power, specifying what governments may *not* do.

New constitutions, and major revisions of existing ones, are usually adopted initially by constitutional conventions—representative bodies especially convened for that purpose. Ordinarily, a constitutional convention writes into the document a procedure under which the constitution must be ratified after being adopted by the convention. Ratification is typically by popular vote or by vote of designated representative bodies. The U.S. Constitution provided that ratification by conventions in nine of the original thirteen states would be sufficient to bring it into effect. Eleven of the states had ratified it before it went into effect in March 1789, and eventually all thirteen did so.

Constitutional *amendments* are normally adopted by legislatures; then they must be ratified. Amendments to the U.S. Constitution may be proposed for ratification by a two-thirds vote in each house of Congress or passage in a national convention called by Congress in response to petitions from two-thirds of the states. Amendments are not effective until ratified by majority vote in either the legislatures or special state constitutional conventions in three-quarters of the states, as proposed by Congress. (See U.S. Constitution, Article V). The amendment process is customarily made cumbersome to discourage frequent or ill-considered tampering with the fundamental law.

The process of formal amendment is not the most important means by which our constitutional law is modified. The federal Constitution has been in effect for about 220 years. In that time—during which the infant mercantile and agrarian nation of 1789 was transformed into the enormously powerful and wealthy industrial giant of today—only twenty-seven amendments have been made to the Constitution. Moreover, ten of these—the so-called Bill of Rights—were proposed by the first Congress in 1789 and ratified in 1791, so may be considered effectively as part of the original Constitution. Some amendments have been important, but certainly no more important than the many changes that Americans have made in their constitutional rules without bothering to amend the Constitution. Sometimes institutions have been created or modified in order to bring about these changes—for example, the development of the two-party system and powerful congressional committees and the greatly reduced importance of the Electoral College. Many changes, however, are the result of the Supreme Court's reinterpretation of key constitutional phrases.

THE SUPREME COURT AS THE FINAL
CONSTITUTIONAL ARBITER

Challenges to the constitutionality of an official act may be raised either in a state court or in a lower federal court. Although these courts must rule on such challenges, their decisions have weight only as tentative interpretations, for the definitive interpretations of the Constitution are made only by the Supreme Court of the United States. This is not to say that the Supreme Court hears only cases that raise constitutional issues. Many of its decisions, such as the *Weber* case in the preceding chapter, involve interpretation of federal statutes. But the Court's best known and, on the whole, most important cases have involved constitutional questions.

The Supreme Court of the United States differs from most other appellate courts in one important respect: it has extremely wide discretion in deciding which cases it will hear. For most types of cases, the only way to secure a hearing before the Court is to persuade it to grant a *writ of certiorari,* an order to a lower court directing it to send up the record of a case for review. Out of the great number of cases that are urged upon it, the Supreme

Court accepts only a hundred or less per year for a full hearing. For the cases it refuses to hear, the decision of the lower court becomes final. This arrangement enables the Court to focus its attention on cases that raise novel and important legal issues.

One might expect that interpreting the words of a constitution would not be too different from interpreting a statute. But the two processes are actually quite different, mainly because of the generality of constitutional language. We have spoken of the deliberate imprecision of some statutory provisions, but few statutes are as imprecise as the key phrases in the federal Constitution. Since the Constitution was designed to endure for centuries, the framers found it advisable to enunciate broad directives in terse, general terms. In effect, the framers delegated to the Supreme Court the responsibility for giving meaning to these provisions by relating them to the particular situations that come before it. Justice Felix Frankfurter commented that the major constitutional phrases have been "purposely left to gather meaning from experience" (*National Mutual Ins. Co. v. Tidewater Transfer Co.*, 337 U.S. 582, 646, 1949). Chief Justice Charles Evans Hughes once put the matter even more baldly: "The Constitution is what the Judges say it is" (1908, 139).

Take, for instance, the power granted to Congress in Article I to "regulate commerce . . . among the several states." Again and again the Court has had to interpret this broad, imprecise provision. What is the power to "regulate"? What is "commerce"? What brings an activity into the category of "among the several states"? At different times the Court has given different answers to each of these questions. There have been periods when the Court has acted as if the commerce clause granted almost unlimited regulatory power to the federal government. During other periods it has interpreted the clause restrictively, invalidating federal statutes for exceeding the power granted to Congress.

The two most important clauses in the Fourteenth Amendment are equally imprecise: "[N]or shall any State deprive any person of life, liberty, or property, without due process of law; nor deny to any person within its jurisdiction the equal protection of the laws." The framers of the amendment probably intended the words "due process of law" as a guarantee of fair treatment in police, prosecuting, and trial procedures. But between the 1890s and the early 1930s, the justices of the Supreme Court used the due-process clause to strike down various state statutes regulating business that they considered arbitrary and unreasonable. During the three decades following, however, the Court abandoned this broad interpretation of the process clause. Similarly, for many years the Court held that the clause guaranteeing "equal protection of the laws" did not stand in the way of officially ordained segregation of the races, as long as the minority races were provided "equal" (though separate) facilities. But more recently the Court has held that the equal-protection clause makes such segregation unconstitutional.

Examples could be multiplied indefinitely. What is important to recognize is that the Court, guided by its own perception of society's changing needs and values, has been able to forge vague constitutional phrases into effective instruments for expanding or limiting official power. This arrangement imposes a heavy responsibility on the justices, and on the whole they have discharged it admirably. With comparatively few amendments, the Constitution has served as our organic law throughout all the changes in the nation's size, wealth, and world position, in the conditions of living, and in the role of government that have far exceeded anything the founders of the Republic could possibly have foreseen.

Some of our state constitutions provide excellent examples of what happens when constitutional documents are *not* deliberately imprecise. These constitutions are lengthy and detailed; often they contain provisions concerning matters too transitory in importance to justify inclusion in a constitution at all. Constitutional provisions that are detailed and specific cannot readily be reinterpreted by a court as the need for change becomes apparent. The needed change is therefore thwarted unless it is possible to amend the constitution. As a result, these state constitutions have needed to be amended much more often than has the federal Constitution, but since the amendment process is usually difficult, many desirable amendments have come about slowly or not at all.

The Power of Judicial Review

The Supreme Court's power to decide constitutional issues includes the power to decide whether or not the act of another agency of government—executive, administrative, or legislative—is permitted by the Constitution. This is often called the power of *judicial review.*

Suppose that an administrative official at the federal, state, or local level performs an act that is challenged in court as violating the federal Constitution. Or suppose that a state court renders a decision that is challenged as conflicting with the federal Constitution. Or suppose that Congress or a state or local legislative body passes a law that is said to be unconstitutional. In all these situations, the Supreme Court of the United States has jurisdiction and may be called upon to decide on the constitutionality of the act, decision, or law in question. If it is found to be unconstitutional, it is invalid.

In a federal system of government like ours, there must be some way to ensure that the officials, courts, and legislatures of the states do not exceed the powers permitted by the federal Constitution. The constitutional compact that the original states adopted in 1789 makes it clear that if the act of any branch of a state or local government ever comes into conflict with the federal Constitution (or with any federal statute or treaty), the latter shall prevail. In the words of Article VI: "This Constitution, and the laws of the United States which shall be made in pursuance thereof; and all treaties made, or which shall be made, under the authority of the United States, shall be the supreme law of the land; and the judges in every state shall be bound thereby, any thing in the Constitution or laws of any state to the contrary notwithstanding."

Although the state courts and lower federal courts have authority to decide constitutional issues, their decisions are not necessarily final. Ever since the Judiciary Act of 1789, the Supreme Court of the United States has had the ultimate authority to decide whether or not the act of a state official or agency is constitutional. The Supreme Court has exercised this power over state acts since the early days of the Republic, and few people today seriously question its legitimacy, although particular exercises of that power have aroused great resentment and hostility to the Court.

The constitutional underpinnings of the Court's power to invalidate the acts of the other two branches of the federal government—that is, of Congress and the President—are somewhat less firm. Nowhere does the Constitution state explicitly that the Supreme Court has the final say in deciding what limits the Constitution imposes on Congress or the President. There is some evidence to suggest that most of the founders of the Republic assumed that if in the course of deciding a case duly brought before it, the Court believed that an act of one of the other branches was contrary to the Constitution, it could deny legal effect to that act. But if this is indeed what the framers had in mind, they never spelled it out.

The argument that each branch of the federal government should be the final interpreter of its own powers is not without merit; it is the position taken in a number of other countries. But the issue was settled otherwise for the United States in 1803, when Chief Justice John Marshal—reasoning from language in the Constitution—declared in the famous case of *Marbury v. Madison* that the Court was empowered to invalidate an act of Congress. The Court has continued to exercise this power (and the related power to invalidate acts of the President) ever since. It has used the power sparingly and, on the whole, with a wise caution. On a few occasions, however, it has seriously impaired its own prestige and effectiveness by unwise invalidations of acts of Congress. The infamous *Dred Scott* decision of 1857, for instance, unquestionably hurt the Court, as did the striking down of much of the New Deal economic legislation in 1935 and 1936.

It is clear today that conflicts over the extent and limits of governmental power were bound to arise, both between federal and state authorities and between the respective branches of the federal government. These conflicts have had to be resolved somehow, and the Supreme Court is probably better able to do the job than any other agency. Judges have always had to interpret and apply the provisions of legal documents; interpreting constitutional provisions differs from other tasks of interpretation performed by appellate courts principally in the remarkably broad discretion granted to the judges and in the unusual importance of the issues at stake.

In one respect the Supreme Court is uniquely suited to act as final arbiter on constitutional issues. In our democratic system, Congress and the President are elected by popular majorities and can be expected to respond to majority desires. But one of the unspoken premises of the Constitution is that the majority of citizens must not be allowed to deprive racial, religious, ideological, and other minority groups of their rights. Since Supreme Court justices are appointed for life, they are relatively insulated from majority pressures. Consequently, they are in a relatively good position to withstand popular opposition when they strike down arbitrary, undemocratic legislation designed to curb or penalize minority groups.

Appointment of Justices

So far we have spoken of the Supreme Court as a unit. We must never forget, however, that the Court is made up of justices who die or retire and are replaced by others, and who have personal philosophies and prejudices, religious affiliations, and political, social, and economic backgrounds that inevitably influence their appraisals of the felt necessities of the time.

According to Article II of the Consitution, vacancies on the Court are filled by the President "with the advice and consent of the Senate." Understandably, he is likely to appoint persons whose political and economic views are not too different from his own. He is certain to nominate individuals with legal training, but there is no tradition requiring that appointees have prior judicial experience, and some of the greatest justices had never previously been judges.

While the President has a good deal of latitude with respect to choosing a nominee, the Senate recognizes the critical importance of the position and takes its "advice and consent" responsibility very seriously. Nominees are called to testify before the Senate Judiciary Committee. The Judiciary Committee can also call any number of witnesses to present information that would be helpful in deciding whether or not a particular nominee should be recommended. For example, one group whose opinion is of particular importance to both the President and the Senate is the American Bar Association's Committee on the Federal Judiciary. Without its support a nominee would face great difficulty in being seated.

Judicial Philosophy

In addition to considering the political and personal characteristics of the nominee and the testimony of witnesses, both the Senate and the President examine the nominee's judicial philosophy. A nominee might believe, for example, that it is the role of the Supreme Court to determine what the framers of the Constitution intended when they drafted the document and to reflect that perspective in the Court's decision-making. This is a position of *judicial restraint.* Former Chief Justice Warren Burger, appointed by President Nixon in 1969, typically made decisions reflecting a position of judicial restraint. He has been called a *strict constructionist* for adhering very closely to the perceived intent of the drafters of the Constitution.

A different approach, *judicial activism,* suggests that the court should reflect and even mold public policy by actively shaping and extending the meaning of the Constitution. The Court under the leadership of Chief Justice Earl Warren, appointed by President Eisenhower in 1953, has been described as particularly activist, or a *loose constructionist.* For example, the Warren Court established rigorous national standards to protect the rights of those accused of committing a crime and vigorously worked to reflect and shape public policy outlawing racial segregation in public schools. We will have more to say about the Supreme Court as a policymaking body later in this chapter.

Once appointed, a justice has indefinite tenure, which is virtually irrevocable. As we have noted, this immunity insulates the justices from direct political pressure and enables them to hand down decisions that they know will be unpopular in some quarters. Immunity has its disadvantages as well. Some justices remained on the bench long after their intellectual powers declined or after their ability to accept new ideas vanished. But for every justice who has sought to stand in the way of change, there have been others who have kept their judicial philosophies superbly attuned to the needs of the times. Some of the most memorable justices have been persistent dissenters from the majority view in their time, only to have history prove them right (e.g., Justices William O. Douglas and Hugo Black); thus their dissenting views have later become the law of the land.

Finally, we must note that the philosophical distinction between judicial "activism" and "restraint" must be maintained and applied with caution. In an often-quoted case, former Supreme Court Justice Harlan Stone suggested that judicial decision-making requires activism some of the time and restraint at other times (*United States v. Carolene Products Co.,* 304 U.S. 144, 1938).

RESTRAINTS ON THE EXERCISE OF JUDICIAL REVIEW

The power to invalidate the legislative and executive acts of popularly elected officials, lodged in the hands of nine justices who are neither chosen by the people nor subject to removal by them, would be intolerable if it were not subject to restraints. In the absence of restraints, nothing would prevent the Court from striking down legislation or executive acts simply because a majority of the justices considered them unfair or unwise. The restraints are of two sorts: external restraints, imposed by the political environment in which the Court operates, and internal restraints, which the justices have traditionally imposed upon themselves.

External Restraints

The effectiveness of the Court's authority depends in large measure on how much prestige it enjoys in the eyes of the American people. In recent years, the Court's prestige has been remarkably high, even when the Court was under strong attack from either conservative or liberal quarters. But there have been periods when its prestige was low: in the years before 1800, for instance, and in the period following the disastrous *Dred Scott* decision of 1857. The Court has no enforcement arm of its own, and the effectiveness of its decisions depends primarily on voluntary compliance by the officials concerned, although the executive branch may, if it is willing, aid in enforcement. A highly unpopular decision may be resisted or ignored. This has not happened often in our history, but on a number of occasions compliance has been far from complete (e.g., implementation of desegregation decisions in public accommodations and schools), and the Court's prestige has suffered. So, although the justices have no obligation to respond to every shift in popular sentiment, they cannot afford to get too far out of step with the nation's mood and desires.

Congress has certain powers that can be used to influence or restrict the Court. For example, it has the power to impeach, and it might impeach a justice of whose philosophy it violently disapproved. No Supreme Court justice has ever been removed by impeachment, however (though an attempt was made in 1804, and a few lower-court judges have been successfully impeached), and the prospect of its ever happening seems remote. But a sharp decline in the Court's prestige might bring this extreme measure within the realm of possibility.

Congress also has the power to decide what types of cases the Court may hear on appeal. If the Court's decisions became irksome to enough legislators, Congress might be induced to curtail the Court's jurisdiction in certain areas. Indeed, several bills designed to exclude the Court from hearing certain kinds of cases have been introduced in Congress within the past two decades; however, the Court's prestige is currently high enough that passage of such legislation seems unlikely. But it has happened before, and it could happen again. In 1868—when the Court's prestige was still at a low ebb following the *Dred Scott* decision—Congress, fearful lest the Court in deciding on the appeal of one McCardle should invalidate some Reconstruction legislation, passed a law that in effect withdrew the Court's appellate jurisdiction in cases such as McCardle's. Although the justices had already heard arguments in the *McCardle* case, they held (in *Ex parte McCardle,* 1869) that they no longer had jurisdiction to decide the case.

Congress also has the power to increase the number of seats on the Court, and if it became sufficiently dissatisfied with the Court's performance, it could authorize the President to appoint enough additional justices to ensure a more favorable line of decisions. Since 1869, however, Congress has left the Court's number of justices at nine. In 1937, President Franklin D. Roosevelt proposed the Court be enlarged. In the preceding two years, the justices had struck down a dozen major New Deal laws, and Roosevelt, fresh from his overwhelming reelection in 1936, was convinced that the justices were using the Constitution to thwart policies that the nation needed and wanted. The Roosevelt court-packing plan, as it was called, aroused violent opposition, however, and in the end was soundly defeated in Congress.

Yet, even though Roosevelt's proposal was defeated, the Court after 1937 stopped declaring federal economic legislation unconstitutional. One explanation may be that Chief Justice Hughes and Justice Owen Roberts, one or both of whom had voted to strike down each of the invalidated New Deal laws, changed sides after realizing that the Court had put itself in the untenable position of standing in the way of policies and programs that most Americans favored. Within the following few years, retirement and death removed three of the justices most firmly opposed to the New Deal philosophy of government, and the President was able to replace them with justices more sympathetic to his policies.

Internal Restraints

More important than these external restraints are the internal restraints imposed by the judicial tradition in general and by the Supreme Court's own tradition in particular. It was to this tradition that Justice (later Chief Justice) Harlan Fiske Stone was alluding in 1936 when he said, in a dissenting opinion, "while unconstitutional exercise of power by the executive and legislative branches of the government is subject to judicial restraint, the only check upon our exercise of power is our own sense of self-restraint."

Traditional Restraints on Judicial Lawmaking

Much of what we said in Chapters 4 and 6 about judicial lawmaking is relevant here. The Constitution is a special sort of enactment, and, as we saw in Chapter 6, judges have rules about how enactments should be interpreted. Many constitutional rules are today embodied in decisional precedents, and as we saw in Chapter 4, judges have rules about building on—and occasionally overruling—precedents.

One of the most basic rules of interpretation is that statutory words whose meaning is plain cannot be ignored. For example, the Constitution provides that "the Senate of the United States shall be composed of two Senators from each State," regardless of the state's size. Under no circumstances could the Court allow a state to elect a third senator. But the constitutional phrases around which most controversies have turned are not so precise. Phrases like "due process of law" do not *in themselves* give the Court much guidance; consequently, they impose no real restraint on the justices' freedom to interpret.

Another basic rule of interpretation is that courts must try to ascertain what those who adopted an enactment meant by the language they used—what general purposes they had in mind. When we study Supreme Court opinions, we find the Court has tried to answer these questions whenever it could. In many opinions the justices have referred back to the recorded deliberations of the Constitutional Convention of 1787 or to the deliberations of the Congress that adopted the various amendments.

The older a constitutional provision becomes, however, the less useful is the guidance provided by its legislative history. Those who adopted and ratified a provision a century or more ago did not and could not have anticipated our modern problems. It seems reasonable to assume that they intended the officials, judges, and lawyers of future generations to accept responsibility for giving the original words a new, more precise meaning suited to current needs.

Thus, neither the actual words of constitutional provisions nor the context of circumstances surrounding their enactment is usually the most important source of restraint on the Court's freedom of interpretation. Far more important are the restraints imposed by previous Court decisions interpreting the provision in question, for these decisions are precedents, and the Court normally feels constrained to follow its own precedents. All the important constitutional phrases have by now been interpreted in many cases, and most modern Supreme Court opinions are discussions, not of the meaning of the constitutional phrases or of the framers' presumed intention, but of the scope and applicability of prior decisions.

As we saw in Chapter 4, no appellate court always adheres to precedents, and the Supreme Court is no exception. The Court, in fact, has felt freer to reverse itself in constitutional cases than would a court applying common-law rules or judicial interpretations of statutes. After all, when an ordinary appellate decision proves to be unwise or becomes outmoded, the legislature can supersede it by passing a statute. But unless the Supreme Court is willing to overrule itself, the only way to nullify a constitutional decision is by the long, uncertain process of constitutional amendment.

Nevertheless, the Supreme Court avoids overruling its precedents directly whenever it can. It prefers to narrow the scope of the unsatisfactory decisions gradually by distinguishing later cases from the unsatisfactory precedent. As it holds that more and more later cases are not covered by the rule of a particular decision, that decision eventually ceases to be significant as a precedent. And when the court does announce that it is overruling an earlier decision, the reversal is rarely unexpected; investigation will usually reveal that the Court has given warning in one or more earlier opinions that it is moving away from the original decision.

As an illustration, let us look at the overruling of *Hammer v. Dagenhart*. In this 1918 case, the Court held that Congress had no power to prohibit the use of child labor in the manufacture of goods to be sold in interstate commerce. It was one of a number of decisions in which the Court restricted the power of legislatures to enact economic regulations. After 1937, the year of President Roosevelt's court-packing proposal, this trend came to an end, and in the next few years an unusually large number of precedents were overruled. The decision that explicitly overruled *Hammer v. Dagenhart* was *United States v. Darby* (1941), which involved a challenge to the constitutionality of the Fair Labor Standards Act of 1938. Speaking for a unanimous Court in the *Darby* case, Justice Stone said:

> The motive and purpose of a regulation of interstate commerce are matters for the legislative judgment upon the exercise of which the Constitution places no restriction and over which the courts are given no control. . . .
>
> [T]hese principles of constitutional interpretation have been so long and repeatedly recognized by this Court as applicable to the Commerce Clause that there would be little occasion for repeating them now were it not for the decision of this Court twenty-two years ago in *Hammer v. Dagenhart,* 247 U.S. 251. In that case it was held by a bare majority of the Court over the powerful and now classic dissent of Mr. Justice Holmes setting forth the fundamental issues involved, that Congress was without power to exclude the products of child labor from interstate commerce. The reasoning and conclusion of the Court's opinion there cannot be reconciled with the conclusion which we have reached. . . .
>
> *Hammer v. Dagenhart* has not been followed. The distinction on which the decision was rested . . . a distinction which was novel when made and unsupported by any provision of the Constitution—has long since been abandoned. . . .
>
> The conclusion is inescapable that *Hammer v. Dagenhart* was a departure from the principles which have prevailed in the interpretation of the Commerce Clause both before and since the decision and that such vitality, as a precedent, as it then had has long since been exhausted. It should be and now is overruled (*United States v. Darby,* 312 U.S. 100, 1941).

As we have remarked before, judicial lawmaking provides both for a degree of certainty and for the possibility of change when change becomes necessary. The Court's normal adherence to precedent creates a large measure of predictability. The more closely woven the web of interpretations becomes, the more unlikely it is that the Court will adopt bold new interpretations. Yet the Court retains the power to distinguish and, if necessary, to overrule undesirable precedents if that proves to be the only way to achieve essential changes in the law.

Other Internal Restraints

In addition to the traditional restraints acting on all appellate judges, there are certain special restraints that the Supreme Court has imposed upon itself in dealing with constitutional issues.

In the first place, the Court has supplemented the constitutional and statutory rules defining its jurisdiction with some self-limiting jurisdictional rules of its own. For example, to implement the constitutional declaration in Article III that the Court's jurisdiction extends to "cases" and "controversies," the justices have spelled out specific standards designed to ensure that the cases it hears are true contests between parties, with each having a genuine interest to protect. That is, the court refuses to address hypothetical situations, and does not issue advisory opinions before a conflict occurs.

The Court has also refused to decide certain cases that present "political questions." It has used this term to describe questions that it considers to be within the special competence of the elected branches of the government, questions that judges are not particularly well equipped to decide or that might bring the Court into open conflict with the other branches. More than once in its history, the Court has lost prestige by rashly involving itself in controversies that brought it into conflict with the other branches of government, and so it has learned to shun situations in which it can perform no useful function. The Court was once asked, for instance, to rule that one of the states did not have "a republican form of government," as required by the Constitution. It ruled instead that the question was one that only the executive and legislative branches could decide, that no judicial intervention was warranted. Until 1962 the Court took a similar position in refusing to rule on the persistent failure of many state legislatures to redraw the boundaries of legislative districts to reflect population shifts, but in that year it ruled that courts may adjudicate such cases.

Sometimes the Court avoids deciding a constitutional issue by disposing of the case before it on nonconstitutional grounds. This practice often disappoints lawyers who hope to get a definitive answer to an unresolved constitutional problem. The Court, however, has nearly always taken the position that when a case turns on several questions of law, the constitutional questions must be decided last—or not at all, if the case can be disposed of on other grounds.

Suppose, for instance, that an administrative official notifies John Jones that he must pay a certain tax. Jones takes the matter to court, arguing that he is exempt from the tax and, moreover, that if the relevant provision in the tax statute were construed to cover him, the provision would be unconstitutional. The justices believe that Jones is probably right: if they interpret the provision broadly enough to make Jones taxable, the statute would probably then be unconstitutional. If, however, they interpret it narrowly enough to exclude Jones, it will pass muster. In such a situation, even if the broad interpretation seems more natural and is probably the one that the legislature intended, the Court is likely to adopt the narrow interpretation in order to avoid invalidating the provision. So the Court rules that the official has misinterpreted the tax law and that it does not apply to Jones. What the justices have done, in effect, is to refer the question of the statute's meaning back to the legislature, with this implicit message: "We, the Supreme Court, presume that you, the legislature, intended to write a constitutionally valid statute. If we were to give this provision a broad interpretation, its constitutionality would be doubtful. To avoid the possibility of having to declare it unconstitutional, we have decided to interpret it narrowly. Now this may not be what you had in mind, but it is up to you either to let our interpretation stand or else to amend the provision to achieve your purpose. If you amend it, we will decide any constitutional issues raised by your amendment when and if they are brought before us."

Even when the Court is willing to consider a constitutional question, it starts from a strong presumption that the challenged official action is constitutional and throws the burden of demonstrating its unconstitutionality on the challenging party. And when the Court does feel compelled to invalidate an official act, it usually does so on the narrowest possible grounds. If, for instance, it can dispose of a case by invalidating only a single statutory section, it will normally say nothing at all about the constitutionality of the other sections.

TAKING PRIVATE PROPERTY FOR PUBLIC PURPOSES

One major area of constitutional interpretation concerns the allocation of rights and liberties between individuals and the community. The following two cases interpret the Fifth Amendment prohibition against taking private property for public use without just compensation. Although both decisions concern takings, *Kelo v. City of New London* focuses on whether a deliberate taking of privately owned land by government with compensation may be appropriate to encourage economic growth in the private sector. In contrast, the second case examines an "unintentional" taking due to enactment of restrictions on the use of land.

In the decision that follows, a closely divided (5–4) U.S. Supreme Court upheld the taking of private property to stimulate local economic development. The city of New London, Connecticut, approved a development plan designed to revitalize its ailing economy. Petitioners brought this state-court action claiming the taking of their properties would violate the "public use" restriction in the Fifth Amendment's takings clause, which says, "nor shall private property be taken for public use, without just compensation." The trial court granted a permanent restraining order prohibiting the taking of some properties, but denying relief as to others. The Connecticut Supreme Court affirmed in part and reversed in part, upholding all proposed takings. Note the court expressed great deference for legislative judgments of both state and local governments. For the sake of brevity, footnotes have been omitted.

Kelo et al. v. City of New London et al.

Supreme Court of the United States
268 Conn. 1 843 A. 2d 500 (2005)

JUSTICE STEVENS delivered the opinion of the Court.

In assembling the land needed for this project, the city's development agent has purchased property from willing sellers and proposes to use the power of eminent domain to acquire the remainder of the property from unwilling owners in exchange for just compensation. . . .

I. [R]espondent New London Development Corporation (NLDC), a private nonprofit entity established . . . to assist the City in planning economic development, . . . finalized an integrated development plan focused on 90 acres of the Fort Trumbull area. . . .

The NLDC intended the development plan to "build momentum for the revitalization of downtown New London," . . . make the City more attractive and . . . create leisure and recreational opportunities on the waterfront and in the park.

The city council approved the plan in January 2000, and designated the NLDC as its development agent in charge of implementation. . . . The city council also authorized the NLDC to purchase property or to acquire property by exercising eminent domain in the City's name. . . . The NLDC successfully negotiated the purchase of most of the real estate in the 90-acre area, but its negotiations with petitioners failed. As a consequence, in November 2000, the NLDC initiated the condemnation proceedings that gave rise to this case.

II. Petitioner Susette Kelo has lived in the Fort Trumbull area since 1997. She has made extensive improvements to her house, which she prizes for its water view. Petitioner Wilhelmina Dery was born in her Fort Trumbull house in 1918 and has lived there her entire life. Her husband Charles (also a petitioner) has lived in the house since they married some 60 years ago. In all, the nine petitioners own 15 properties in Fort Trumbull . . . Ten of the parcels are occupied by the owner or a family member; the other five are held as investment properties. There is no allegation that any of these properties is blighted or otherwise in poor condition; rather, they were condemned only because they happen to be located in the development area.

In December 2000, petitioners brought this action in the New London Superior Court. They claimed, among other things, that the taking of their properties would violate the "public use" restriction in the Fifth Amendment. . . .

We granted certiorari to determine whether a city's decision to take property for the purpose of economic development satisfies the "public use" requirement of the Fifth Amendment. . . .

III. Two polar propositions are perfectly clear. On the one hand, it has long been accepted that the sovereign may not take the property of A for the sole purpose of transferring it to another private party B, even though A is paid just compensation. On the other hand, it is equally clear that a State may transfer property from one private party to another if future "use by the public" is the purpose of the taking; the condemnation of land for a railroad with common-carrier duties is a familiar example. Neither of these propositions, however, determines the disposition of this case.

As for the first proposition, the City would no doubt be forbidden from taking petitioners' land for the purpose of conferring a private benefit on a particular private party. . . . Nor would the City be allowed to take property under the mere pretext of a public purpose, when its actual purpose was to bestow a private benefit. The takings before us, however, would be executed pursuant to a "carefully considered" development plan. 268 Conn., at 54, 843 A. 2d, at 536. The trial judge and all the members of the Supreme Court of Connecticut agreed that there was no evidence of an illegitimate purpose in this case. Therefore, as was true of the statute challenged in *Midkiff*, 467 U.S., at 245, the City's development plan was not adopted "to benefit a particular class of identifiable individuals."

On the other hand, this is not a case in which the City is planning to open the condemned land—at least not in its entirety—to use by the general public. Nor will the private lessees of the land in any sense be required to operate like common carriers, making their services available to all comers. But although such a projected use would be sufficient to satisfy the public use requirement, this "Court long ago rejected any literal requirement that condemned property be put into use for the general public." Id., at 244. Indeed, while many state courts in the mid-19th century endorsed "use by the public" as the proper definition of public use, that narrow view steadily eroded over time. Not only was the "use by the public" test difficult to administer (e.g., what proportion of the public need have access to the property? at what price?), but it proved to be impractical given the diverse and always evolving needs of society. Accordingly, when this Court began applying the Fifth Amendment to the States at the close of the 19th century, it embraced the broader and more natural interpretation of public use as "public purpose." See, e.g., *Fallbrook Irrigation Dist. v. Bradley*, 164 U.S. 112, 158–164 (1896). Thus, in a case upholding a mining company's use of an aerial bucket line to transport ore over property it did not own, Justice Holmes' opinion for the Court stressed "the inadequacy of use by the general public as a universal test." *Strickley v. Highland Boy Gold Mining Co.*, 200 U.S. 527, 531 (1906). We have repeatedly and consistently rejected that narrow test ever since.

The disposition of this case therefore turns on the question whether the City's development plan serves a "public purpose." Without exception, our cases have defined that concept broadly, reflecting our longstanding policy of deference to legislative judgments in this field.

In *Berman v. Parker*, 348 U.S. 26 (1954), this Court upheld a redevelopment plan targeting a blighted area of Washington, D.C., in which most of the housing for the area's 5,000 inhabitants was beyond repair. Under the plan, the area would be condemned and part of it utilized for the construction of streets, schools, and other public facilities. The remainder of the land would be leased or sold to private parties for the purpose of redevelopment, including the construction of low-cost housing.

The owner of a department store located in the area challenged the condemnation, pointing out that his store was not itself blighted and arguing that the creation of a "better balanced, more attractive community" was not a valid public use. Id., at 31. Writing for a unanimous Court, Justice Douglas refused to evaluate this claim in isolation, deferring instead to the legislative and agency judgment that the area "must be planned as a whole" for the plan to be successful. Id., at 34. The Court explained that "community redevelopment programs need not, by force of the Constitution, be on a piecemeal basis—lot by lot, building by building." Id., at 35. The public use underlying the taking was unequivocally affirmed:

> We do not sit to determine whether a particular housing project is or is not desirable. The concept of the public welfare is broad and inclusive. . . . The values it represents are spiritual as well as physical, aesthetic as well as monetary. It is within the power of the legislature to determine that the community should be beautiful as well as healthy, spacious as well as clean, well balanced as well as carefully patrolled. In the present case, the Congress and its authorized agencies have made determinations that take into account a wide variety of values. It is not for us to reappraise them. If those who govern the District of Columbia decide that the Nation's Capital should be beautiful as well as sanitary, there is nothing in the Fifth Amendment that stands in the way. Id., at 33. . . .

Viewed as a whole, our jurisprudence has recognized that the needs of society have varied between different parts of the Nation, just as they have evolved over time in response to changed circumstances. Our earliest cases in particular embodied a strong theme of federalism, emphasizing the "great respect" that we owe to state legislatures and state courts in discerning local public needs. . . . For more than a century, our public use jurisprudence has wisely eschewed rigid formulas and intrusive scrutiny in favor of affording legislatures broad latitude in determining what public needs justify the use of the takings power.

IV. Those who govern the City were not confronted with the need to remove blight in the Fort Trumbull area, but their determination that the area was sufficiently distressed to justify a program of economic rejuvenation is entitled to our deference. The City has carefully formulated an economic development plan that it believes will provide appreciable benefits to the community, including—but by no means limited to—new jobs and increased tax revenue. . . . To effectuate this plan, the City has invoked a state statute that specifically authorizes the use of eminent domain to promote economic development. Given the comprehensive character of the plan, the thorough deliberation that preceded its adoption, and the limited scope of our review, it is appropriate for us, as it was in Berman, to resolve the challenges of the individual owners, not on a piecemeal basis, but rather in light of the entire plan. Because that plan unquestionably serves a public purpose, the takings challenged here satisfy the public use requirement of the Fifth Amendment.

To avoid this result, petitioners urge us to adopt a new bright-line rule that economic development does not qualify as a public use. Putting aside the unpersuasive suggestion that the City's plan will provide only purely economic benefits, neither precedent nor logic supports petitioners' proposal. Promoting economic development is a traditional and long accepted function of government. There is, moreover, no principled way of distinguishing economic development from the other public purposes that we have recognized. In our cases upholding takings that facilitated agriculture and mining, for example, we emphasized the importance of those industries to the welfare of the States in question, see, e.g., *Strickley*, 200 U.S. 527; in Berman, we endorsed the purpose of transforming a blighted area into a "well-balanced" community through redevelopment, 348 U.S., at 33; . . . It would be incongruous to hold that the City's interest in the economic benefits to be derived from the development of the Fort Trumbull area has less of a public character than any of those other interests. Clearly, there is no basis for exempting economic development from our traditionally broad understanding of public purpose. . . .

Alternatively, petitioners maintain that for takings of this kind we should require a "reasonable certainty" that the expected public benefits will actually accrue. Such a rule, however, would represent an even greater departure from our precedent. "When the legislature's purpose is legitimate and its means are not irrational, our cases make clear that empirical debates over the wisdom of takings—no less than debates over the wisdom of other kinds of socioeconomic legislation—are not to be carried out in the federal courts." *Midkiff*, 467 U.S., at 242. . . . The disadvantages of a heightened form of review are especially pronounced in this type of case. Orderly implementation of a comprehensive redevelopment plan obviously requires that the legal rights of all interested parties be established before new construction can be commenced. A constitutional rule that required postponement of the judicial approval of every condemnation until the likelihood of success of the plan had been assured would unquestionably impose a significant impediment to the successful consummation of many such plans. . . .

In affirming the City's authority to take petitioners' properties, we do not minimize the hardship that condemnations may entail, notwithstanding the payment of just compensation. We emphasize that nothing in our opinion precludes any State from placing further restrictions on its exercise of the takings power. . . . This Court's authority, however, extends only to determining whether the City's proposed condemnations are for a "public use" within the meaning of the Fifth Amendment to the Federal Constitution. Because over a century of our case law interpreting that provision dictates an affirmative answer to that question, we may not grant petitioners the relief that they seek.

The judgment of the Supreme Court of Connecticut is affirmed.

STEVENS, J., delivered the opinion of the Court, in which KENNEDY, SOUTER, GINSBURG, and BREYER, JJ., joined. KENNEDY, J., filed a concurring opinion. O'CONNOR, J., filed a dissenting opinion, in which REHNQUIST, C.J., and SCALIA and THOMAS, JJ., joined. THOMAS, J., filed a dissenting opinion.

Questions

1. Why do you think the Court in *Kelo* expressed such great deference for the judgment of the legislature? Were there "political questions" the Court did not wish to address? If so, what were they, and why should they be left to legislative judgment?

2. Do you think defining economic growth in the private sector as a "public use" may be based in part on a cultural bias in favor of capitalism?
3. If there is no legal distinction between private and public purposes in stimulating economic growth, does this decision invite the capture of government decision-making for private business purposes?

Unlike the previous decision, in which a taking and payment of compensation were deliberate, *Lucas v. South Carolina Coastal Council* considered when an "unintentional" taking due to enactment of restrictions on the use of privately owned land may require compensation. Unlike the previous case, in this decision the court expressed a notable lack of deference for judgments of the state legislature.

Lucas bought two residential lots on a South Carolina barrier island in 1986, intending to build single-family homes such as those on adjacent parcels. At that time, Lucas's lots were not subject to state coastal zone building permit requirements. In 1988, the state legislature enacted the Beachfront Management Act, which barred Lucas from erecting any permanent habitable structures on his parcels. He filed suit against the South Carolina Coastal Council, a state agency, contending the ban on construction deprived him of all "economically viable use" of his property and therefore constituted a taking under the Fifth Amendment that required payment of just compensation. The state trial court agreed, finding the ban rendered Lucas's parcels "valueless," and entered an award exceeding $1.2 million. In reversing, the state supreme court held itself bound, in light of Lucas's failure to attack the Beachfront Act's validity, to accept the legislature's "uncontested . . . findings" that new construction in the coastal zone threatened a valuable public resource. That court ruled that when a regulation is designed to prevent "harmful or noxious uses" of property akin to public nuisances, no compensation is owed regardless of the regulation's effect on the property's value. The U.S. Supreme Court (6–3) reversed for Lucas, reasoning that because the Fifth Amendment implies that title to real estate is always held subject to a government's potential decision to eliminate a viable use, a regulation that actually does eliminate all economic value requires just compensation. For the sake of brevity, footnotes once again have been omitted from this abridged decision. We have italicized certain key passages.

Lucas v. South Carolina Coastal Council

Supreme Court of the United States
505 U.S. 1003 (1992)

JUSTICE SCALIA delivered the opinion of the Court.

Prior to Justice Holmes' exposition in *Pennsylvania Coal Co. v. Mahon*, 260 U.S. 393 (1922), it was generally thought that the Takings Clause reached only a "direct appropriation" of property, Legal Tender Cases, 12 Wall. 457, 551 (1871), or the functional equivalent of a "practical ouster of [the owner's] possession." *Transportation Co. v. Chicago*, 99 U.S. 635, 642 (1879). . . . Justice Holmes recognized in *Mahon*, however, that if the protection against physical appropriations of private property was to be meaningfully enforced, the government's power to redefine the range of interests included in the ownership of property was necessarily constrained by constitutional limits. 260 U.S., at 414–415. If, instead, the uses of private property were subject to unbridled, uncompensated qualification under the police power, "the natural tendency of human nature [would be] to extend the qualification more and more until at last private property disappear[ed]." Id., at 415. These considerations gave birth in that case to the oft-cited maxim that, "while property may be regulated to a certain extent, if regulation goes too far it will be recognized as a taking." Ibid.

Nevertheless, our decision in *Mahon* offered little insight into when, and under what circumstances, a given regulation would be seen as going "too far" for purposes of the Fifth Amendment. In 70 odd years of succeeding "regulatory takings" jurisprudence, we have generally eschewed any "'set formula'" for determining how far is too far, preferring to "engag[e] in . . . essentially ad hoc, factual inquiries," *Penn Central Transportation Co. v. New York City*, 438 U.S. 104, 124 (1978). . . . We have, however, described at least two discrete categories of regulatory action as compensable without case specific inquiry into the public interest advanced in support of the restraint. The first encompasses regulations that compel the property owner to suffer a physical "invasion" of his property. In general (at least with regard to permanent invasions), no matter how minute the intrusion, and no matter how weighty the public purpose behind it, we have required compensation. . . .

The second situation in which we have found categorical treatment appropriate is where regulation denies all economically beneficial or productive use of land. . . . As we have said on numerous occasions, the Fifth Amendment is violated when land use regulation "does not substantially advance legitimate state interests or denies an owner economically viable use of his land." . . .

We have never set forth the justification for this rule. Perhaps it is simply, as Justice Brennan suggested, that total deprivation of beneficial use is, from the landowner's point of view, the equivalent of a physical appropriation. . . .

On the other side of the balance, affirmatively supporting a compensation requirement, is the fact that regulations that leave the owner of land without economically beneficial or productive options for its use—typically, as here, by requiring land to be left substantially in its natural state—carry with them a heightened risk that private property is being pressed into some form of public service under the guise of mitigating serious public harm. . . . The many statutes on the books, both state and federal, that provide for the use of eminent domain to impose servitudes on private scenic lands preventing developmental uses, or to acquire such lands altogether, suggest the practical equivalence in this setting of negative regulation and appropriation. . . .

We think, in short, that there are good reasons for our frequently expressed belief that when the owner of real property has been called upon to sacrifice all economically beneficial uses in the name of the common good, that is, to leave his property economically idle, he has suffered a taking.

It is correct that many of our prior opinions have suggested that "harmful or noxious uses" of property may be proscribed by government regulation without the requirement of compensation. For a number of reasons, however, we think the South Carolina Supreme Court was too quick to conclude that that principle decides the present case. The "harmful or noxious uses" principle was the Court's early attempt to describe in theoretical terms why government may, consistent with the Takings Clause, affect property values by regulation without incurring an obligation to compensate—a reality we nowadays acknowledge explicitly with respect to the full scope of the State's police power. . . . We made this very point in *Penn Central Transportation Co.*, where, in the course of sustaining New York City's landmarks preservation program against a takings challenge, we rejected the petitioner's suggestion that *Mugler* and the cases following it were premised on, and thus limited by, some objective conception of "noxiousness":

> [T]he uses in issue in *Hadacheck, Miller,* and *Goldblatt* were perfectly lawful in themselves. They involved no 'blameworthiness, . . . moral wrongdoing or conscious act of dangerous risk taking which induce[d] society] to shift the cost to a pa[rt]icular individual.' . . . These cases are better understood as resting not on any supposed 'noxious' quality of the prohibited uses but rather on the ground that the restrictions were reasonably related to the implementation of a policy—not unlike historic preservation—expected to produce a widespread public benefit and applicable to all similarly situated property. 438 U.S., at 133–134, n. 30.

"Harmful or noxious use" analysis was, in other words, simply the progenitor of our more contemporary statements that "land use regulation does not effect a taking if it 'substantially advance[s] legitimate state interests.' . . ." *Nollan, supra*, at 834 (quoting *Agins v. Tiburon*, 447 U.S., at 260); see also *Penn Central Transportation Co., supra*, at 127; *Euclid v. Ambler Realty Co.*, 272 U.S. 365, 387–388 (1926).

The transition from our early focus on control of "noxious" uses to our contemporary understanding of the broad realm within which government may regulate without compensation was an easy one, since the distinction between "harm preventing" and "benefit conferring" regulation is often in the eye of the beholder. It is quite possible, for example, to describe in either fashion the ecological, economic, and aesthetic concerns that inspired the South Carolina legislature in the present case. One could say that imposing a servitude on Lucas's land is necessary in order to prevent his use of it from "harming" South Carolina's ecological resources; or, instead, in order to achieve the "benefits" of an ecological preserve. . . . Whether one or the other of the competing characterizations will come to one's lips in a particular case depends primarily upon one's evaluation of the worth of competing uses of real estate. . . . A given restraint will be seen as mitigating "harm" to the adjacent parcels or securing a "benefit" for them, depending upon the observer's evaluation of the relative importance of the use that the restraint favors. . . . Whether Lucas's construction of single family residences on his parcels should be described as bringing "harm" to South Carolina's adjacent ecological resources thus depends principally upon whether the describer believes that the State's use interest in nurturing those resources is so important that any competing adjacent use must yield. . . .

When it is understood that "prevention of harmful use" was merely our early formulation of the police power justification necessary to sustain (without compensation) any regulatory diminution in value; and that the distinction between regulation that "prevents harmful use" and that which "confers benefits" is difficult, if not impossible, to discern on an objective, value free basis; it becomes self evident that noxious use logic cannot serve as a touchstone to distinguish regulatory "takings"—which require compensation—from regulatory deprivations that do not require compensation. A fortiori the legislature's recitation of a noxious use justification cannot be the basis for departing from our categorical rule that total regulatory takings must be compensated. If it were, departure would virtually always be allowed. The South Carolina Supreme Court's approach would essentially nullify *Mahon's* affirmation of limits to the noncompensable exercise of the police power. Our cases provide no support for this: None of them that employed the logic of "harmful use" prevention to sustain a regulation involved an allegation that the regulation wholly eliminated the value of the claimant's land. . . .

Where the State seeks to sustain regulation that deprives land of all economically beneficial use, we think it may resist compensation only if the logically antecedent inquiry into the nature of the owner's estate shows that the proscribed use interests were not part of his title to begin with. This accords, we think, with our "takings" jurisprudence, which has traditionally been guided by the understandings of our citizens regarding the content of, and the State's power over, the "bundle of rights" that they acquire when they obtain title to property. *It seems to us that the property owner necessarily expects the uses of his property to be restricted, from time to time, by various measures newly enacted by the State in legitimate exercise of its police powers;* "[a]s long recognized, some values are enjoyed under an implied limitation and must yield to the police power." [emphasis added] *Pennsylvania Coal Co. v. Mahon*, 260 U.S., at 413. And in the case of personal property, by reason of the State's traditionally high degree of control over commercial dealings, he ought to be aware of the possibility that new regulation might even render his property economically worthless. . . . In the case of land, however, we think the notion pressed by the Council that title is somehow held subject to the "implied limitation" that the State may subsequently eliminate all economically valuable use is inconsistent with the historical compact recorded in the Takings Clause that has become part of our constitutional culture.

Where "permanent physical occupation" of land is concerned, we have refused to allow the government to decree it anew (without compensation), no matter how weighty the asserted "public interests" involved, *Loretto v. Teleprompter Manhattan CATV Corp.*, 458 U.S., at 426. . . . We believe similar treatment must be accorded confiscatory regulations, i.e., regulations that prohibit all economically beneficial use of land: *Any limitation so severe cannot be newly legislated or decreed (without compensation),* [emphasis added] but must inhere in the title itself, in the restrictions that background principles of the State's law of property and nuisance already place upon land ownership. A law or decree with such an effect must, in other words, do no more than duplicate the result that could have been achieved in the courts—by adjacent landowners (or other uniquely affected persons) under the State's law of private nuisance, or by the State under its complementary power to abate nuisances that affect the public generally, . . .

The "total taking" inquiry we require today will ordinarily entail (as the application of state nuisance law ordinarily entails) analysis of, among other things, the degree of harm to public lands and resources, or adjacent private property, posed by the claimant's proposed activities, . . . and the relative ease with which the alleged harm can be avoided through measures taken by the claimant and the government (or adjacent private landowners) alike. . . . The fact that a particular use has long been engaged in by similarly situated owners ordinarily imports a lack of any common law prohibition. . . . So also does the fact that other landowners, similarly situated, are permitted to continue the use denied to the claimant.

It seems unlikely that common law principles would have prevented the erection of any habitable or productive improvements on petitioner's land; they rarely support prohibition of the "essential use" of land, *Curtin v. Benson*, 222 U.S. 78, 86 (1911). The question, however, is one of state law to be dealt with on remand. We emphasize that to win its case South Carolina must do more than proffer the legislature's declaration that the uses Lucas desires are inconsistent with the public interest, or the conclusory assertion that they violate a common law maxim such as *sic utere tuo ut alienum non laedas*. As we have said, a "State . . . may not transform private property into public property without compensation. . . ." *Webb's Fabulous Pharmacies, Inc. v. Beckwith*, 449 U.S. 155, 164 (1980). Instead, as it would be required to do if it sought to restrain Lucas in a common law action for public nuisance, South Carolina must identify background principles of nuisance and property law that prohibit the uses he now intends in the circumstances in which the property is presently found. Only on this showing can the State fairly claim that, in proscribing all such beneficial uses, the Beachfront Management Act is taking nothing.

The judgment is reversed and the cause remanded for proceedings not inconsistent with this opinion.

SCALIA, J., delivered the opinion of the Court, in which REHNQUIST, C.J., and WHITE, O'CONNOR, and THOMAS, JJ., joined. KENNEDY, J., filed an opinion concurring in the judgment. BLACKMUN, J., and STEVENS, J., filed dissenting opinions. SOUTER, J., filed a separate statement.

Questions

1. Can you think of any other economically viable use of Lucas's shorefront land that does not require construction of a dwelling?
2. If protecting human life and property is an appropriate concern of government policy, should homes ever be built on barrier islands?
3. Do you think the result in *Lucas* may have stemmed from a poorly worded statute? Might *Lucas* be a case poorly prepared and presented to the trial court by lawyers for the state? Why?
4. Why do you think the court displayed so little deference to the judgment of the legislature in *Lucas* and so much deference in *Kelo*?
5. Does the decision suggest that statutory regulations can only prohibit uses of land that were previously prohibited at common law without payment of just compensation? Might the sheer expense of such compensation restrict desirable social and legal change?

THE SUPREME COURT AS POLICYMAKER

When, in the early days of the Republic, Chief Justice John Marshall had to interpret the scope of the federal power to regulate interstate commerce, he found little guidance in the sixteen words of the Constitution that make up the commerce clause. Essentially, he had to make a policy decision: would a broad or narrow interpretation of the federal power best suit the needs of the country? When the Supreme Court today has to decide whether the conduct of a certain sheriff or police officer or jailer meets the requirement of "due process of law," the constitutional phrase in itself is of no use as a standard of measurement. According to Justice Felix Frankfurter, the concept of due process in matters of procedure "expresses a demand for civilized standards of law. It is thus not a stagnant formulation of what has been achieved in the past but a standard for judgment in the progressive evolution of the institutions of society." The judgment "must move within the limits of accepted notions of justice" (*Adamson v. California*, 332 U.S. 46, 1947). The Court, then, must decide what the currently accepted notions of justice are.

Past decisions may be of some use in suggesting criteria against which the official's conduct can be measured, but the Court's job is essentially to decide whether the official's conduct was within the limits of what is fair or just under standards set for an agent of government in today's democratic society. This is a policymaking, lawmaking function.

Sometimes an official act seems valid with reference to one constitutional principle but invalid with reference to another. Then the Court is compelled to establish a priority between the two principles. Some statutes designed to restrict picketing by labor unions have raised this problem. Viewed as a potential interference with property rights, picketing would seem to be subject to regulation under the states' "police power"; viewed as an exercise of free speech by the unions, however, it would seem to be protected from legislative interference by the First and Fourteenth Amendments (which together restrict the power of states to interfere with freedom of expression). Sometimes the Court has given priority to one of these competing values and sometimes to the other, depending on the form of regulation and the purpose of the picketing. It should be clear that the Court can take no position on a question of this sort without making a *policy decision*—without, that is, making a choice between conflicting social aims and values.

But when acting as a policymaker, a Supreme Court justice must display infinitely more objectivity and self-restraint than is demanded of legislative or executive policymakers. No matter how broad the discretion granted, the justice's task is never to ask: How do *I* feel about the wisdom of this statute or the fairness of this official act? It is only to ask: Is this official act—however unwise it may seem to me—within the limits of what the Constitution permits? And since, as we have seen, the words of the Constitution usually provide no direct answer, the task is to interpret the *spirit* of the Constitution and to relate that spirit to the changing needs and values of an evolving society. Finally, the justice may have to explain and justify the decision in a written opinion that, when published, should clarify and illuminate the constitutional principles in question.

The justices of the Supreme Court have not always practiced such perfect self-restraint. On occasion, both conservative and liberal members of the Court have confused their personal convictions with the law of the land. But some of our greatest justices have resisted this temptation. In the first half of the twentieth century, Justices Holmes and Stone stood as outstanding examples of judicial self-restraint. Neither was enthusiastic about many of the laws regulating business that came before the Court during his tenure, yet each dissented again and again when his colleagues voted to strike down those laws. Although they each believed that many of the enactments were ill conceived and futile, they could find nothing in the Constitution to justify the assumption that judges were better qualified than the people's elected representatives to decide what was good for a state or for the nation. Unless a legislature has clearly exceeded the express or implied powers granted to it by the Constitution, they insisted, the Court must not override its enactments, however unwise they may seem. As Justice Stone once put it, "For the removal of unwise laws from the statute books, appeal lies not to the courts but to the ballot and to the processes of democratic government. . . . Courts are not the only agency of government that must be assumed to have capacity to govern" (*United States v. Butler*, 297 U.S. 1, 87, 1936).

From time to time the Court has misused its power by acting as a sort of superlegislature. But not every attack made on the Court for abuse of power has been justified. The underlying cause of most of the attacks on the Court has been acute disappointment over the outcome of particular cases. It is not surprising that in 1935–1936, when so many New Deal programs were being struck down, the Court's most vocal critics tended to be those who favored the New Deal programs. Today a different set of issues is being brought before the Court, and now many of the groups that in the 1930s deplored the Court's decisions are its most ardent defenders, while its former friends are among its critics.

Like other democratic institutions, the Supreme Court is not exempt from criticism, and constructive criticism (as distinguished from personal attacks on particular justices) can serve a useful purpose. Even intemperate attacks on the Court made during the late 1950s may have encouraged people to reflect on the values and limitations of the Court as a political institution and on the moral issues implicit in the cases it was deciding. Indeed, the Court's decisions on such major issues as equal rights for minorities, limits of free speech, and separation of church and state do not achieve their fullest effect until they have been studied and understood by the nation's citizens. Only when they have been accepted not just as the law, but also as just and right, are they truly effective.

FREE SPEECH AND FLAG BURNING

The First Amendment to the Constitution of the United States reads: "Congress shall make no law respecting an establishment of religion, or prohibiting the free exercise thereof; or abridging the freedom of speech, or of the press; or of the right of the people peaceably to assemble, and to petition the Government for a redress of grievances."

This amendment is designed to protect some of the most treasured aspects of life in the United States. Freedom of speech has long been seen as one of the cornerstones of our system of government. The ability to exchange religious, political, economic, and other ideas freely and openly is particularly coveted, even if some of those ideas are offensive. It is through the free exchange of ideas that our government remains responsive and open. In fact, at least with respect to political ideas, the Supreme Court has held that the First Amendment has a preferred position. This implies that when rights come into conflict, First Amendment rights should prevail.

In the case that follows, rights did indeed come into conflict and the Supreme Court had to make a difficult choice. Gregory Johnson participated in a political demonstration protesting the policies of the Reagan administration. While chanting protests, he burned an American flag. Although no one was physically injured, a number of people were offended by his action. Johnson was charged with a crime, and ultimately the Supreme Court was faced with balancing the conflicting rights to free speech and public order.

Texas v. Johnson

Supreme Court of the United States
1095 S.Ct. 2533 (1989)

JUSTICE BRENNAN delivered the opinion of the Court.

After publicly burning an American flag as a means of political protest, Gregory Lee Johnson was convicted of desecrating a flag in violation of Texas law. This case presents the question whether his conviction is consistent with the First Amendment. We hold that it is not. . . .

While the Republican National Convention was taking place in Dallas in 1984, respondent Johnson participated in a political demonstration. . . .

The demonstration ended in front of Dallas City Hall, where Johnson unfurled the American flag, doused it with kerosene, and set it on fire. While the flag burned, the protestors chanted, "America, the red, white, and blue, we spit on you." . . .

Of the approximately 100 demonstrators, Johnson alone was charged with a crime. The only criminal offense with which he was charged was the desecration of a venerated object in violation of Tex. Penal Code Ann. §42.09(a)(3)(1989) . . .

The Court of Appeals . . . affirmed Johnson's conviction, . . . but the Texas Court of Criminal Appeals reversed, . . . holding that the State could not, consistent with the First Amendment, punish Johnson for burning the flag in these circumstances. . . .

Johnson was convicted of flag desecration for burning the flag rather than for uttering insulting words. This fact somewhat complicates our consideration of his conviction under the First Amendment. We must first determine whether Johnson's burning of the flag constituted expressive conduct, permitting him to invoke the First Amendment in challenging his conviction. See, e.g., *Spence v. Washington*, 418 U.S. 405, 409–411 (1974). If his conduct was expressive, we next decide whether the State's regulation is related to the suppression of free expression. . . .

If the State's regulation is not related to expression, then the less stringent standard we announced in *United States v. O'Brien* for regulations of noncommunicative conduct controls. . . . If it is, then we are outside of *O'Brien*'s test, and we must ask whether this interest justifies Johnson's conviction under a more demanding standard. . . .

The First Amendment literally forbids the abridgement only of "speech," but we have long recognized that its protection does not end at the spoken or written word. . . .

In deciding whether particular conduct possesses communicative elements to bring the First Amendment into play, we have asked whether "[a]n intent to convey a particularized message was present, and [whether] the likelihood was great that the message would be understood by those who viewed it." . . .

Especially pertinent to this case are our decisions recognizing the communicative nature of conduct relating to flags. Attaching a peace sign to the flag, . . . displaying a red flag, . . . we have held, all may find shelter under the First Amendment. See also *Smith v. Goguen*, 415 U.S. 566, 588 (1974). . . . That we have had little difficulty identifying an expressive element in conduct relating to flags should not be surprising. The very purpose of a national flag is to serve as a symbol of our country; it is, one might say, "the one visible manifestation of two hundred years of nationhood." . . .

The Government generally has a freer hand in restricting expressive conduct than it has in restricting the written or spoken word. . . . It is, in short, not simply the verbal or nonverbal nature of the expression, but the governmental interest at stake, that helps to determine whether a restriction on that expression is valid.

Thus, although we have recognized that where "'speech' and 'nonspeech' elements are combined in the same course of conduct, a sufficiently important governmental interest in regulating the nonspeech element can justify incidental limitations on First Amendment freedoms." *O'Brien, supra*, at 376, . . .

In order to decide whether *O'Brien*'s test applies here, therefore, we must decide whether Texas has asserted an interest in support of Johnson's conviction that is unrelated to the suppression of expression.

Texas claims that its interest in preventing breaches of the peace justifies Johnson's conviction for flag desecration. However, no disturbance of the peace actually occurred or threatened to occur because of Johnson's burning of the flag. . . .

The State's position, therefore, amounts to a claim that an audience that takes serious offense at particular expression is necessarily likely to disturb the peace and that the expression may be prohibited on this basis. Our precedents do not countenance such a presumption. . . .

Nor does Johnson's expressive conduct fall within that small class of "fighting words" that are "likely to provoke the average person to retaliation, and thereby cause a breach of the peace." . . . No reasonable onlooker would have regarded Johnson's generalized expression of dissatisfaction with the policies of the Federal Government as a direct personal insult or an invitation to exchange fisticuffs. . . .

We thus conclude that the State's interest in maintaining order is not implicated on these facts. . . .

The State also asserts an interest in preserving the flag as a symbol of nationhood and national unity. . . . The State apparently, is concerned that such conduct will lead people to believe either that the flag does not stand for nationhood and national unity, but instead reflects other, less positive concepts, or that the concepts reflected in the flag do not in fact exist, that is, we do not enjoy unity as a Nation. These concerns blossom only when a person's treatment of the flag communicates some message and thus are related "to the suppression of free expression" within the meaning of *O'Brien*. We are thus outside of *O'Brien*'s test altogether. . . .

It remains to consider whether the State's interest in preserving the flag as a symbol of nationhood and national unity justifies Johnson's conviction. . . . Johnson was not, we add, prosecuted for the expression of just any idea; he was prosecuted for his expression of dissatisfaction with the policies of this country, expression situated at the core of our First Amendment values. . . .

Moreover, Johnson was prosecuted because he knew that his politically charged expression would cause "serious offense." . . . The Texas law is thus not aimed at protecting the physical integrity of the flag in all circumstances, but is designed instead to protect it only against impairments that would cause serious offense to others. Texas concedes as much: "Section 42.09(b) reaches only those severe acts of physical abuse of the flag carried out in a way likely to be offensive." . . .

Whether Johnson's treatment of the flag violated Texas law thus depended on the likely communicative impact of his expressive conduct. Our decision in *Boos v. Barry, supra*, tells us that this restriction on Johnson's expression is content-based. In *Boos*, we considered the constitutionality of a law prohibiting "the display of any sign within 50 feet of a foreign embassy if that sign tends to bring that foreign government into 'public odium' or 'public disrepute.'" *Id.*, at 315. Rejecting the argument that the law was content-neutral because it was justified by "our international law obligation to shield diplomats from speech that offends their dignity," *id.*, at 820, we held that "[t]he emotive impact of speech on its audience is not a 'secondary effect'" unrelated to the content of the expression itself. . . .

According to the principles announced in *Boos*, Johnson's political expression was restricted because of the content of the message he conveyed. We must therefore subject the State's asserted interest in preserving the special symbolic character of the flag to "the most exacting scrutiny." *Boos v. Barry,* 485 U.S., at 321.

Texas argues that its interest in preserving the flag as a symbol of nationhood and national unity survives this close analysis. Quoting extensively from the writings of this Court chronicling the flag's historic and symbolic role in our society, the State emphasizes the "'special place'" reserved for the flag in our Nation. . . .

[T]he State's claim is that it has an interest in preserving the flag as a symbol of *nationhood* and *national unity,* a symbol with a determinate range of meanings. . . . According to Texas, if one physically treats the flag in a way that would tend to cast doubt on either the idea that nationhood and national unity are the flag's referents or that national unity actually exists the message conveyed thereby is a harmful one and therefore may be prohibited.

If there is a bedrock principle underlying the First Amendment, it is that the Government may not prohibit the expression of an idea simply because society finds the idea itself offensive or disagreeable. . . .

We have not recognized an exception to this principle even where our flag has been involved. In *Street v. New York,* 394 U.S. 576 (1969), we held that a State may not criminally punish a person for uttering words critical of the flag. . . . Nor may the Government, we have held, compel conduct that would evince respect for the flag. "To sustain the compulsory flag salute we are required to say that a Bill of Rights, which guards the individual's right to speak his own mind, left it open to public authorities to compel him to utter what is not on his mind." . . .

In short, nothing in our precedents suggests that a State may foster its own view of the flag by prohibiting expressive conduct relating to it. To bring its argument outside our precedents, Texas attempts to convince us that even if its interest in preserving the flag's symbolic role does not allow it to prohibit words or some expressive conduct critical of the flag, it does permit it to forbid the outright destruction of the flag. The State's argument cannot depend here on the distinction between written or spoken words and nonverbal conduct. That distinction, we have shown, is of no moment where the nonverbal conduct is expressive, as it is here, and where the regulation of that conduct is related to expression, as it is here. . . .

Texas' focus on the precise nature of Johnson's expression, moreover, misses the point of our prior decisions; their enduring lesson, that the Government may not prohibit expression simply because it disagrees with its message, is not dependent on the particular mode in which one chooses to express an idea. . . .

We never before have held that the Government may ensure that a symbol be used to express only one view of that symbol or its referents. . . .

There is, moreover, no indication—either in the text of the Constitution or in our cases interpreting it—that a separate juridical category exists for the American flag alone. Indeed, we would not be surprised to learn that the persons who framed our Constitution and wrote the Amendment that we now construe were not known for their reverence for the Union Jack. The First Amendment does not guarantee that other concepts virtually sacred to our Nation as a whole—such as the principle that discrimination on the basis of race is odious and destructive—will go unquestioned in the marketplace of ideas. . . . We decline, therefore, to create for the flag an exception to the joust of principles protected by the First Amendment.

It is not the State's ends, but its means, to which we object. It cannot be gainsaid that there is a special place reserved for the flag in this Nation, and thus we do not doubt that the Government has a legitimate interest in making efforts to "preserve the national flag as an unalloyed symbol of our country." . . .

The way to preserve the flag's special role is not to punish those who feel differently about these matters. It is to persuade them that they are wrong. "To courageous, self-reliant men, with confidence in the power of free and fearless reasoning applied through the processes of popular government, no danger flowing from speech can be deemed clear and present, unless the incidence of the evil apprehended is so imminent that it may befall before there is opportunity for full discussion. If there be time to expose through discussion the falsehood and fallacies, to avert the evil by processes of education, the remedy to be applied is more speech, not enforced silence." *Whitney v. California,* 274 U.S. 375, 877 (1927) (Brandeis, J., concurring). And, precisely because it is our flag that is involved, one's response to the flagburner may exploit the uniquely persuasive power of the flag itself. We can imagine no more appropriate response to burning a flag than waving one's own, no better way to counter a message than by saluting the flag that burns, no surer means of preserving the dignity even of the flag that burned than by—as one witness here did—according its remains a respectful burial. We do not consecrate the flag by punishing its desecration, for in so doing we dilute the freedom that this cherished emblem represents. . . .

Johnson was convicted for engaging in expressive conduct. The State's interest in preventing breaches of the peace does not support his conviction because Johnson's conduct did not threaten to disturb the peace. Nor does the State's interest in preserving the flag as a symbol of nationhood and national unity justify his criminal conviction for engaging in political expression. The judgment of the Texas Court of Criminal Appeals is therefore [affirmed].

Chief Justice Rehnquist, with whom Justice White and Justice O'Connor join, dissenting.

In holding this Texas statute unconstitutional, the Court ignores Justice Holmes' familiar aphorism that "a page of history is worth a volume of logic." *New York Trust Co. v. Eisner,* 256 U.S. 345, 349 (1921). For more than 200 years, the American flag has occupied a unique position as the symbol of our Nation, a uniqueness that justifies a governmental prohibition against flag burning in the way respondent Johnson did here . . .

But the Court insists that the Texas statute prohibiting the public burning of the American flag infringes on respondent Johnson's freedom of expression. Such freedom, of course, is not absolute. See *Schenck v. States,* 249 U.S. 47 (1919). In *Chaplinsky v. New Hampshire,* 315 U.S. 568 (1942), a unanimous Court said:

> Allowing the broadest scope to the language and purpose of the Fourteenth Amendment, it is well understood that the right of free speech is not absolute at all times and under all circumstances. There are certain well-defined and narrowly limited classes of speech, the prevention and punishment of which have never been thought to raise any Constitutional problem. These include the lewd and obscene, the profane, the libelous and the insulting or 'fighting' words—those that by their very utterance inflict injury or tend to incite an immediate breach of the peace. It has been well observed that such utterances are no essential part of any exposition of ideas, and are of such slight social value as a step to truth that any benefit that may be derived from them is clearly outweighed by the social interest in order and morality. *Id.,* at 571–572 (footnotes omitted). . . .

Here it may equally well be said that the public burning of the American flag by Johnson was no essential part of any exposition of ideas, and at the same time it had a tendency to incite a breach of the peace. . . .

The Court could not, and did not, say that Chaplinsky's utterances were not expressive phrases—they clearly and succinctly conveyed an extremely low opinion of the addressee. The same may be said of Johnson's public burning of the flag in this case; it obviously did convey Johnson's bitter dislike of his country. But his act, like Chaplinsky's provocative words, conveyed nothing that could not have been conveyed and was not conveyed just as forcefully in a dozen different ways. As with "fighting words," so with flag burning for purposes of the First Amendment: It is "no essential part of any exposition of ideas and [is] of such slight social value as a step to truth that any benefit that may be derived from [it] is clearly outweighed" by the public interest in avoiding a probable breach of the peace. The highest courts of several States have upheld state statutes prohibiting the public burning of the flag on the grounds that it is so inherently inflammatory that it may cause a breach of public order. . . .

The result of the Texas statute is obviously to deny one in Johnson's frame of mind one of many means of "symbolic speech." Far from being a case of "one picture being worth a thousand words," flag burning is the equivalent of an inarticulate grunt or roar that, it seems fair to say, is most likely to be indulged in not to express any particular idea, but to antagonize others. Only five years ago we said in *Los Angeles City Council v. Taxpayers for Vincent,* 466 U.S. 789, 812 (1984), that "the First Amendment does not guarantee the right to employ every conceivable method of communication at all times and in all places." The Texas statute deprived Johnson of only one rather inarticulate symbolic form of protest—a form of protest that was profoundly offensive to many—and left him with a full panoply of other symbols and every conceivable form of verbal expression to express his deep disapproval of national policy.

Questions

1. Briefly outline the court's reasoning. Are there any points with which you disagree? Why?
2. Was there any actual disturbance of the peace in this case? Did that fact make a difference in the majority opinion that was discounted in the dissenting opinion?
3. Do you believe that speech that is critical of the government—even disrespectful—should be protected? Why?
4. Should the government be allowed to place restrictions of time or place on acts such as flag burning? Why?

CHAPTER PROBLEM:
"ARE WE READY FOR TRUTH IN JUDGING?"

The constant reader of constitutional cases soon comes to know that many of the important decisions of the Supreme Court of the United States are not based on law, in the popular sense of that term.

The Court endeavors to identify constitutional clauses on which to hang its pronouncements, but some key words and phrases in the Constitution are so highly indeterminate that they cannot qualify as law in any usual sense. They are semantic blanks—verbal vacuums that may be filled readily with any one of many possible meanings. It should not be surprising that different judges over a period of time, as well as at the same time, choose to fill them with their own meanings. . . .

In the present scheme of things, the Supreme Court's nature is not primarily that of a court. Its role and function are more closely akin to that of a legislative body or of an executive oligarchy. Perhaps it is our central committee. The search for analogues is an interesting one. But comparatists tell me there is no exact copy—now or in political history.

But note well that it is not an act of condemnation or disapproval to say that the institution is not primarily a court. It is a matter of healthy recognition that a new kind of governmental institution has evolved—one probably unique in the history of governmental institutions. It is an institution that has thus far been highly successful as an instrument of political action despite the fact that in combining legislative, judicial, and executive powers it has contradicted the basic warnings of the doctrine of separation of powers, and the apprehensions against concentrated power expressed by the framers of the Constitution.

By honestly and accurately identifying what we have wrought through the development of this singular institution, the American people may more wisely evaluate and observe its workings in the exercise of great and concentrated power. That power, vast as it has become, is still contained within a proved system of checks and balances and within a working structure of constitutional government that vest the ultimate power of choice and direction in the American people.

The merit of our "Legiscourt" in our democratic framework is worthy of further straightforward analysis and evaluation, particularly in relation to long-range effects. The maintenance of this body as the designated protector of minorities against the will of the majority is a strong point in its favor. But the tendency of the body to venture into other areas of government, where the necessity to safeguard minorities is not present or ambiguous, may be less favorable. There is much to study and to think about. But the first thing to do is to identify and reveal the true nature of the institution.

Source: Excerpted with permission from Forrester (1977, 1212).

Questions

1. What does the author of this article mean by the term *Legiscourt?*
2. How is the Supreme Court acting like a new kind of governmental institution? Can you give an example?
3. Do you agree with the author of this article that the Supreme Court exercises "great and concentrated power"? Why or why not?

QUESTIONS FOR REVIEW

1. To better understand the process of constitutional amendment, research the history and progress of the proposed Equal Rights Amendment. How did its history differ from that of other constitutional amendments?
2. How does the Supreme Court decide which cases to hear among all those that are sent to it for consideration?
3. The text suggests the Supreme Court is uniquely suited to act as final arbiter on constitutional issues. Do you agree with this claim? Why or why not?
4. Why do you suppose the Supreme Court has nearly always taken the position that, when a case turns on several questions of law, the constitutional questions must be decided last—or not at all, if the case can be disposed of on other grounds?
5. What types of restraints are imposed on the actions of the Supreme Court?
6. Do you agree that Supreme Court justices should have indefinite tenure and should be virtually unremovable from office? Explain your answer.

BIBLIOGRAPHY

Forrester, William R. 1977. "Are We Ready for Truth in Judging?" *American Bar Association Journal* 63 (September): 1212–1216.
Hughes, Charles Evans, and Jacob Gould Shurman. 1908. *Addresses and Papers of Charles Evans Hughes, Governor of New York, 1906–1908.* New York: G.P. Putnam.

CHAPTER 8

Administrative Lawmaking
and Adjudication

To many Americans, the influence of administrative officials seems far more pervasive than that of judges and legislators. Not only do these officials execute the laws, but also together they create more legal rules than all the legislatures and try more cases than all the courts. The body of law that controls their activity is known as *administrative law.* We consider some of the most important principles of administrative law in this chapter.

Administrators perform a great variety of functions. The following examples will suggest the sorts of rulemaking and adjudicative activities with which this chapter is concerned.

1. Administrators determine the value of taxable property. They issue regulations defining what must be included in taxpayers' income declarations, and they review declarations of taxable income. They negotiate disputes over tax liability with particular taxpayers. They staff a special federal tax court that adjudicates controversies over liability when negotiation has failed.
2. Administrators grant (and may deny, suspend, or revoke) a great variety of licenses, permits, franchises, charters, and patents. Most citizens are familiar, for example, with the process involved in renewing a driver's license at a state administrative agency.
3. Administrators establish the rates charged by transportation, communications, and public utility companies and supervise the services these companies provide.
4. Administrators serve as both prosecutors and judges in proceedings to determine whether laws prohibiting unfair competition, unfair labor practices, and racial discrimination in housing and employment have been violated. They also rule on alleged violations of laws setting standards for wages and hours and for the quality of food and drugs.
5. Administrators investigate crimes and terrorist threats to national security, screen passengers at airports, issue summonses for traffic violations, extinguish fires, and supervise cleanup of hazardous waste sites.
6. Administrators determine whether certain persons should be excluded from government or defense-industry jobs and whether others should be deported from the country.
7. Administrators hear and rule on the claims of employees who have suffered injuries while at work.

THE EMERGENCE OF ADMINISTRATIVE AGENCIES

There have always been administrators, but they have not always had the breadth of discretionary power that many of them have today. How has it happened that nonelective officials now make rules governing conduct and that officials outside the judicial tradition hear and decide cases?

The power of modern administrators is a product of economic developments that began in the years following the Civil War, when the United States was transformed with remarkable speed from a farming and trading nation into an industrial nation. A vigorous generation of entrepreneurs created great manufacturing, railroad, and financial empires. The resulting concentration of power in private hands brought widespread abuses that, in turn, provoked a popular demand for government regulation of business practices deemed harmful to the general interest.

Traditionally, when a legislature decided to lay down a new set of rules regulating private conduct, it simply adopted a statute setting standards in terms as specific or as general as the circumstances warranted. Courts were left to fill in gaps in the law as cases—criminal prosecutions or civil suits, depending on the remedies provided by statute—were brought before them. This was the pattern of lawmaking set in 1890, for example, with enactment of the Sherman Act, discussed previously. Thus the body of federal antimonopoly rules was the joint creation of Congress and the federal courts. A third participant was the Antitrust Division of the Department of Justice, which influenced the growth of antitrust law by deciding which violators to prosecute and by choosing which legal arguments to present to the judges. In this limited sense, administrators participated in lawmaking even under the traditional arrangements, as laws and regulations developed in response to abuses of the market by a few innovative business managers and entrepreneurs.

Legislatures came to realize that lawmaking under such regulatory programs would not be a one-shot affair: it would require continuous attention and enough flexibility to allow lawmakers to readily change the rules as new problems (including new techniques of evading the law) emerged. It soon became clear, however, that legislatures had neither the time nor the knowledge to undertake this large, continuing responsibility for making and modifying rules. Neither could the courts be saddled with primary responsibility for filling in the gaps in new regulatory statutes: judges were little better equipped than legislators to acquire the knowledge and experience—and to give the continuous attention—necessary for dealing with complex, rapidly changing problems.

Hence a new pattern of regulation emerged. Administrative officials began to receive much larger discretionary powers and to perform a variety of functions previously reserved for legislatures and courts. As Benjamin Franklin is reputed to have stated, "Necessity is the mother of invention." In this instance, new administrative powers were invented because they were necessary for effective governance of human behavior in society.

This new pattern emerged at the federal level in 1887 with enactment of the Interstate Commerce Act. The original purpose of this statute was to eliminate inequities in setting rates and other practices in interstate rail transportation. The statute resembled the

Sherman Act in that it provided for criminal prosecutions and civil suits against business practices declared to be unlawful. It also established a new agency, the Interstate Commerce Commission (ICC), and gave it general responsibility for making day-to-day policy decisions pertaining to regulation of railroads. The ICC had authority, among other things, to investigate complaints by shippers against the railroads, to hold hearings at which witnesses could be compelled to testify, and, if necessary, to issue formal orders that the courts were expected to enforce—that is, that had the force of law.

For almost twenty years, hostile courts interpreted the assigned powers of the ICC and state railway commissions, created at about the same time for similar purposes, so restrictively as to deny them any real authority. Eventually, however, this obstacle was overcome by new legislation strengthening the ICC and by abatement of judicial hostility. Thereafter, new techniques of economic regulation by administrative agencies were increasingly relied on at both the federal and the state levels, in addition to a great deal of social regulation. As the name implies, social regulation is less concerned with the economy than with values such as safety and health. Such regulation may, for example, establish entitlement programs such as Social Security and agencies such as the Occupational Health and Safety Administration, the Consumer Product Safety Commission, and the Environmental Protection Agency, charged with protecting citizens inside and outside the workplace.

Social and economic regulations emerged from a bureaucracy that in 2006 totaled about 2.6 million national government civilian employees. When we speak of administrative officials in this chapter, we are referring to officials in the executive branch of government. While this category includes the President, state governors, mayors, and other elected officials, we are concerned here primarily with activities of the nonelected officials subordinate to them. The category specifically includes those who staff the so-called regulatory commissions, even though these agencies are commonly described as independent regulatory agencies, as if they were outside the executive branch. These administrative officials we call *bureaucrats,* but not in any pejorative sense—just because they often work for bureaus, offices, services, and other administrative subunits of the executive branch. Figure 8.1 illustrates the number, complexity, and size of this national bureaucracy in the executive branch of the U.S. government.

The powers of modern regulatory agencies tend to be greater than those of nineteenth-century administrators in three respects:

1. Their purely executive powers are greater. Modern agencies have broader authority to investigate, to insist that private concerns keep certain kinds of records, to negotiate settlements with regulated parties, and to initiate enforcement action.
2. Many agencies have the expressly delegated rulemaking authority to elaborate the meaning of statutes couched in general terms. Many of these general enabling statutes do no more than indicate a policy objective, define a set of abuses to be dealt with, and prescribe in broad terms the standards against which private or official acts are to be measured. By issuing specific regulations in these circumstances, the agency becomes the real lawmaker.

Figure 8.1 The Executive Branch of Government

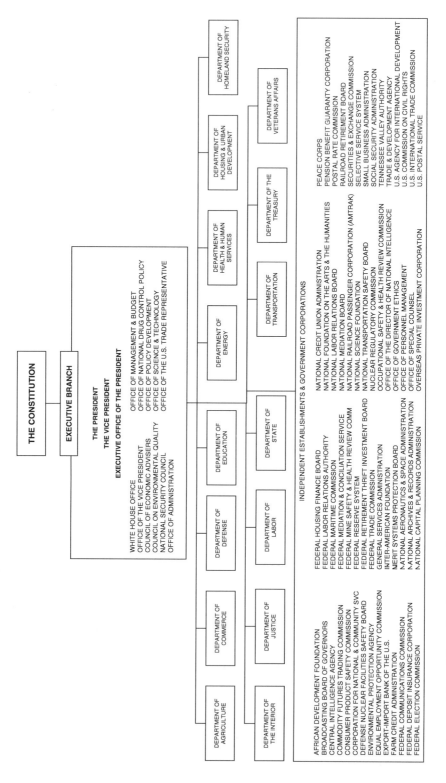

Source: Adapted from the chart "The Government of the United States" in National Archives and Records Administration (2006). *The United States Government Manual 2006–2007,* 21. www.gpoaccess.gov/gmanual/browse-gm-06.html.

3. Many agencies have the authority to hold trial-like hearings to determine facts and adjudicate particular controversies. The decisions that result from these hearings are subject to review by a court, but the scope of that review is limited; it is more like an appeal than a new trial.

It is these last two types of authority—rulemaking and adjudication—that are the subject of the rest of this chapter. In addition to the formal powers outlined above, federal bureaucrats wield a good deal of power by virtue of their expertise. In practice, both the President and Congress regularly call upon various parts of the bureaucracy for advice about particular pieces of public policy. Over time, employees of the various agencies come to know the industries they regulate or the social concerns they deal with at a level of detail that is very helpful to legislators.

LEGISLATIVE RULEMAKING BY ADMINISTRATORS

In Chapter 1 we mentioned that legal rules are either *legislative* or *decisional* in origin. There we stated a legislative rule is embodied in an authoritative, official text. A decisional rule is a precedent, the by-product of a decision handed down in an adjudicated case.

Statutes passed by legislatures are the most familiar embodiments of *legislative* rules. Executive orders issued by presidents and governors and detailed regulations issued by administrative agencies are also examples of legislative rules with authoritative texts. So how do we label a legislative rule made by someone other than a legislature? Often when such rules are made by executives or administrators, they are described as *quasi-legislative* rules to distinguish them from acts of legislatures.

Used broadly, *adjudication* refers to any proceeding in which, after an examination of evidence and arguments, a finding of facts is made and a decision is reached by applying rules to the facts found. Adjudication produces decisional rules. The court trial is the best known, but not the only example of adjudication. The most familiar decisional rules are precedents established by appellate courts, but decisions of administrative agencies adjudicating cases also establish precedents and hence are decisional rules. To distinguish adjudicative proceedings of administrative agencies from those of courts, often the former are described as *quasi-judicial* proceedings.

Let us first consider the process of legislative rulemaking by agencies. An administrative agency supplements general policies enunciated in the statutes it administers by interpreting them and issuing a variety of pronouncements of its own. The most formal and important of these are usually known as *regulations*. If an agency has explicit authority to issue such regulations and if it exercises that authority in a valid manner, its regulations are just as much "law," just as likely to be honored by the courts, as any statute.

Discretion is the freedom to choose any one of two or more possible alternatives when a decision is made. Administrative law scholar Kenneth Culp Davis argued persuasively that rulemaking authority is necessarily implicit in statutory mandates for functions that entail the exercise of discretion: "Any officer who has discretionary power necessarily also has the power to state publicly the manner in which he will exercise it, and any such public statement can be adopted through a rulemaking procedure, whether or not the legislative body has separately conferred a rulemaking power on the officer" (Davis 1976, 68).

Regulations are normally published, allowing affected parties (or at least their lawyers) to learn about them. An agency is free to amend its regulations after publishing them, of course, but they remain binding so long as they have not been formally amended or repealed. To have legal force, all regulations of federal agencies must be published in a daily journal called the *Federal Register* (which also publishes presidential proclamations and executive orders, as well as certain other documents). Periodically, federal regulations are codified and republished in the *Code of Federal Regulations*. Some, but not all, states have similar arrangements.

Challenges to the Validity of Regulations

Under what circumstances might a court hold a regulation to be invalid and hence not entitled to enforcement?

Judges do not ask themselves whether they consider a regulation wise, fair, and likely to produce the desired result. Doing that would make judges the ultimate legislators. Legislative power has been delegated to administrators presumably because of their technical knowledge and specialized experience. Therefore, their exercise of judgment is usually no more an issue before the court than would be the judgment of the legislature in passing a statute: courts display great deference to the judgment of administrators within their areas of expertise.

The first question judges must ask in deciding on the validity of a regulation is whether the authority delegated to an agency is broad enough to cover that particular regulation. Has the agency done what it was told to do? Is there a reasonable correspondence between the regulation and the policies and standards enunciated in a statute? If the answer to these questions is negative, then the agency has acted *ultra vires* (beyond its powers), and its action is invalid.

The degree of discretion delegated to administrators varies. As we have already remarked, enabling statutes frequently state policies and prescribe standards in extremely general terms. Often, for instance, a legislature will instruct an agency to establish standards that are "fair and equitable" or "in the public interest" or that "serve the public convenience and necessity" or that "effectuate the purposes of this Act." Obviously such general phrases leave great discretion to agency administrators.

These broad delegations of authority raise a significant constitutional issue. After all, U.S. constitutions assign to the legislative branch the basic responsibility for legislating. The national Constitution says, "All legislative Powers herein granted shall be vested in a Congress of the United States." Are there no limits to the power of legislatures to delegate this responsibility?

A few judicial decisions, mostly by state courts, have invalidated executive and administrative acts on the ground that they were based on delegations of authority deemed to be excessive. The best-known federal decision of this sort struck down the New Deal's

National Industrial Recovery Act in 1935. But most courts today seem willing to uphold laws that contain extremely general statements of policy and standards.

One issue in the case of *Yakus v. United States* was whether Congress had made an unconstitutional delegation of power to a federal administrative agency. The following excerpts from the Supreme Court's majority opinion are worth reading with care, for the opinion is both a statement of the Court's position on the delegation-of-authority issue and an example of how it interprets regulations that are often issued under the modern regulatory statute.

Under wartime laws designed to check inflation, the Office of Price Administration (OPA) was empowered to set maximum price levels for specified commodities and services. When administrators fix maximum prices or rates, they are making rules: establishing standards, enforceable by the courts, for the future conduct of a class of persons. Unlike some regulatory statutes, the price-control law did not provide for administrative adjudication of alleged violations; instead, those charged with violations were criminally prosecuted. The defendants in *Yakus* were tried and convicted of selling beef at prices above levels prescribed in the regulations. In their appeal to the Supreme Court of the United States, the defendants challenged the constitutionality of the basic statute.

Yakus v. United States

Supreme Court of the United States
321 U.S. 414, 64 S.Ct. 660 (1944)

MR. CHIEF JUSTICE STONE delivered the opinion of the Court.

[The Chief Justice first identified the statutes and policies underlying them.]

The Emergency Price Control Act provides for the establishment of the Office of Price Administration under the direction of a Price Administrator appointed by the President, and sets up a comprehensive scheme for the promulgation by the Administrator of regulations or orders fixing such maximum prices of commodities and rents as will effectuate the purpose of the Act and conform to the standards which it prescribes. The Act was adopted as a temporary wartime measure and provides in §1(b) for its termination on June 30, 1943, unless sooner terminated by Presidential proclamation or concurrent resolution of Congress. By the amendatory act of October 2, 1942, it was extended to June 30, 1944.

Section 1(a) declares that the Act is "in the interest of the national defense and security and necessary to the effective prosecution of the present war," and that its purposes are:

> to stabilize prices and to prevent speculative, unwarranted, and abnormal increases in prices and rents; to eliminate and prevent profiteering, hoarding, manipulation, speculation, and other disruptive practices resulting from abnormal market conditions or scarcities caused by or contributing to the national emergency; to assure that defense appropriations are not dissipated by excessive prices; to protect persons with relatively fixed and limited incomes, consumers, wage earners, investors, and persons dependent on life insurance, annuities, and pensions, from undue impairment of their standard of living; to prevent hardships to persons engaged in business, . . . and to the Federal, State, and local governments, which would result from abnormal increases in prices; to assist in securing adequate production of commodities and facilities; to prevent a post-emergency collapse of values . . .

[The Court then identified the standards prescribed in the two statutes and in a presidential executive order:]

The standards which are to guide the Administrator's exercise of his authority to fix prices, so far as now relevant, are prescribed by §2(a) and by §1 of the amendatory Act of October 2, 1942, and Executive Order 9250.... By §2(a) the Administrator is authorized, after consultation with representative members of the industry so far as practicable, to promulgate regulations fixing prices of commodities which "in his judgment will be generally fair and equitable and will effectuate the purposes of this Act" when, in his judgment, their prices "have risen or threaten to rise to an extent or in a manner inconsistent with the purposes of this Act."

This section also directs that

> So far as practicable, in establishing any maximum price, the Administrator shall ascertain and give due consideration to the prices prevailing between October 1 and October 15, 1941 (or if, in the case of any commodity, there are no prevailing prices between such dates, or the prevailing prices between such dates are not generally representative because of abnormal or seasonal market conditions or other cause, then to the prices prevailing during the nearest two-week period in which, in the judgment of the Administrator, the prices for such commodity are generally representative) ... and shall make adjustments for such relevant factors as he may determine and deem to be of general applicability, including ... [s]peculative fluctuations, general increases or decreases in costs of production, distribution, and transportation, and general increases or decreases in profits earned by sellers of the commodity or commodities, during and subsequent to the year ended October 1, 1941.

By the Act of October 2, 1942, the President is directed to stabilize prices, wages and salaries "so far as practicable" on the basis of the levels which existed on September 15, 1942, except as otherwise provided in the Act. By Title I, §4 of Executive Order No. 9250, he has directed "all departments and agencies of the Government ... to stabilize the cost of living in accordance with the Act of October 2, 1942."

[The relevant administrative regulation was then summarized:]

Revised Maximum Price Regulation No. 169 was issued December 10, 1942, under authority of the Emergency Price Control Act as amended and Executive Order No. 9250. The Regulation established specific maximum prices for the sale at wholesale of specified cuts of beef and veal. As is required by §2(a) of the Act, it was accompanied by a "statement of the considerations involved" in prescribing it. From the preamble to the Regulation and from the Statement of Considerations accompanying it, it appears that the prices fixed for sales at wholesale were slightly in excess of those prevailing between March 16 and March 28, 1942, and approximated those prevailing on September 15, 1942. Findings that the Regulation was necessary, that the prices that it fixed were fair and equitable, and that it otherwise conformed to the standards prescribed by the Act, appear in the Statement of Considerations. ...

[The Court then explained why the delegation of legislative power to the agency was not unconstitutional:]

Congress enacted the Emergency Price Control Act in pursuance of a defined policy and required that the prices fixed by the Administrator should further that policy and conform to standards prescribed by the Act. The boundaries of the field of the Administrator's permissible action are marked by the statute. It directs that the prices fixed shall effectuate the declared policy of the Act to stabilize commodity prices so as to prevent war-time inflation and its enumerated disruptive causes and effects. In addition the prices established must be fair and equitable, and in fixing them the Administrator is directed to give due consideration, so far as practicable, to prevailing prices during the designated base period, with prescribed administrative adjustments to compensate for enumerated disturbing factors affecting prices. ...

The Act is thus an exercise by Congress of its legislative power. In it Congress has stated the legislative objective, has prescribed the method of achieving that objective—maximum price fixing—and has laid down standards to guide the administrative determination of both the occasions for the exercise of the price-fixing power, and the particular prices to be established. ...

The Constitution as a continuously operative charter of government does not demand the impossible or the impracticable. It does not require that Congress find for itself every fact upon which it desires to base legislative action [emphasis added], *or that it make for itself detailed determinations which it has declared to be* prerequisite to the application of the legislative policy to particular facts and circumstances impossible for Congress itself properly to investigate. *The essentials of the legislative function are the determination of the legislative policy and its formulation and promulgation as a defined and binding rule of conduct* [emphasis added]—here the rule, with penal sanctions, that prices shall not be greater than those fixed by maximum price regulations which conform to standards and will tend to further the policy which Congress has established. These essentials are preserved when Congress has specified the basic conditions of fact upon whose existence or occurrence, ascertained from relevant data by a designated administrative agency, it directs that its statutory command shall be effective. It is no objection that the determination of facts and the inferences to be drawn from them in the light of the statutory standards and declaration of policy call for the exercise of judgment, and for the formulation of subsidiary administrative policy within the prescribed statutory framework. . . .

Nor does the doctrine of separation of powers deny to Congress power to direct that an administrative officer properly designated for that purpose have ample latitude within which he is to ascertain the conditions which Congress has made prerequisite to the operation of its legislative command. Acting within its constitutional power to fix prices, it is for Congress to say whether the data on the basis of which prices are to be fixed are to be confined within a narrow or a broad range. In either case the only concern of courts is to ascertain whether the will of Congress has been obeyed. . . .

Congress is not confined to that method of executing its policy that involves the least possible delegation of discretion to administrative officers. . . . It is free to avoid the rigidity of such a system, which might well result in serious hardship, and to choose instead the flexibility attainable by the use of less restrictive standards. . . . *Only if we could say that there is an absence of standards for the guidance of the administrator's action, so that it would be impossible in a proper proceeding to ascertain whether the will of Congress has been obeyed, would we be justified in overriding its choice of means for effecting its declared purpose of preventing inflation* [emphasis added].

[Finally, the Court compared the standards of the price-control statutes with those prescribed in other laws that had been upheld by the Court in earlier decisions:]

The standards prescribed by the present Act, with the aid of the "statement of the considerations" required to be made by the Administrator, are sufficiently definite and precise to enable Congress, the courts and the public to ascertain whether the Administrator, in fixing the designated prices, has conformed to those standards. . . . Hence we are unable to find in them an unauthorized delegation of legislative power. The authority to fix prices only when prices have risen or threaten to rise to an extent or in a manner inconsistent with the purpose of the Act to prevent inflation is no broader than the authority to fix maximum prices when deemed necessary to protect consumers against unreasonably high prices . . . or the authority to take possession of and operate telegraph lines whenever deemed necessary for the national security or defense . . . or the authority to suspend tariff provisions upon findings that the duties imposed by a foreign state are "reciprocally unequal and unreasonable." . . .

The directions that the prices fixed shall be fair and equitable, that in addition they shall tend to promote the purposes of the Act, and that in promulgating them consideration shall be given to prices prevailing in a stated base period, confer no greater reach for administrative determination than the power to fix just and reasonable rates . . . or the power to approve consolidations in the "public interest" . . . or the power to regulate radio stations engaged in chain broadcasting "as public interest, convenience or necessity requires" . . . or the power to prohibit "unfair methods of competition" not defined or forbidden by the common law . . . or the direction that in allotting marketing quotas among states and producers due consideration be given to a variety of economic factors . . . or the similar direction that in adjusting tariffs to meet differences in costs of production the President "take into consideration" "in so far as he finds practicable" a variety of economic matters . . . or the similar authority, in making classifications within an industry, to consider various named and unnamed "relevant factors" and determine the respective weights attributable to each. . . .

Affirmed.

Questions

1. Based on your reading of this case, what are the limits on the power of legislatures to delegate their responsibilities?
2. As social circumstances change, public administrators must respond in new ways. How can a legislature give these administrators leeway to respond flexibly without running afoul of the delegation doctrine?

Although the courts rarely invalidate administrative regulations on the ground they have been issued under unconstitutional delegations of power, regulations are sometimes invalidated because they fail to satisfy other constitutional standards. Regardless of how much authority a legislature grants to an agency, the agency is not permitted to issue a regulation that represents an unconstitutional exercise of government power. For example, a federal agency whose regulatory authority is constitutionally based on the commerce clause may not attempt to regulate purely *intrastate* (i.e., in-state) commerce. Nor may any agency issue a regulation that serves to "deprive any person of life, liberty, or property without due process of law." Several early efforts by railroad commissions to establish rates foundered on the due-process restriction in the Fourteenth Amendment; the Supreme Court decided that the rates set were so low that they deprived the railroads of property (profits) without due process. Similarly, an administrative rule establishing a discriminatory classification might be invalidated under the Fourteenth Amendment's equal-protection clause.

Finally, in deciding on the validity of administrative regulations, the courts ask whether an agency has followed proper procedures in adopting the regulations. A major purpose of procedural requirements is to ensure fair treatment to private persons who are likely to be affected by an agency's rules. Are such persons entitled, for example, to receive notice that a new rule is under consideration and to have an opportunity to express themselves on its contents? Ordinarily, an agency's failure to give notice and to hold a hearing before issuing a regulation is not considered a denial of constitutional rights. Still, many statutes under which administrative agencies operate require the agency to publish notice of proposed regulations and give interested parties an opportunity to express their views.

Less Formal Administrative Pronouncements

Administrative agencies issue a variety of pronouncements, less formal and binding than their legislative regulations, that are designed to clarify laws they administer.

Some of these pronouncements are described as *interpretive regulations*, meaning precisely that they are designed to provide the public either with notice of a new rule or with an explanation of an existing rule. Others, issued in response to inquiries, are advisory rulings that interpret the law with reference to particular types of situations. In addition, some agencies also publish instructions, guides, explanatory pamphlets, and so forth.

In approaching federal income-tax problems, for instance, lawyers will look first at the Internal Revenue Code and at voluminous regulations of the Treasury Department and the Internal Revenue Service (IRS). But they will also look at other interpretations and guides the IRS publishes. These have some qualities of legal rules. They indicate how an agency interprets the law it is administering, and hence they form a basis for predicting its position in particular cases. The courts accord considerable respect to these informal pronouncements, particularly if they seem to be reasonable elaborations of policies and standards of the statute.

ADJUDICATION AND DECISIONAL RULEMAKING BY ADMINISTRATORS

So far we have discussed how administrators *create* rules—that is, how they issue authoritative directives designed to influence the future conduct of whole categories of persons. Now let us consider how administrators *apply* rules to particular cases. Rules are applied through adjudication to determine facts and through decisional rulemaking that interprets the law.

Administrative Adjudication

Administrators have always engaged in fact finding. In order to determine whether a law is being complied with, for example, or whether an applicant is entitled to a license or a franchise, administrators have always had to investigate, inspect, ask questions, and insist that their questions be answered. But only with the emergence of the modern regulatory agency has the trial-like hearing, at which testimony and documents may be presented and challenged with the aid of counsel, come into widespread use.

One of the most important categories of administrative adjudication is the so-called *enforcement proceeding.* This is a proceeding to adjudicate charges that standards established by a particular law have not been complied with. The National Labor Relations Board, for example, conducts enforcement proceedings to determine whether an unfair labor practice has been committed. And state employment practices commissions hold enforcement proceedings to determine whether an employer's hiring and promoting practices have involved racial or religious discrimination.

An agency's enforcement officials, acting either on their own initiative or in response to a private complaint (depending on what the statute provides), inquire into possible violations. If they find evidence of wrongdoing, they usually try first to negotiate settlements with violators under which they agree to comply with the law and pay a reduced fine. Many violations are brought to an end by negotiation, and administrative intervention goes no further. But if negotiation proves fruitless, the agency files a complaint and holds a public hearing.

Many procedures of the court trial have been taken over for the administrative hearing (perhaps partly because officials who participate in the hearings are usually lawyers). But one difference is noteworthy: in administrative hearings the functions of both prosecutor and judge are normally performed by officials of the same agency and occasionally by the same official. In large agencies, cases are generally heard by a trial examiner (often trained as an administrative law judge), whose decision is later reviewed by top officials of the agency (usually referred to collectively as a commission or governing board). If the commission sustains the enforcement official's contentions, it usually issues an agency order to the accused party. If this order is not voluntarily obeyed, the agency must obtain a court order to enforce it.

Other types of administrative hearings are held to determine, for example, whether a license should be revoked, or which of several parties should be awarded a franchise, or whether a person accused of past wrongdoing should be discharged from government service or deported from the country. Some hearings in which one private party presses a claim against another are very similar to civil proceedings—as, for example, when an employee comes before a workers' compensation board to claim damages from an employer for an injury sustained while at work.

Judicial Review

Administrative decisions affecting named individuals or organizations are often made after a hearing, but this is not always required or necessary. For instance, a registrar of motor vehicles does not have to hold a hearing before it can grant or deny a driver's license to a new applicant. Regardless of whether an agency has acted on the basis of an administrative hearing, the law normally gives to affected persons a right to contest the agency's action in the courts. This is another aspect of the power of judicial review discussed in Chapter 7. The court may be asked to rule on such issues as the statute's constitutionality, the agency's jurisdiction, or the regularity of procedures followed in reaching a decision. Individuals can always persuade the courts to reverse an administrative decision if they can prove prejudice or corruption. To cut the private party off from this access to the courts might well be a denial of constitutional due process.

Over the centuries, judges and legislators have devised a variety of procedures by which an individual may challenge administrative acts in the courts (we need not enumerate them here). It is not always necessary, moreover, for an individual to take the initiative. Since, with a few exceptions, administrators have no power to enforce their own decisions (i.e., to compel private persons to obey their orders or to punish them for not complying), an individual is often able to contest a decision simply by defying it and forcing an administrator to take the case to court.

Having an administrative hearing does not deprive a person of the right to judicial review, but as administrative fact-finding procedures have improved, the scope of judicial review has narrowed. As legislators and judges gained confidence in the fairness of administrative procedures, they abandoned their earlier insistence on judicial reexamination of an agency's findings of fact. The reviewing court may be either a trial court or an appellate court (depending on what the relevant statute provides), but in either event a review proceeding ordinarily resembles an appeal rather than a new trial.

The court does not rehear the evidence; it merely reviews the record of agency proceedings to determine whether the prescribed procedure was actually followed and whether the decision was "arbitrary, capricious, an abuse of discretion, or otherwise not in accordance with law" as prohibited by the Administrative Procedure Act (5 *U.S. Code* §706). Usually judicial review is limited to nondiscretionary acts: those decisions which by law an administrator is specifically required to make, usually described in statutory language using the word "shall," which indicates something is mandatory, not optional (e.g., "the Secretary of Commerce shall . . ."). Nondiscretionary decisions are distinguishable from discretionary acts, which are often described in statutory language giving administrators freedom to decide between alternatives (e.g., "the Secretary may issue a permit, deny the permit application, or issue a permit with conditions . . ."). However, even a discretionary act can be challenged in court if it appears to be "arbitrary, capricious, an abuse of discretion, or otherwise not in accordance with law."

If there appears to be "substantial evidence in the whole record" to support an agency's decision, the judges will not overturn it, even though they might have drawn different conclusions from the evidence if they personally had heard the case in the original hearing. That is, an administrative decision must be consistent with a reasonable interpretation of the record, grounded in and related to "substantial evidence" presented by the parties, or it will be considered arbitrary and capricious. The judges do, of course, review all the agency's conclusions of law, but they often acknowledge that an agency, through its knowledge and experience, is far better equipped than they to work out implications of statutory policy. Hence, if an agency's conclusions of law seem to be a reasoned and reasonable elaboration of the statute's objectives, most courts are inclined to accept them. The result is substantial deference by courts for administrative judgments.

This requirement is significant during the setting of regulatory standards as well as in adjudication. For example, to withstand court challenge, a regulatory standard designed to protect human health from toxic air or water pollution must be based on substantial scientific research concerning the level of a contaminant that may be detrimental to living beings. The standard need not be identical to some threshold level of exposure at which human cell damage begins, but it must be related to scientific evidence establishing such a level, perhaps with a small additional margin for error to allow for variations in health between individuals and the imprecision of scientific results.

The availability of judicial review undoubtedly makes administrators less arbitrary in their decisions and more careful in construing their legal powers. This is so, even though only a tiny percentage of each year's administrative decisions are actually reviewed in the courts.

Decisional Rulemaking

To decide cases, agencies must interpret the law as well as determine the facts. Their interpretations appear in opinions that accompany agency decisions, many of which are published. Most agencies, though they do not feel rigidly bound by *stare decisis,* still tend to follow their own precedents, for the same reasons that courts follow theirs. Hence, adjudicative decisions give interested parties a fairly reliable basis for predicting an agency's future position on similar issues and circumstances. Of course, an agency ruling ceases to be controlling if it is appealed and a court reverses it. As we have just seen, though, most agency decisions are not appealed, and, of those few that are, most are upheld by the courts.

In short, agency decisions become, in effect, decisional rules: They channel future conduct. If, for instance, a company wishes to know how far it must go in bargaining with a union in order to satisfy the statutory requirement of "bargaining in good faith," it can do no better than to study the National Labor Relations Board's decisions (plus the relatively few court decisions) in which the requirement has been interpreted.

Since many agencies have power both to issue regulations and to adjudicate cases, they can choose between these two methods of rulemaking when action is warranted. When an agency believes the time has come to formulate a policy decision in an official text, it can draft and issue a regulation. But if an agency prefers to wait until the contours of a problem become clearer, it can continue to deal with the problem on a case-by-case basis, formulating a series of decisional rules couched in terms that ensure continuing flexibility. That is, rulemaking tends to constrain future administrative decisions to parameters of a rule, while case-by-case decision-making maximizes discretion. Consequently, some administrative agencies that wish to continue making decisions with maximum flexibility tend to prefer case-by-case decision-making, even if explicitly authorized by statute to make rules. Furthermore, an agency, unlike a court, does not have to wait passively for cases to be brought before it. Its enforcement officials can go out looking for cases that will raise issues on which its adjudicating officials want to rule. And since the agency can decide which enforcement proceedings to initiate, it can choose cases that present issues in such a way that the courts will be likely to uphold the agency's ruling if that ruling is appealed. Strategic thinking does enter into administrative decision-making in such matters.

An Illustrative Case

Generally, the courts exercise remarkable self-restraint in reviewing decisions of administrative agencies. Yet, as the following case illustrates, the courts are willing to exercise their power of judicial review when necessary. The case of *Board of Governors of the Federal System v. Dimension Financial Corporation* deals with a challenge to the Federal Reserve Board's attempt to extend the definition of *bank* to apply to institutions that provide services similar to those provided by a bank.

Board of Governors of the Federal System
v. Dimension Financial Corporation

U.S. Supreme Court
474 U.S. 361 (1986)

CHIEF JUSTICE BURGER delivered the opinion of the Court.

We granted certiorari to decide whether the Federal Reserve Board acted within its statutory authority in defining "banks" under 2(c) of the Bank Holding Company Act of 1956, 12 U.S.C. 1841 *et seq.*, as any institution that (1) accepts deposits that "as a matter of practice" are payable on demand and (2) engages in the business of making "any loan other than a loan to an individual for personal, family, household, or charitable purposes" including "the purchase of retail installment loans or commercial paper, certificates of deposit, bankers' acceptances, and similar money market instruments." 12 CFR 225.2(1)(1) (1985). . . .

This case is about so-called "nonbank banks"—institutions that offer services similar to those of banks but which until recently were not under Board regulation because they conducted their business so as to place themselves arguably outside the narrow definition of "bank" found in 2(c) of the Act. Many nonbank banks, for example, offer customers NOW (negotiable order of withdrawal) accounts which function like conventional checking accounts but because of prior notice provisions do not technically give the depositor a "legal right to withdraw on demand." 12 U.S.C. 1841(c)(1) . . .

The Bank Holding Company Act of 1956, 12 U.S.C. 1841 *et seq.*, vests broad regulatory authority in the Board over bank holding companies "to restrain the undue concentration of commercial banking resources and to prevent possible abuses related to the control of commercial credit." . . .

The breadth of that regulatory power rests on the Act's definition of the word "bank." . . .

Since 1970 the statute has provided that a bank is any institution that

(1) accepts deposits that the depositor has a legal right to withdraw on demand, and
(2) engages in the business of making commercial loans. 12 U.S.C. 1841(c). . . .

In 1984, the Board initiated rulemaking to respond to the increase in the number of nonbank banks. After hearing views of interested parties, the Board found that nonbank banks pose three dangers to the national banking system. *First,* by remaining outside the reach of banking regulations, nonbank banks have a significant competitive advantage over regulated banks despite the functional equivalence of the services offered. *Second,* the proliferation of nonbank banks threatens the structure established by Congress for limiting the association of banking and commercial enterprises. . . .

The Board amended its definition of "demand deposit" primarily to include within its regulatory authority institutions offering NOW accounts. A NOW account functions like a traditional checking account—the depositor can write checks that are payable on demand at the depository institution. The depository institution, however, retains a seldom exercised but nevertheless absolute right to require prior notice of withdrawal. Under a literal reading of the statute, the institution—even if it engages in full-scale commercial lending—is not a "bank" for the purposes of the Holding Company Act because the prior notice provision withholds from the depositor any "legal right" to withdraw on demand. The Board in its amended definition closes this loophole by defining demand deposits as a deposit, not that the depositor has a "legal right to withdraw on demand," but a deposit that "as a matter of practice is payable on demand."

In determining whether the Board was empowered to make such a change, we begin, of course, with the language of the statute. If the statute is clear and unambiguous, "that is the end of the matter, for the court, as well as the agency, must give effect to the unambiguously expressed intent of Congress." . . .

The traditional deference courts pay to agency interpretation is not to be applied to alter the clearly expressed intent of Congress [emphasis added].

[1] Application of this standard to the Board's interpretation of the "demand deposit" element of 2(c) does not require extended analysis. By the 1966 amendments to 2(c), Congress expressly limited the Act to regulation of institutions that accept deposits that "the depositor has a legal right to withdraw on demand." 12 U.S.C. 1841(c). The Board would define "legal right" as meaning the same as "a matter of practice." But no amount of agency expertise—however sound may be the result—can make the words "legal right" mean a right to do something "as a matter of practice." A *legal* right to withdraw on demand means just that: a right to withdraw deposits without prior notice or limitation. Institutions offering NOW accounts do not give the depositor a legal right to withdraw on demand; rather, the institution itself retains the ultimate legal right to require advance notice of withdrawal. The Board's definition of "demand deposit," therefore, is not an accurate or reasonable interpretation of 2(c) . . .

[3] Unable to support its new definitions on the plain language of 2(c), the Board contends that its

new definitions fall within the "plain purpose" of the Bank Holding Company Act. Nonbank banks must be subject to regulations, the Board insists, because "a statute must be read with a view to the 'policy of the legislation as a whole' and cannot be read to negate the plain purpose of the legislation." The plain purpose of the legislation, the Board contends, is to regulate institutions "functionally equivalent" to banks. Since NOW accounts are the functional equivalent of a deposit in which the depositor has a legal right to withdraw on demand and money market transactions involve the extension of credit to commercial entities, institutions offering such services should be regulated as banks.

The "plain purpose" of legislation, however, is determined in the first instance with reference to the plain language of the statute itself. *Richards v. United States* 369 U.S. 1, 9, 82 S.Ct. 585, 590, 7 L.Ed.2d 492 (1962). Application of "broad purposes" of legislation at the expense of specific provisions ignores the complexity of the problems Congress is called upon to address and the dynamics of legislative action. Congress may be unanimous in its intent to stamp out some vague social or economic evil; however, because its Members may differ sharply on the means for effectuating that intent, the final language of the legislation may reflect hard-fought compromises. Invocation of the "plain purpose" of legislation at the expense of the terms of the statute itself takes no account of the processes of compromise and, in the end, prevents the effectuation of congressional intent.

Without doubt there is much to be said for regulating financial institutions that are the functional equivalent of banks. NOW accounts have much in common with traditional payment-on-demand checking accounts; indeed we recognize that they generally serve the same purpose. Rather than defining "bank" as an institution that offers the functional equivalent of banking services, however, Congress defined with specificity certain transactions that constitute banking subject to regulation. *The statute may be imperfect, but the Board has no power to correct flaws that it perceives in the statute it is empowered to administer. Its power is limited to adopting regulations to carry into effect the will of Congress as expressed in the statute* [emphasis added].

If the Bank Holding Company Act falls short of providing safeguards desirable or necessary to protect the public interest, that is a problem for Congress, and not the Board or the courts, to address. Numerous proposals for legislative reform have been advanced to streamline the tremendously complex area of financial institution regulation. See, e.g., Blueprint for Reform: Report of the Task Group on Regulation of Financial Services (July 1984). Our present inquiry, however, must come to rest with the conclusion that the action of the Board in this case is inconsistent with the language of the statute for here, as in *TVA v. Hill*, 437 U.S. 153, 194, 98 S.Ct. 2279, 2301, 57 L.Ed.2d 117 (1978) "[o]nce the meaning of an enactment is discerned . . . the judicial process comes to an end."

Questions

1. How might an administrative agency "correct flaws" that it finds in its statutory charge?
2. Do you think the Supreme Court should have exercised more self-restraint in this case in order to allow the Federal Reserve Board to extend its reach? Why or why not?

ACHIEVEMENTS AND DISAPPOINTMENTS

As legislative decisions were made to create larger numbers of specialized administrative agencies, they were given broader powers than administrators had traditionally exercised. These powers included the power to issue regulations having the force of law and the power to hear and decide cases—powers previously reserved to legislatures and courts.

It was recognized by legislators that granting these powers held some dangers.

Bureaucrats who received new rulemaking power did not have to face the salutary test of standing for election every few years, and the new adjudicators were not heirs to a long and honorable professional tradition. But various safeguards existed—particularly judicial review, which, it was hoped, would curb arbitrariness, oppression, and corruption on the part of officials.

Regulatory agencies have had a mixed record of performance. Some of the hopes of those who framed early legislation have been disappointed. For one thing, too few regulatory agencies have become effective formulators of long-range policy. Establishing a specialized agency with broad authority to create new rules is only a beginning. An agency must be staffed by officials who are bold and imaginative, farsighted in their planning and yet ready to renounce policy formulations made obsolete by changing conditions, and capable of running an efficient agency without letting daily routine obscure the needs of the future. Such administrators have always been in short supply, and their absence has made the agencies only partially effective.

Over the years, the criticisms leveled against administrative agencies have changed. In the 1940s, when some of the most important agencies were still young, critics complained that administrators were high-handed zealots, often suspicious of or downright hostile toward the economic group whose practices they were supposed to regulate. In those days the main focus of criticism was on the assignment to some agencies of both enforcement and adjudicative functions. Some of these earlier criticisms have been met over the years.

Today, criticism takes different forms. One major area of debate concerns the extent of government regulation. Only a few persons argue for elimination of all government regulation, but a powerful argument has been made that at least some industries, such as airlines and trucking, have been overregulated, and in 1978 airlines, at least, were deregulated. Business interests have tried to demonstrate that excessive regulation is costly to business and consumers and that overregulation hurts the competitive position of the United States and distorts operations of markets. Thus, since the Reagan presidency of the 1980s, the government has moved toward deregulation in several policy areas. However, it is difficult to discern to what extent such criticism may have been motivated by the desire for competitive advantage, ideology, or negative responses to regulation that is actually effective in attaining protective goals.

On the other hand, many people argue that deregulation has hurt consumer and business interests, claiming, for example, that the airline industry has been substantially damaged by deregulation. Airline profits were down even before the catastrophic events of September 11, 2001; consumers, travel agents, and others find the industry much less rational and air travel much more cumbersome and unpleasant than before deregulation. Critics also vigorously argue that a deregulated marketplace simply does not provide adequate standards of service to protect consumers or the general public.

In addition to debates about the merits of regulation, a loud political outcry claims that public bureaucracies are wasteful and poorly run. Public administration scholar Charles Goodsell reviewed the evidence on this score with what some consider surprising findings:

Client surveys, exit interviews, and mailed questionnaires all repeat the same basic finding: The large majority of encounters are perceived as satisfactory, with many highly rated. Bureaucracy is reported as *very often* providing the services sought and expected. *Most of the time* it lives up to acceptable standards of efficiency, courtesy, and fairness. Sometimes government agencies perform poorly, of course; innumerable acts of sloth, injustice, incompetence, and common rudeness are committed daily in government offices around the country. No one is claiming perfection for bureaucracy. At the same time, the basic conclusion of satisfactory citizen treatment as the *norm* rather than the *exception* flies radically in the face of most literature on the subject. That success is normal in American public administration is substantiated, moreover, by quantifiable evidence obtained from measures of bureaucratic performance having nothing to do with citizen perceptions, such as on-time measures, error rates, external observation of transactions, and productivity data.

The relatively good performance of American bureaucracy is made even clearer when we study it comparatively. . . . Even the most convincing negative stereotypes (e.g., condescending application forms and dreary welfare waiting rooms) are seen on close examination to vary enormously. Then too, the long-standing expectation by political liberals that urban bureaucracies systematically discriminate against the poor and racial minorities is discovered to be not merely an oversimplification but plain wrong. The commonly accepted view of political conservatives that government never performs as well as business is also shown to be a patent falsehood. Moreover, a comparison of American bureaucracy to that of other countries reveals that we experience one of the best levels of service in the world, light years ahead of that endured by most national populations. (Goodsell 1994, 166; emphasis in original)

The National Performance Review led by Vice President Al Gore during the Clinton administration generated literally hundreds of suggestions for improving government performance—many of them suggested by bureaucrats (Hamilton 1996)—and many of them were implemented.

Ironically, another criticism leveled at bureaucracy is the opposite of that leveled at overzealous agencies in the 1940s. Now the charge is that agencies sometimes become far too cozy with the very interest groups they are called upon to regulate. In effect, Congress, the government bureaucracy, and private interest groups may form an *iron triangle* (also called a subgovernment, subsystem, or issue network) or powerful mutual benefit society, which may or may not be responsive to wider public needs. One prominent example of such an alliance is the relationship between a few committees of Congress, the Defense Department, and defense contractors (Adams 1981); another concerns alliances between committees of Congress, several executive branch agencies, and the tobacco industry (Fritschler and Rudder 2007). That such alliances occur is testimony to the strong influence of Congress and interest groups on administrative agencies that require viable bases of continuing political support for their existence and activities.

In conclusion, we must acknowledge that although some expectations for government performance have been disappointed, many have been realized. And it is difficult to see how more of the original objectives in legislation could have been achieved—within the limitations imposed by democratic principles, the federal system, and long-standing constitutional arrangements—by any governmental arrangement substantially different from the system of administrative agencies that now forms such a large and crucial part of American government.

CHAPTER PROBLEM: RED TAPE AND REGULATORY REFORM

In his now classic book *Red Tape: Its Origins, Uses and Abuses,* Herbert Kaufman reviewed four strategies for reducing the burden of regulation and red tape that have been either attempted or proposed in recent years: shrinking the government, devolving federal power, concentrating authority, and manipulating financial incentives. He concluded that all four were unsatisfactory:

> The surest way to get rid of the red tape associated with the federal government is to shrink the federal government itself, but the prospects of shrinking it to even its size in the early twentieth century are not bright; the disadvantages would be too great for too many people. Devolution likewise is not free of costs balancing many of its gains, and some of the frustrations of decentralization can match those caused by federal red tape. Concentration of authority, on the other hand, undeniably is often responsible for congestion at the center, layering of administrative levels, and long lines of communication; its disadvantages, too, are discouraging. And even the ingenious proposal for taking advantage of private incentives through taxes and subsidies would apparently result in just as much government paper and procedural complexity as the currently prevailing techniques of government intervention in social and economic relations.
>
> To make things still more complicated, the quantity of red tape is not fixed; it is always growing. For red tape tends to beget more red tape. When the government enters upon a program of protecting people from one another or from their officials, or takes steps to assure the integrity of its own processes, or refines its system of taxation, its pronouncements inevitably entail ambiguities. The way ambiguities are resolved determines whether specific people or groups are entitled to particular benefits or subject to particular constraints. For that reason, the government, through all forms of law—statutes, regulations, judicial decisions, and executive orders—is constantly clarifying categories. But each clarification in turn leaves areas of uncertainty at the new definitional borders even as it clears up the old ones. So the growth of the corpus of provisions goes on and on.
>
> The more extensive the corpus of provisions becomes, the more extensive the policing must be to ensure compliance. That alone means more red tape for the affected clients. More extensive policing requires more enforcement agents, which in turn mean intensified measures to deter abuses of power and trust. Ultimately the result is more internal and external red tape. . . .

That is not to say the termination, transfer, or concentration of specific governmental activities or the manipulation of pecuniary incentives is never followed by their intended effects. On the contrary, they may reduce red tape significantly in specific instances, at least for a time. But it does not follow that they will succeed everywhere if they are applied wholesale. . . . Their respective advocates sometimes give the impression that their favored formulas are remedies for red tape that, if taken in large doses, would reduce it to negligible proportions. For the reasons cited, such claims must be taken with a grain of salt. There is no panacea.

But there are ways of keeping red tape under control and endurable. They are not spectacular or glamorous. They work no miracles. Nevertheless, they can provide relief.

Treating Symptoms

Those ways are the normal methods of politics. The political system responds to pointed demands for specific actions, not to grand visions or all-embracing lamentations. Grand visions and ill-defined complaints, of course, often determine the particulars of demands. But until and unless they are translated into concrete measures that officials can act on, they seldom evoke any governmental response. They may win offers of sympathy, expressions of shared outrage, and even symbolic gestures of solidarity and support. But not tangible benefits. . . .

Similarly, railing against all red tape or advancing some panacea that will purportedly dispose of it once and for all avails nothing; *an attack on a particular procedure in a particular agency or on a designated tax or application form or on a specified requirement long since out of date is much more likely to get results.* . . . [emphasis added].

Source: Kaufman (1977, 85–88). Reprinted with permission from the Brookings Institution Press.

Questions

1. If it is true that in politics the squeaking wheel gets the grease, does Kaufman's prescription seem plausible?
2. What are some examples of regulatory measures from which you personally benefit?
3. Do you think that administrative agencies have, as a general rule, overstepped their authority? Why or why not?

QUESTIONS FOR REVIEW

1. How does Congress justify its decision to delegate legislative power to administrative agencies?

2. What power do the courts have to review administrative decisions? Should the courts have greater or lesser powers than they currently have?

3. Can you see any potential for conflicts of interest in administrative agencies? Keep in mind that agencies often act as judge, prosecutor, and jury.

4. Individuals now have the right to be represented by counsel at administrative hearings. Do you think this rule should be changed? Explain.

5. How have opponents of administrative agencies changed the grounds of their criticism over the past fifty years? Do you think the form and function of these agencies is likely to change in the future? In what ways?

BIBLIOGRAPHY

Adams, Gordon. 1981. *The Iron Triangle: The Politics of Defense Contracting.* New York: Council on Economic Priorities.

Davis, Kenneth Culp. 1976. *Discretionary Justice: A Preliminary Inquiry.* Chicago: University of Illinois Press.

Fritschler, A. Lee, and Catherine Rudder. 2007. *Smoking and Politics: Bureaucracy-Centered Politics.* 6th ed. Upper Saddle River, NJ: Pearson/Prentice Hall.

Goodsell, Charles T. 1994. *The Case for Bureaucracy.* 3rd ed. Chatham, NJ: Chatham House.

Hamilton, Michael S. 1996. "The Career Service and Presidential Transition: From Bush to Clinton to National Performance Review." *Public Administration Quarterly* 20 (Spring): 52–70.

Kaufman, Herbert. 1977. *Red Tape: Its Origins, Uses and Abuses.* Washington, DC: Brookings Institution.

National Archives and Records Administration. 2006. *The United States Government Manual, 2006–2007.* Washington, DC: U.S. Government Printing Office.

CHAPTER 9

Private Contributions to the Legal System

In this book, *law* is defined to include only those guides to conduct that are created by officials; hence, *lawmaking* is defined to cover only the creation of rules by officials. Some scholars use a broader definition that includes "private lawmaking": the many arrangements that private individuals and groups work out among themselves that have the same effect as legal rules.

Our narrower definition of lawmaking corresponds more closely to what most people understand by the term. But we cannot on that account ignore contributions made by private persons to the legal system. These contributions are discussed in this chapter. First, we consider very briefly the contributions of private persons and groups to the legal fabric that is continuously being woven by legislators, judges, and administrators. Then we consider at much greater length contributions that private groups make to social ordering by creating their own systems of private rules. As an example of such a system, we shall study the *government under law* that has been developed in industry by employers and organized labor under collective bargaining agreements.

PRIVATE CONTRIBUTIONS TO LAWMAKING

In a democratic society, the major aim of government and law is to provide a setting in which individuals can pursue their own objectives. For example, the United States continues to rely to a great extent on decisions of private producers and consumers to determine what gets produced, how, and by whom. Law establishes the framework within which such private decision-making takes place. But the reverse relationship is equally important: patterns of private conduct play a part in forming law. What the rules permit largely determines what people do, but what people do (and aspire to do) largely determines the problems with which officials must deal and thus the content of the rules they make.

How, specifically, does private conduct affect the content of legal rules?

1. *Private controversies produce decisional rules.* Those who prosecute cases in the courts or in administrative hearings influence the shaping of decisional rules by choosing which cases to contest and which legal arguments to present in those cases. The character of decisions that emerge from court and agency adjudications is largely determined by the way in which legal issues are presented for decision,

which in turn depends on the facts of a particular case and arguments advanced by the parties. In short, as private persons go about settling their disputes, they provide the cases and grounds by which decisional laws are made.

2. *Group pressures produce legislative rules.* Legislative rules are enacted because of a felt need for legislative action. This felt need is usually stimulated by actions of private persons and political pressures of organized interest groups. In a free society, such pressures are inevitable and desirable. Often an interest group will not only point out the need but also propose a remedy. It may even come up with a draft bill for enactment, and when the subject matter is technical, legislators tend to rely heavily on such drafts. Clearly, what private groups do about creating the need for legislative action and then pushing for specific enactments plays a part in creating law.

3. *Private arrangements become legal standards.* In the eighteenth century, the privately enforced rules and usages (practices) that merchants had been developing since the Middle Ages were absorbed into English law. English judges had long been willing to accept evidence of merchants' usages as aids in interpreting commercial contracts, but eighteenth-century judges went further and declared these nonofficial arrangements to be a part of the law of England. Many of our modern rules of commercial law thus had their origins in a privately developed body of rules.

This process continues in modern times. Suppose someone wishes to exercise a legal power in such a way as to secure certain results while avoiding certain other results. Perhaps she wants to complete a certain transaction while incurring the minimum possible tax liability. Or she may want to make an airtight contract with someone she does not wholly trust. Or she may want to create an ownership interest in a business with only a limited right of control. In any such case, she goes to a lawyer and presents her problem. The lawyer discovers none of the standard tools in his kit is exactly what is needed. So he invents a solution: a new arrangement, a new type of document, or a new combination of words especially designed to achieve the desired result. His invention may eventually be challenged and tested in court. If it survives and if it is shown to accomplish what the client wanted, other lawyers will learn of it and copy it. Before long the new device is likely to be given a standardized form and a label. Judges will acknowledge it as an approved method of exercising a legal power. Drafters of legislation on tax laws, for example, will take it into account and make provisions for it. And finally it will take its place among tools in the kit of every competent lawyer.

The terms of standardized sales contracts, deeds, mortgages, leases, corporate charters, and bylaws were largely created by lawyers in this manner, as were such arrangements of relatively recent origin as the employee pension trust and the stock option for corporate executives. Moreover, many customs and usages that have no status as authoritative rules are regularly taken into account by courts deciding cases. A trade practice may illuminate the probable intentions of parties to a commercial contract, for instance. Furthermore, when a court must decide whether a business or professional person has acted with due care, it measures that person's action against the traditional standards and practices of the trade or profession.

ALTERNATIVE DISPUTE RESOLUTION

When a power is exercised by private persons in such a way as to determine rights and duties of a large number of people, the process has much in common with lawmaking as we have defined it; hence, we can say that such an exercise of power creates private supplements to law. Take, for example, the Major League Agreement that controls activities of professional baseball teams forming the two major leagues. In form, this agreement is a contract drawn up by club owners and subscribed to by all major-league players. But it might also be described as the constitution of a system of private self-government in which club owners are the legislators, league presidents the executives, and the commissioner of baseball a judge. The actual division of functions is not quite so neat, of course. Yet it is interesting to note that the first commissioner of baseball in the 1920s, Kenesaw Mountain Landis, was a former federal judge.

It would be most undesirable, if not impossible, for a state to try to prescribe all the rules governing private conduct. Our innumerable private associations—corporations, labor unions, clubs, schools, churches, and families, to name only a few—all have their own rules, and the state relies on these private rules to channel much of the conduct of its citizens.

Part of the job of these private rules is resolution of disputes among group members. In Chapter 3 we examined the usefulness of arbitration as a technique to resolve differences without resorting to the formal legal system. It is important to note again there are desirable alternatives to the legal system available for resolving disputes. In the sections that follow, we examine in detail the elaborate system of labor-management self-government. Special emphasis is placed on the handling of disputes under labor agreements. The purpose of this exploration is twofold: to examine how private lawmaking activity takes place in groups such as can be found in the workplace, and to see exactly how one *alternative dispute resolution* (ADR) mechanism, called the *grievance procedure*, works.

ADR complements labors of the courts by easing the onerous backlog of work that continues to build. In fact, so valuable have these systems become that the formal legal system has encouraged and even required parties to use ADR. In the *McMahon* case in Chapter 3, we saw how one form of ADR, arbitration, is used in the workplace and in consumer transactions. Many states today require mandatory arbitration or mediation (negotiation with assistance of an independent third party) for a broad variety of disputes. Other states have created opportunities for mini-trials or *summary jury trials*. In such cases, a jury is impaneled and a summary of a case is presented by attorneys before a neutral third party. Rules of procedure and evidence are more leniently adhered to, and ultimately the jury comes up with an advisory opinion. The hope is that such a mini-trial will allow litigants to appreciate the likely outcome of a regular trial and thus encourage them to settle the case without a full court procedure.

Despite the apparent benefits of ADR, a number of criticisms have been leveled at the process (see, for example, Goldberg, Green, and Sander 1986, 291–299). First, the process inherently lacks some of the legal protections available in a more formal court proceeding. Second, many potential users are unaware that ADR procedures are available for their circumstances. Third, the competence of people conducting ADR proceedings is variable and may at times be inadequate to ensure fairness for all parties.

Nonetheless, it is increasingly clear that private and public legal systems supplement and complement each other. Essentially, the legal system provides a framework, and a backstop if they fail, for operation of these private rules and procedures.

COLLECTIVE BARGAINING AGREEMENTS: AN EXAMPLE OF INDUSTRIAL SELF-GOVERNMENT

A particularly interesting illustration of a supplementary legal system is the labor-management relationship established under a collective bargaining agreement. Such agreements have some characteristics of contracts, but in many ways they resemble constitutions. When the United Steelworkers of America and the major steel companies sign an agreement, for example, they put into effect a set of basic rules governing the relationships of hundreds of thousands of employees with their employers. The agreement contains not only rules governing conduct of the parties, but also rules establishing institutions and procedures under which disputes arising between parties will be handled while the agreement is in force. This type of supplementary system is the subject of the remainder of this chapter.

Relations between an employer and organized employees are carried on under a system of rules that they have created for themselves, acting within a framework provided by law. Among these rules are *collective bargaining agreements* (of which more than 150,000 are now in operation in the United States), which might be described as the "constitutions" of an industrial community. Such communities have other "legislative" rules, too, some of them laid down by the employer alone, but most of them the product of negotiations carried on under provisions of an agreement. The agreement also establishes a procedure for settling disputes between employer and employees. The final stage in that procedure is usually arbitration, a form of adjudication. Arbitration produces decisions that have some of the quality of decisional rules for the industrial community.

Let us first consider the bargaining that leads up to a collective agreement, and then the agreement itself and arrangements established under it.

Conditions of Collective Bargaining

What conditions are essential to effective bargaining? We must keep in mind that a bargain is an exchange. First, each party must have something that the other wants, so coming to terms will be to their mutual advantage. Second, each party must be in a position to exercise the alternative of *not* exchanging what he or she has if the terms offered are too unfavorable. If a party lacks either one of these prerequisites, he has no bargaining power, and there can be no real bargaining.

Bargaining between management and labor boils down to the exchange of labor for work opportunities for workers. An employer may make jobs available or may close down the workplace (an act known as a *lockout*). Organized workers may do the employer's work or may refuse as a group to go on working (an act known as a *strike*). Although choosing the second alternative in both cases is an act of desperation entailing immediate sacrifices, this alternative is essential to each party's bargaining position in the long run. In the days when most employees had to negotiate singly with an employer, they usually were unable to bargain at all. Their individual services were rarely indispensable to an employer, since the supply of labor for most types of work was relatively abundant. Even if workers possessed skills that were in short supply, they could afford to quit a job only if they could start at once on another job, since they normally had little or no savings and no union strike fund standing ready to aid them. It was only when workers joined a union that they could bargain, because then others would join them in refusing to work if their terms were not met. And even a union would be unable to bargain effectively if the law prevented it from going out on strike or using other means of pressure on an employer.

To promote bargaining, modern labor law has tried to lessen inequalities between the parties and to bring them together around a bargaining table. But it also permits private sector employees to strike and employers to close down their workplaces. (Government employees often are denied the right to strike by state laws.) Both rights are subject to limitations, however, as are other weapons in the industrial struggle: labor's picketing and boycotts, and various techniques that management has developed to resist union pressures. Collective bargaining agreements negotiated by employers and unions usually contain self-imposed limitations on the right of the parties to use coercive pressures against each other during the life of an agreement, and these limitations, too, are backed up by law.

The law has, of course, never sought to ensure that bargaining parties would be of exactly equal strength. To do so would be quite impossible, for the outcome of any negotiation depends on subtle and shifting factors, including the skill of negotiating representatives and external circumstances such as economic conditions at the time of a negotiation. A union's bargaining position is obviously stronger, for instance, in a period when demand for a company's product is strong and workers are scarce than in a period of slack demand and widespread unemployment.

The first step in the bargaining process is formation and recognition of a union or bargaining unit. This is normally accomplished using procedures specified in national and state legislation that require a favorable vote by persons to be included in the bargaining unit. These laws provide that a favorable vote requires management to recognize the union as the exclusive bargaining agent for all persons holding positions classified as included in the bargaining unit. The vote creates a permanent relationship that can be terminated only by another special vote of members of the recognized bargaining unit under specified procedures, and management is usually limited in how actively it can encourage such a vote.

Thereafter, the most important step in the bargaining process is to secure an agreement. Since agreements must be renewed periodically, there will be further bargaining when revisions to an agreement are proposed by one party or the other. Bargaining goes on even while an agreement is in operation: New problems may appear in a production process, and disputes may arise over the meaning and application of an agreement. Contrary to the impression given by news reports, however, the orderly settlement of differences at all these stages is the rule, and resort to economic warfare such as a strike is an exception.

The Contents of Collective Bargaining Agreements

What matters do collective bargaining agreements cover? Agreements have no standard form, of course. Those negotiated in small establishments are likely to be much briefer than those negotiated in giant firms, and relatively weak unions are often unable to win the commitments from management that strong unions can secure. However, almost all agreements have five major sections: (1) union security and management rights, (2) the wage and effort bargain, (3) individual security, (4) employee participation, and (5) contract administration (Beal and Begin 1989, 327–334). Each is discussed below.

A Shared Management Process: Union Security and Management Rights

Fifty years ago, a basic principle of any collective bargaining agreement, whether or not it was made explicit, was that an employer is responsible for managing an enterprise and directing the labor force. Over time, in both private and public sectors, the trend has been toward greater sharing of control over what once were considered strictly management prerogatives in running the workplace. Labor-management relations today represent a form of organizational participation in which individuals and groups other than formal leaders have a voice in directing an organization. Thus, labor-management relations today may be characterized as structured relationships between formally organized participants in a shared management process (Milakovich and Gordon 2007, 323).

Many agreements contain a section specifying that management is responsible for scheduling production, making work assignments, hiring, promoting, demoting, transferring, discharging, classifying, and disciplining personnel for just cause. In all these matters, management has the initiative. But agreements today increasingly describe qualifications or limitations on the prerogatives of management. As an example, the employer's power to lay off workers during a period of reduced production may be qualified by seniority provisions, specifying criteria to be used in deciding who is laid off first and rehired last. Or an employer's power to discharge workers for disciplinary reasons may be qualified by a provision that disciplinary discharges must be for *just cause*. This provision allows the union to file a grievance and have a case fully reviewed if it believes that an employee has been fired without just cause.

Every union is understandably anxious to hold onto its members, to collect members' dues regularly, and to make members of as many employees as it can. Many employers actually help unions achieve these goals, usually on the ground that if the union feels secure, it is more likely to be reasonable and responsible. Unless prohibited by the law of the state in which a workplace is located, the employer has the right under federal legislation to agree to a *union shop* clause, in which the employer promises to discharge any employee who fails to join the union within a set period of time (usually thirty days) after being employed or who fails to continue as a member thereafter.

The Wage and Effort Bargain

Many people consider this section of the labor contract the most important of all. It deals with the total amount of compensation paid by an employer to employees in return for their work effort. In addition to information about standard rates of pay, this section of the contract provides employees with explanations of fringe benefits like earned sick leave, paid health insurance, premium pay, retirement contributions, holidays, and earned vacation days.

Individual Security

The individual-security section of a contract deals with an employee's ability to keep his or her job. One standard technique employed by unions to establish individual security is job seniority. This system guarantees that in the event of a work shortage, the least senior individual will be required to leave first and the most senior person to leave last.

The individual-security section of the contract also contains information about a grievance procedure, which is used to resolve disputes that frequently occur on the job. Some contracts also describe sanctions for particular forms of misbehavior. Shortly, we shall discuss in detail how disputes are settled under an agreement, so as to clarify how private legal systems perform quasi-judicial functions.

Employee Participation

This section of a contract discusses the procedures and standards for establishing rules to provide employees broader forms of participation in organizational decision-making than was previously typical of collective bargaining. It specifies alternative procedures for securing employee input (e.g., quality circles), the types of issues for which those procedures may be used, and the level of authority to be exercised by employees (e.g., advisory, shared decision-making, or final decision). In these provisions, collective bargaining agreements have increasingly devised innovations for shared management of organizations.

Contract Administration

The final section of a contract deals with procedures for implementing other parts of the agreement. For example, it states which agency will be hired to perform any arbitration work that might be needed. It also specifies the powers of people such as shop stewards and grievance officers (employees elected to speak for a union in the basic production unit) in resolving contract questions.

Dispute Settlement

No matter how good relations are between a company and its employees, events that produce disagreements are bound to occur. For example, Brown is discharged for misconduct on the job and claims that he did not do what he is accused of, that it was not misconduct, or that discharge is too severe a penalty. Or Jones is promoted, whereupon Smith says that the promotion should have been hers because she has been with the company longer than Jones. Or management lowers the classification and wage rate on a certain job because a newly installed machine has made the job less hazardous, and affected workers protest.

One of the major pieces of federal labor law, the Taft-Hartley Act of 1947, makes it clear that management and labor still have a legal obligation to negotiate after they have signed a collective bargaining agreement. The act established a Federal Mediation and Conciliation Service to aid companies and unions in settling their disputes, but Section 203(d) clearly indicates that Congress wants them to settle their disputes in their own way whenever possible. The act stated, "Final adjustment by a method agreed upon by the parties is hereby declared to be the desirable method for settlement of grievance disputes arising over the application or interpretation of an existing collective bargaining agreement."

As has already been noted, nearly all agreements make some provision for a grievance procedure. In principle, employees, the union, and management all have the right to file grievances, but the procedures are usually based on the assumption that virtually all grievances will be filed by employees, with the support of their union representatives. Management will probably take the position that in running a workplace it may make any decision it sees fit, subject only to its commitments under the agreement, and that any employee who believes that any management decision violates the agreement must file a grievance. This throws the initiative for filing a grievance onto employees, though of course the employer can indirectly take the initiative by doing something that forces the union to file a grievance.

We have spoken of the grievance procedure as an alternative to labor-management strife, as indeed it is. We must recognize, however, that handling grievances is far from easy; indeed, it should be thought of as an extension of the hardheaded bargaining that produced an agreement. In negotiating an agreement, the employer probably fought to define as narrowly as possible the area falling under a grievance procedure, because there is a strategic advantage to keeping the area of unrestricted management discretion as broad as possible. For opposite reasons, the union probably fought to have the grievance area broadly defined. The outcome is to some degree a reflection of the bargaining power and skill of the two parties. Once the grievance machinery is in operation, the volume of complaints at any given time is likely to be determined not merely by events in the workplace but by union tactics: is this a good time to press hard, or should the union ease up? Whether management adopts a hard or a conciliatory position on complaints filed by a union is likely to be influenced by similar tactical considerations.

Grievance settlements contribute to what is known as the *law of the plant* (i.e., workplace). The outcome of a proceeding (particularly if the final stage, arbitration, is reached) has significance for the law of the industrial community roughly comparable to the significance of a judicial or administrative decision. The precedent it establishes has no binding effect, but due to "equal treatment" requirements of the U.S. Constitution, in many circumstances it will influence patterns of future conduct. The parties are well aware of this likelihood. When negotiators of a collective bargaining agreement cannot agree on the wording of a provision, they often put in some vague words, counting on the grievance procedure to fill in the gaps as an area of dispute is illuminated by actual cases. The rule that grows out of a grievance settlement may prove so satisfactory to both parties that they will formalize it as a new provision in the next revision of the contract.

In agreements negotiated with large companies, the grievance procedure consists of a series of meetings between union and management representatives at successively higher levels of authority in the company. The first step is usually for the shop steward or griev- ance officer to present a grievance to the shop foreman immediately concerned. If no settlement can be reached at that level, the union's elected grievance committee presents the grievance to the divisional superintendent. If this step does not produce a settlement, one or more further appeals are carried to managers at higher levels; the final appeal is to a representative of top management. For each step (after the first) there is usually a deadline both for filing and for responding to an appeal, so that a succession of appeals up to the top management level ordinarily does not take more than a few weeks at most.

Most grievances are disposed of (or abandoned) at one of these stages. But in a small minority of cases a final stage is reached: the union asks that a grievance be submitted to a neutral third party for arbitration.

Arbitration

What is arbitration? When two parties submit a dispute to arbitration, they are asking one or more disinterested outsiders to hear and judge a controversy, on the understand- ing that the parties will accept whatever decision is reached. Arbitration is thus a special form of adjudication. Its procedures and such law as exists concerning it (mostly on the enforceability of agreements to arbitrate and of arbitral awards) have developed largely as a result of its widespread use under commercial contracts. Employers making such contracts often include a provision binding themselves to arbitrate any dispute that may arise under the contract, in the belief that arbitration is cheaper, speedier, and more private than litigation in the courts. Recently many banks have attempted to impose on consum- ers provisions requiring binding arbitration for disputes about charges to personal credit cards, in a manner that may deprive some consumers of access to the courts. Arbitration has also been used in settling certain kinds of international disputes.

Arbitration, as a form of adjudication, is to be distinguished from fact-finding and mediation. *Arbitrators* are called upon to determine a solution to a particular problem. The parties agree ahead of time to be bound by the arbitrator's decision, and the arbitra- tor decides who wins what.

Fact-finding is a limited version of arbitration, in which an independent person or board makes a binding determination about a particular version of disputed facts, but does not decide who wins or loses what. Fact-finding is similar to what a jury does at a trial when sifting through various versions of what happened in order to decide issues of fact. Fact-finding, which may be performed by persons other than an arbitrator, is often a preliminary step toward arbitration.

A *mediator* is a neutral third party called in to facilitate negotiations between the parties to explore and reconcile their differences. In mediation, the disputants are not bound to a third-party decision: they may either accept or reject suggestions made by the mediator, who has no authority to impose a particular version of disputed facts or a solution to any problem. The mediator may suggest solutions to problems or simply play the role of an active listener, suggesting alternative strategies for resolving a dispute; essentially, the mediator acts as a catalyst, to keep the parties talking to each other until they resolve their own disagreements. Sometimes mediation, which is often performed by persons other than arbitrators, is a preliminary step before fact-finding.

The conceptual distinction between arbitration and mediation is important, but in practice arbitrators sometimes act as mediators, and mediators may be tempted to act as if they were arbitrators. Thus, references to a "mediator with clout" actually describe a form of intervention more akin to arbitration or fact-finding than mediation (Hamilton 1991, 171). A similar conceptual confusion sometimes afflicts judges; perhaps the best example is the judge in a domestic-relations court who makes a practice of trying to help married couples patch up their differences before considering a petition for divorce. Judges who conduct pretrial conferences also act as mediators on occasion.

Although some mediating by adjudicators to encourage a settlement is probably inevitable, many students of our legal institutions feel that combining the two roles should be kept to a minimum. They argue that performing both functions may cause confusion, foster abuses of power, or otherwise prevent an adjudicator from performing either role properly.

Various methods have been devised for selecting an arbitrator acceptable to both parties. One method is to invite an outside agency to submit a list of three or five names to the parties, who then take turns at eliminating a name until only one is left. Lists of persons available and qualified to serve as labor arbitrators are maintained by the Federal Mediation and Conciliation Service (a government agency) and the American Arbitration Association (a private, nonprofit organization).

Most labor arbitrators are chosen to hear only a single case (although an arbitrator whose work satisfies the parties may be chosen again by them). But a large company faced with a substantial flow of grievance cases often joins with the union representing its employees in hiring one or more arbitrators on a continuing basis. Sometimes the company and the union arrange *tripartite arbitration*: each party names one arbitrator and then both parties jointly name a third, who heads the group. Under all these arrangements, the costs of arbitration are usually shared equally by the parties.

Special Problems of the Labor Arbitrator

Although labor arbitrators perform functions that in many ways resemble those of both the commercial arbitrator (whose job is to resolve problems involving business transactions) and the trial judge, their role is unique in a number of respects.

Labor arbitrators, unlike judges, are not public officials whose authority is imposed on the parties by the state and whose decision will be enforced by other officials. Arbitrators are hired and paid by the parties to the agreement (who may discharge them if their performance is unsatisfactory). Their assigned task is not to seek justice in any general sense, but to perform a function in the system of self-government the parties have created, to apply rules established by their agreement.

The job of labor arbitrators is different from that of commercial arbitrators because collective bargaining agreements are not like ordinary commercial contracts, in which the parties have normally come together only to carry out a single transaction. Management and labor are bound together by the strongest of ties. However bitter their occasional differences may be, each needs the other, and each has the same ultimate concern for maintaining the flow of production. Under these circumstances, the task of adjudicating one of their disputes often requires rare skill. It may be particularly challenging for the temporary, one-time arbitrator, who somehow must rapidly acquire an awareness of the total relationship between the parties. If, failing to acquire such an awareness, the arbitrator comes up with a decision that is formally impeccable but leaves one side bitter and relations tenser than ever, the arbitration can hardly be deemed a success. After all, a major aim of the grievance procedure is to eliminate causes of tension. "Let justice be done though the heavens fall" is not an appropriate slogan for a labor arbitrator.

Labor arbitrators must also bear in mind that arbitration is the last step in a settlement procedure, to be taken only after all attempts at negotiated settlement have failed. If a commercial arbitrator cannot render a satisfactory decision, a dispute can be carried to the courts. But litigation is not always a practical alternative to grievance arbitration. True, the law provides that parties to a collective agreement may sue in the courts for alleged breaches of contract. But such suits are, and must always be, exceptional. There are too many grievances, and litigation is too costly. Prompt settlement of most grievances is imperative, and litigation is slow. Finally, courts, being courts of *law,* have to apply doctrines of law when they are relevant, but some of these doctrines may be quite inappropriate for the handling of grievances.

Labor arbitrators can never forget, then, that the alternative to an acceptable award is likely to be not a lawsuit but a strike, or at least continued unrest and dissatisfaction that may impair organizational productivity. A party is sometimes able to take a dispute arising under a collective bargaining agreement to the National Labor Relations Board by complaining that the other party is guilty of an unfair labor practice (for instance, refusing to bargain in good faith). But constant resort to administrative adjudication is no more a practical alternative to grievance proceedings than constant resort to the courts would be.

Identifying Rules to Apply

Perhaps the greatest difference between labor arbitration and other forms of adjudication stems from the unique character of the *body of principle* on which labor arbitrators must base their decisions.

The arbitration clause in a collective bargaining agreement usually specifies that arbitrators are authorized to settle only those grievances that are related to "the interpretation and application of this agreement" and that the arbitrators may not add to, subtract from, or modify the agreement. But if these phrases make the arbitrators' job of identifying the rules to apply sound easy, they are deceptive.

We have already compared collective bargaining agreements with constitutions. Like most other constitutional documents, agreements tend to be notably imprecise and incomplete. They are usually pounded out by negotiators working against a deadline—the expiration date of the current contract. When accord on a particular issue seems remote as the deadline draws near, the parties may be tempted to say nothing about the issue at all or else to include a fuzzy provision that satisfies both sides because it means so little. Nor is the agreement couched in carefully chosen, legalistic words characteristic of commercial contracts. Sometimes lawyers play no part in the drafting. A major aim of negotiators is to produce a relatively brief document that can be distributed to employees with some expectation of their understanding it. Finally, even when negotiators try to be precise, they may still stumble into traps presented to all drafters by the undetected ambiguity of some words and by the impossibility of predicting the future.

As a consequence, arbitrators have a wide measure of discretion. Although they cannot alter the words of an agreement, they are often able to choose from among a variety of possible meanings. For instance, when a case raises the question of whether the disciplinary discharge of a certain employee was for "just cause," an arbitrator will not get very far by simply trying to define the phrase "just cause." Instead, it is necessary to give meaning to this empty phrase by formulating a standard against which a particular discharge can be measured.

When an agreement is not clear, where do arbitrators look for help in setting up such a standard? If they have had legal training, they may turn to relevant legal doctrines. They may also try to find out what other arbitrators have done in similar cases in the past. Although there is no tradition that arbitral precedents must be followed, arbitrators—most of whom are lawyers who respect legal traditions—are understandably prone to strive for some degree of consistency in interpretation of a particular agreement, and the absence of a *stare decisis* rule does not deter arbitrators from looking for ideas in the records of earlier awards. However, only a minority of arbitral awards are published, and those are usually unaccompanied by written opinions.

Even more important than such precedents, then, may be relevant circumstances in the "legislative history" of negotiations that produced an agreement and relevant practices within an enterprise (sometimes referred to as the common law of the plant or workplace). Arbitrators are also influenced by their own views on what is consistent with sound industrial practice and with national labor policy and by their own notions of what is just and reasonable.

Arbitrability

Occasionally one party resists submission of a grievance to arbitration. This party usually argues that under the arbitration clause of a collective bargaining agreement, the arbitrator can hear only grievances involving interpretation and application of the agreement and that the grievance in question is not covered by any provision. To contest the arbitrability of a grievance in this way is somewhat like contesting the jurisdiction of a court to hear a case.

Here is an example. A collective bargaining agreement contains no provision on the company's ability to contract work out to other firms. Either it has never occurred to the parties that a dispute might arise over subcontracting or else they tried but were unable to agree on a formula. Even though some of its own employees are working only part-time, the company subcontracts some work that might have been done in the workplace.

The union files a grievance. It claims that subcontracting is a violation of the *implied* terms of the agreement. It points out that the agreement recognizes the union as the representative of *all* the company's production and maintenance workers, and it contends that provisions concerning layoffs and part-time labor constitute an implied promise that work will not be turned over to outsiders while employees are idle.

The company retorts that the union's arguments are farfetched and that making decisions about subcontracting is clearly management's prerogative. Furthermore, the company insists that since the contract is silent about subcontracting, the arbitrator has no authority over the matter under terms of the arbitration clause. After all, concludes the company, when we agreed to this arbitration procedure we did not agree to having every little gripe the union comes up with submitted to arbitration.

Most arbitrators are reluctant to refuse to arbitrate. After all, the result of a refusal to arbitrate is that the dispute goes back to the parties, who have already been unable to settle it in earlier stages of the grievance procedure. Moreover, a refusal to arbitrate usually has the effect of a decision against the grievant. If, however, the arbitrators feel that the union's attempt to relate a dispute to some provision in the agreement is completely farfetched, or if they get the impression—from the general tone of the agreement or from what they know of its legislative history—that this agreement should be interpreted literally rather than liberally, they probably will refuse to arbitrate.

If one party feels strongly enough that a dispute is not arbitrable, it can try to prevent arbitration by simply refusing to participate in the hearing. The law now provides, however, that a party desiring arbitration may ask a court to order the other to submit to it, on grounds that the refusal to do so is a breach of contract.

One might think such a suit would compel a court to decide whether the matter in dispute was covered by the agreement. But in three cases decided in 1960 the Supreme Court of the United States made it clear the role of the federal courts, at least, would be much more modest. The Court held that unless the arbitration clause of an agreement makes it perfectly clear that a particular dispute could not under any possible interpretation be covered by the agreement, the lower court must order the dispute submitted to arbitration, thus letting arbitrators decide whether to arbitrate. Nor can a lower court refuse to order a reluctant party to submit to arbitration merely because it feels the grievance in question is frivolous and certain to be rejected. The Court also ruled that when a party that has submitted to arbitration under protest later refuses to comply with an award and the other party asks a lower court to order compliance, the court may not refuse to do so merely because it disagrees with the arbitrators' interpretation of the contract; if their interpretation has any possible justification, the court must accept it. The parties, the Court pointed out, bargained for the arbitrators' interpretation of the contract, not for a judge's interpretation. The prestige and usefulness of labor arbitrators were unquestionably enhanced by these Supreme Court decisions.

Collective Bargaining and National Policy

The national policy on labor-management relations is to allow employers and employees to work out for themselves the rules and procedures under which their relations will be carried on. The principal aim of the legal rules in this area is to foster conditions favorable to negotiation of collective bargaining agreements and to settlement of disputes arising under them. There are also legal rules that restrict the use of economic weapons and the terms parties may agree to, and each party is given the right to seek assistance in the courts if the other party breaches an agreement. Within this legal framework, labor and management are expected to work out the details of their relationship in each industrial community.

Underlying the national policy is a presupposition that in a free society it is ordinarily desirable for private individuals and groups to work out their own contractual arrangements. They will be better citizens if they have to bear this responsibility themselves, and they will probably devise more imaginative and flexible rules and procedures to govern their affairs than would even the wisest of public officials. This is our government's policy not only for labor-management relations but also for the internal affairs of such private associations as corporations, unions, churches, educational institutions, and clubs; legal rules merely establish a framework within which the complex behaviors of voluntary private relationships take their course.

On the whole, we can say the record of labor-management industrial communities in setting up and operating their own systems of self-government has justified the national presupposition. Thousands of arrangements have been negotiated, and under them large numbers of grievances are settled year after year. Strikes, lockouts, picketing, and boycotts are resorted to in only a tiny minority of instances in which contract negotiations or grievance procedures have failed. In many industries it is clear that labor-management relations are no longer marked by the bitterness that characterized the era before collective bargaining was introduced.

Underlying the national policy on industrial relations is another presupposition: that occasional results of the bargaining process that seem contrary to *the public interest* are a price worth paying for industrial self-government. From time to time negotiations are bound to break down and produce work stoppages that are inconvenient to the public and harmful to the economy. From time to time a company and a union will sign an agreement containing provisions (most often relating to wages) that seem likely to interfere with such national goals as price stability and rapid growth. The presupposition of our national policy is that, at least in time of peace, such occurrences are worth enduring for the sake of preserving a system of collective bargaining.

In recent years, strikes and inflationary wage settlements in basic U.S. industries have raised questions about this second presupposition. A balancing of values is involved, and some people wonder whether the government should not have more effective means to prevent these undesirable occurrences, even though government intervention would lessen the freedom to bargain collectively.

A further exploration of the issues raised by recent proposals for an expanded government role in industrial relations would carry us far beyond the subject of this chapter. But this proposed increase in government intervention in industries like railroads and shipping does raise some important questions: What would be the effect of such intervention (either to prevent a work stoppage or to prevent adoption of a particular term in a collective agreement) on the persistence with which bargaining—both agreement negotiation and dispute settlement—would be pursued? For instance, is there a danger that parties who know that the government may step in to prevent a strike will stop doing their utmost to settle the differences between them? And if the possibility of government intervention does weaken bargaining processes in a particular industry, may not this result be more undesirable in the long run than the misfortunes that government intervention was designed to prevent? We should give serious thought to these questions before making any radical changes in national policies regarding labor-management relations.

CHAPTER PROBLEM: UNIVERSITY OF NORTH DAKOTA RULES AND PROCEDURES

Academic Honesty: Each student is expected to be honest in his academic work. Dishonesty in examinations, papers, or other work is considered an extremely serious offense by the faculty and students.

Financial Obligation of the Student: It is the responsibility of the student to make satisfactory arrangements for the settling of accounts with the University.

Failure to settle a University account will result either in cancellation of the student's enrollment or the placing of a "hold" on the student's official records and future registration.

The intentional passing of worthless checks to the University or the failure to redeem promptly a worthless check passed unintentionally to the University is considered sufficient cause for stringent disciplinary action.

Falsification of Documents: The falsification, defacing, altering, or mutilating of any official University document—I.D. card, receipt, transcript, etc.—or the withholding or falsification of information on an admissions application, subjects the student to cancellation of registration.

Keys: The possession of keys to University buildings by students who have not been authorized to use such keys is strictly forbidden. The duplication of a key issued to a student by the University is prohibited.

Hazing: Hazing is prohibited on or off-campus. Hazing is defined to include any actions, activities, or situation intentionally created to produce unnecessary or undue mental or physical discomfort, embarrassment, harassment, ridicule, excessive fatigue, interference with scholarship or personal lives, or exposure to situations wherein one's physical or mental well-being may be endangered.

Drugs: The University unequivocally disapproves of, and will not condone, the illegal possession or professionally unsupervised use of hallucinogenic or narcotic drugs by any member of the University community. It is considered an especially serious offense to sell, provide, share, or distribute such drugs illegally.

Disorderly Behavior: Behavior which is disturbing or disorderly, e.g., physical or verbal abuse of another person, obscene language or actions, disrespect for the rights or privileges of others, or drunkenness, detracts from the academic environment and is therefore contrary to the best interests of the University community.

Disorderly behavior by students or non-students at public events on-campus, athletic contests, or University Center programs, subjects the violator(s) to arrest and referral to civil authorities.

Cheating or Plagiarism: These words refer to the use of unauthorized books or notes or otherwise securing help in a test; copying tests, assignments, reports or term papers; or being in unauthorized places like offices, buildings after hours, or a professor's office without his permission. These forms of dishonesty are very serious matters in a University.

In cases of cheating or plagiarism, the instructor shall refer the case to his academic dean. After meeting with the instructor and student involved, the academic dean shall have the authority to act.

A student has the right to appeal the academic dean's action to the Student Relations Committee. The student's appeal is initiated with his academic dean.

Source: Extracted from rules and procedures of the University of North Dakota in Holmes (1971, 289–292).

Questions

1. Does this code constitute a complete legal system for the University of North Dakota? Explain. (Referring back to Chapter 2 concerning elements of a legal system may be helpful.)
2. Suppose that Jim, a student, slips and falls at an athletic event and in the process shouts an obscenity. May he be punished for disorderly behavior? Describe at least four other situations for which the university's code provides no clear sanctions.
3. Design a list of sanctions for the situations you described in question 2. Be prepared to justify your list.

QUESTIONS FOR REVIEW

1. State an example of an interaction between a private legal system and the public legal system.

2. Examine your university's legal system. Does it have a clear statement of rules and procedures? If you find the system unclear, give three examples of this lack of clarity.

3. Define the term *collective bargaining*. Is collective bargaining an adequate tool for maintaining industrial peace? Why or why not?

4. Discuss the five major sections found in most collective bargaining agreements.

5. What is a grievance procedure? Can you think of any examples of how a grievance procedure might be used other than for labor disputes?

BIBLIOGRAPHY

Beal, Edwin F., and James P. Begin. 1989. *The Practice of Collective Bargaining.* 8th ed. Homewood, IL: R.D. Irwin.

Goldberg, Stephen B., Erick D. Green, and Frank E. Sander. 1986. "ADR Problems and Prospects: Looking to the Future." *Judicature* 69 (February–March): 291–299.

Hamilton, Michael S. 1991. "Environmental Mediation: Requirements for Successful Institutionalization." In *Resolving Disputes in the Public Sector*, ed. Miriam K. Mills. Chicago: Nelson-Hall.

Holmes, Grace, ed. 1971. *Law and Discipline on Campus.* Ann Arbor, MI: Institute of Continuing Legal Education.

Milakovich, Michael E., and George J. Gordon. 2007. *Public Administration in America.* 9th ed. Belmont, CA: Thomson/Wadsworth.

CHAPTER 10

Law in Society
A Conclusion

The emphasis throughout this book has been on the processes and institutions of the law rather than on the aims and policies that law seeks to implement. It is important to remember that the legal system is not a machine that runs for its own sake; it exists to serve the purposes of the community. Law is not a set of restrictions imposed on a community by some external power; it is a system of rules, institutions, and procedures a community itself establishes to achieve its many and varying objectives.

This is not to say, of course, that every member of a community likes and approves of every legal rule that restricts freedom. But experience shows that in a democratic community a rule is rarely effective unless a substantial majority of those affected are willing, however reluctantly, to accept the restraints that the rule imposes. Persistent disobedience has nullified many a law, and political pressures have brought about repeal of many others. The rules that remain in effect are accepted because most people feel they are necessary—or at least acknowledge the difficulties involved in devising or enforcing better ones.

We do well not to forget that while some rules command and prohibit, many rules merely permit us to do certain things, and other rules provide means that enable people to achieve their objectives. Rules that create liberties merely say, "If you choose to act in this way, public officials will not interfere with you" (as in attending church). Rules that create powers say, "If you choose to act in this way, you can alter your legal position; you can create for yourself and others new rights and duties, provided only that you follow the prescribed procedures" (as in writing a will).

We are most aware of the legal system when it deals with breakdowns in normal social relations: when it provides for punishment of wrongdoers, for compensation of those who have been wronged, for the enjoining of further wrongdoing, or for settlement of disputes. And these are important functions of the law. Even more important, however, is its function of channeling conduct in such a way that most clashes of competing interests are resolved without resort to coercive powers of the system. In a well-ordered community, adjustment of differences without resort to litigation and prosecution is the normal pattern of life; disruptions requiring remedial action are the rare exception.

Moreover, while the legal system is a powerful mechanism for exercise of social control, it is certainly not the only system. In Chapter 9, we looked at labor relations as an example of a social-control mechanism in the workplace. Families, schools, churches, and social organizations all exercise private control where official intervention would be undesirable or futile.

A perpetual problem of any legal system is how to reconcile a need for certainty, predictability, and stability with the inevitable need for continuing social change. We have stressed again and again that a legal system cannot serve as an effective instrument of social control unless people can be sure that, under most circumstances, yesterday's rules still apply today. Without some stability in the law, people would have no way of foreseeing the legal consequences of their acts. Nonetheless, continual changes in legal rules are inevitable. Some of these may be relatively minor adjustments to take account of new combinations of facts, but some of them will be major innovations made necessary by changes in the social, economic, and technological environment and in the attitudes and values of a dynamic society. Chapters 4 through 9 all dealt with means by which the legal system maximizes certainty wherever possible, yet makes possible continuous modification of the law as the need for change arises.

As legal rules impinge upon our lives, we may be able to understand them better if we understand the workings of interacting processes and institutions from which the rules emerge; if we recognize the difficulties of combining a maximum of individual freedom and private self-government with an indispensable element of coercive public control; and if we acknowledge the value of reconciling the need for stability and the need for change. Finally, we may understand legal rules better if we recognize that the legal system is a *process*—a never-ending, trial-and-error process of distilling a community's shared purposes from its many competing purposes and of translating those shared purposes into effective guides to human conduct.

CHAPTER PROBLEM:
TOO MUCH LAW—OUR NATIONAL DISEASE

As a final problem, consider the following controversial statement by legal scholar Bayless Manning:

> By any index or measure that you might choose to apply, our law is exploding. We are inundated by waves of new regulations, by judicial decision, by legislation. Whole new areas of the law have sprung out of the ground overnight—environmental regulation is an example—and familiar areas like good old-fashioned property law have undergone a process of infinite fission. We have increasing numbers of statutory codes that are becoming increasingly particularistic: commercial law and taxation are two examples. The truth is we are simply drowning in law.
>
> All this law is irritating, annoying, and a nuisance. But I would like to suggest that it is much more serious than that and that a great deal more is at stake than the irritations we all feel as citizens and as lawyers in wrestling with this mass of material.

Source: Manning (1977, 435).

Questions

1. How would you respond to Manning's statement?
2. Should more power be turned over to private organizations, such as churches and social clubs? Do you think these organizations could satisfactorily replace the public legal system in many areas? Why or why not?

BIBLIOGRAPHY

Manning, Bayless. 1977. "Too Much Law: Our National Disease." *Business Lawyer* 33 (November): 435–440.

Bibliographic Note

The body of literature about legal processes and institutions is enormous. This note lists a very limited number of works that will be particularly useful to the student wishing to inquire further into the subjects treated in the text. Books available in paperback editions are marked with an asterisk (*).

LAW AND SOCIETY

In *Social Control Through Law* (New Brunswick, NJ: Transaction Publishers, 1997), Roscoe Pound, a former dean of Harvard Law School, discourses on the nature of law and its role in society. Of the many books written to introduce the beginning law student to the nature of law, perhaps the most penetrating is Karl N. Llewellyn's *The Bramble Bush*, found in *Karl N. Llewellyn on Legal Realism* (Birmingham, AL: Legal Classics Library, 1986). *The Nature and Functions of Law,* 6th ed., by Harold J. Berman, William R. Greiner, and Samir N. Saliba (New York, NY: Foundation Press, 2004) is an interesting collection of cases and other materials designed for use in general legal-studies courses. A useful collection of readings brought together by social scientists is *Law and the Behavioral Sciences,* 2nd ed., by Lawrence Friedman and Stewart Macaulay (Indianapolis: Bobbs-Merrill, 1977).

JURISPRUDENCE

Books of interest concerning jurisprudence include M.D.A. Freeman, *Lloyd's Introduction to Jurisprudence,* 7th ed. (London: Sweet and Maxwell, 2001); Allan C. Hutchinson, ed., *Critical Legal Studies* (Totowa, NJ: Rowan & Littlefield, 1989); and Howard Zinn, *Declarations of Independence: Cross-Examining American Ideology* (New York: Harper Collins, 1990). For a more philosophical treatment, see John Rawls's *A Theory of Justice,* rev. ed. (Cambridge: Harvard University Press, 1999).

LEGAL PROCESSES AND INSTITUTIONS

Next to be recommended are some books in which all or most of the legal processes and institutions examined throughout this text are discussed. *The Law in America* by Bernard

Schwartz (New York: American Heritage, 1974) considers the evolution of U.S. legal institutions from 1790. Also helpful is *Introduction to Law, Legal Process, and Procedure* by Cornelius F. Murphy (St. Paul, MN: West, 1977), prepared for first-year law students. Also interesting are Frederick G. Kempin Jr., *Legal History: Law and Social Change* (Englewood Cliffs, NJ: Prentice-Hall, 1963), and H. Richard Hartzler, *Justice, Legal Systems, and Social Structure* (Port Washington, NY: Kennikat Press, 1976).

JUDICIAL PROCESS

Among the many books about the judicial process, *The Nature of the Judicial Process** (New Haven: Yale University Press, 1998) by Benjamin N. Cardozo is a timeless classic, first published in 1921, and still widely regarded as the best description ever written of how appellate judges decide cases. Its author was one of the United States' greatest judges and legal scholars. Justice Cardozo was also author of two essays reprinted from the pages of *Harvard Law Review* that its editors brought together in a valuable collection under the title *An Introduction to Law** (Cambridge: Harvard Law Review Association, 1957); among the authors represented are eight who were (or later became) distinguished judges. A rare and revealing memoir about the workings of the U.S. Supreme Court by one of its most distinguished contemporary justices, Thurgood Marshall, is *Thurgood Marshall: His Speeches, Writings, Arguments, Opinions and Reminiscences* (Chicago: Lawrence Hill Books, 2001). A classic, penetrating analysis of the reasoning process by which appellate judges arrive at decisions is found in Edward H. Levi's *An Introduction to Legal Reasoning** (Chicago: University of Chicago Press, 1949). On this subject see also William Zelermyer's *The Legal System in Operation** (St. Paul, MN: West, 1977). Jerome Frank's *Law and the Modern Mind** (Birmingham, AL: Legal Classics Library, 1985) is a classic on judicial process.

Other interesting contemporary works in judicial process are *Politics, Democracy and the Supreme Court: Essays on the Future of Constitutional Theory* by Arthur S. Miller (Westport, CT: Greenwood Press, 1985) and *God Save This Honorable Court: How the Choice of Supreme Court Justices Shapes Our History* by Laurence Tribe (New York: Random House, 1985).

JUDICIAL ADMINISTRATION

A useful book dealing with problems of judicial administration is *The High Cost and Effect of Litigation*, 3 vols., by Kenneth Feinberg, Jack Kress, Gary McDowell, and Warren E. Burger (Washington, DC: National Legal Center for the Public Interest, 1986).

SPECIAL TOPICS

We come finally to a few works on special topics that were considered in this book. On the role of the lawyer, see Richard L. Abel, *American Lawyers* (New York: Oxford University Press, 1989), and *Law and Lawyers in the United States* by Erwin N. Griswold

(Buffalo, NY: W.S. Hein, 1996). Griswold was dean of Harvard Law School. One of the best descriptions of a lawyer's practice is to be found in Louis Nizer's *My Life in Court** (New York: Jove, 1978). Eminently readable biographies of innovative trial lawyers include *Clarence Darrow for the Defense* by Irving Stone (Garden City, NY: Garden City, 1943), about a lawyer who largely invented the insanity defense, with a humorous chapter titled "Can a Lawyer Be an Honest Man?" Another is *A Lawyer's Journey* (Chicago: American Bar Association, 2001) by Morris Dees, founder of the Southern Poverty Law Center. Dees earned his reputation putting white supremacist organizations and Ku Klux Klan chapters out of business by using litigation to seize their property for civil damages and turn it over to their victims. For an unusually fine short treatment of some problems of ethics and law, see Eugene V. Rostow, *The Ideal in Law* (Chicago: University of Chicago Press, 1978).

Perhaps the most fascinating of many books for the layperson about the Supreme Court is Anthony Lewis's *Gideon's Trumpet* (Birmingham, AL: Notable Trials Library, 1991). For a short historical interpretation, see Robert G. McCloskey and Sanford Levinson, *The American Supreme Court*, 4th ed.* (Chicago: University of Chicago Press, 2005). On administrative law, see *Administrative Law and Government* by Kenneth Culp Davis (St. Paul, MN: West, 1975). For two comprehensive but very different approaches to administrative law, see Kenneth Culp Davis and John P. Wilson, *Administrative Law: Cases, Texts, Problems*, 6th ed. (St. Paul, MN: West, 1977), and *Administrative Law: Cases and Comments* 8th ed., by Walter Gellhorn et al. (Mineola, NY: Foundation Press, 1987, Supp. 1993).

Index

About the Authors

Michael S. Hamilton (PhD 1984, Colorado State University) is a professor of political science at the University of Southern Maine, specializing in public policy and administration. He started and managed a retail and light manufacturing business as an undergraduate and has served in various capacities in local, state, and national government. His book, *Mining Environmental Policy: Comparing Indonesia and the USA,* was named Best Book of Public Administration Scholarship published in 2004 and 2005 by the American Society for Public Administration.

George W. Spiro (JD 1974, Syracuse University) was a professor of management and associate dean in the Isenberg School of Management, University of Massachusetts–Amherst, until his untimely death in 1997. He spearheaded a business-writing course, and the George W. Spiro '71 Business Communication Program at Amherst honors his memory. He was known for giving students a basic platform of skills and teaching them to think critically, using business law to train their minds.